**BLACK LEGACY PRESS™**
WWW.BLACKLEGACYPRESS.ORG

SLAVE NARRATIVES

VOLUME XIV
SOUTH CAROLINA NARRATIVES
PART 1

By
United States.
Work Projects Administration

Copyright © 2024 by BLACKLEGACYPRESS.ORG

All rights reserved. No part of this publication may be reproduced or transmitted in any form or by any means electronic or mechanical, including information storage and retrieval systems without permission in writing from the publisher, except for student research using the appropriate citations.

ISBN: 978-1-63652-198-5

# SLAVE NARRATIVES

A Folk History of Slavery in the United States. From Interviews with Former Slaves

**UNITED STATES.
WORK PROJECTS ADMINISTRATION**

TYPEWRITTEN RECORDS PREPARED BY
THE FEDERAL WRITERS' PROJECT
1936-1938
ASSEMBLED BY
THE LIBRARY OF CONGRESS PROJECT
WORK PROJECTS ADMINISTRATION
FOR THE DISTRICT OF COLUMBIA
SPONSORED BY THE LIBRARY OF
CONGRESS
WASHINGTON 1941

# VOLUME XIV
## SOUTH CAROLINA NARRATIVES PART 1

Prepared by
The Federal Writers' Project of
The Works Progress Administration
For the State of South Carolina

# CONTENTS

| | |
|---|---|
| MRS. M. E. ABRAMS | 1 |
| EZRA ADAMS | 7 |
| MARY ADAMS | 13 |
| VICTORIA ADAMS | 15 |
| FRANK ADAMSON | 19 |
| FRANCES ANDREWS | 25 |
| FRANCES ANDREWS | 27 |
| UNCLE PETER | 29 |
| JOSEPHINE BACCHUS | 31 |
| WILLIAM BALLARD | 37 |
| CHARLEY BARBER | 41 |
| ED BARBER | 47 |
| MILLIE BARBER | 53 |
| ANDERSON BATES | 57 |
| MILLIE BATES | 63 |
| UNCLE WELCOME BEES | 67 |
| ANNE BELL | 71 |
| MISS CAROLINE BEVIS | 75 |
| MAGGIE BLACK | 79 |
| GORDON BLUFORD | 85 |
| SAMUEL BOULWARE | 89 |
| MR. JOHN BOYD | 95 |
| JANE BRADLEY | 101 |
| ANDY BRICE | 103 |

| | |
|---|---|
| GEORGE BRIGGS | 109 |
| GEORGE BRIGGS | 119 |
| GEORGE BRIGGS | 123 |
| JOSEPHINE BRISTOW | 129 |
| ANNE BROOME | 135 |
| HAGAR BROWN | 139 |
| HAGAR BROWN | 143 |
| HAGAR BROWN | 147 |
| HENRY BROWN | 151 |
| HENRY BROWN | 155 |
| JOHN C. BROWN AND ADELINE BROWN | 161 |
| MARY FRANCES BROWN | 167 |
| MARY FRANCES BROWN | 171 |
| MOM SARA BROWN | 175 |
| SARA BROWN | 179 |
| AUNT MARGARET BRYANT | 183 |
| SAVILLA BURRELL | 187 |
| C. B. BURTON | 191 |
| GEORGE ANN BUTLER | 193 |
| ISAIAH BUTLER | 195 |
| SOLBERT BUTLER | 201 |
| GRANNY CAIN | 207 |
| GRANNY CAIN | 211 |
| LAURA CALDWEL | 213 |
| SOLOMON CALDWELL | 215 |
| NELSON CAMERON | 219 |
| THOMAS CAMPBELL | 225 |

| | |
|---|---|
| SYLVIA CANNON | 229 |
| SYLVIA CANNON | 235 |
| UNCLE ALBERT CAROLINA | 245 |
| SILVIA CHISOLM | 249 |
| TOM CHISOLM | 251 |
| MARIA CLELAND | 255 |
| PETER CLIFTON | 257 |
| HENRY COLEMAN | 263 |
| TUFF COLEMAN | 271 |
| MOM LOUISA COLLIER | 273 |
| JOHN COLLINS | 279 |
| BOUREGARD CORRY | 283 |
| CALEB CRAIG | 287 |
| DINAH CUNNINGHAM | 293 |
| LUCY DANIELS | 297 |
| JOHN N. DAVENPORT | 299 |
| MOSES DAVENPORT | 305 |
| CHARLIE DAVIS | 307 |
| CHARLIE DAVIS'S MUSINGS. | 313 |
| HEDDIE DAVIS | 319 |
| HENRY DAVIS | 325 |
| JESSE DAVIS | 329 |
| LIZZIE'S 'SPONSIBILITY | 335 |
| LIZZIE DAVIS | 357 |
| LIZZIE DAVIS | 363 |
| LOUISA DAVIS | 369 |
| WALLACE DAVIS | 375 |

| | |
|---|---|
| WALLACE DAVIS | 379 |
| WILLIAM HENRY DAVIS | 383 |
| ELIAS DAWKINS | 389 |
| WILL DILL | 397 |
| THOMAS DIXON | 403 |
| ISABELLA DORROH | 407 |
| LAURENCE DOWNING | 411 |
| WASHINGTON DOZIER | 413 |
| ALICE DUKE | 419 |
| AUNT SILVA DURANT | 421 |
| SYLVIA DURANT | 427 |

Project 1885-1
From Field Notes.
District No. 4.
April 27, 1937

Edited by:
Elmer Turnage

# MRS. M. E. ABRAMS
## Folk Lore: Folk TaLES (Negro).

"Marse Glenn had 64 slaves. On Sat'day night, de darkies would have a little fun on de side. A way off from de big house, down in de pastur' dar wuz about de bigges' gully what I is ebber seed. Dat wuz de place whar us collected mos' ev'ry Sa'day night fer our lil' mite o' fun frum de white folks hearin'. Sometime it wuz so dark dat you could not see de fingers on yo' han' when you would raise it fo' your face. Dem wuz sho' schreechy nights; de schreechiest what I is ever witnessed, in all o' my born natu'al days. Den of cose, dar wuz de moonlight nights when a darky could see; den he see too much. De pastur' wuz big and de trees made dark spots in it on de brightest nights. All kind o' varmints tuck and hollered at ye as ye being gwine along to reach dat gully. Cose us would go in droves sometime, and den us would go alone to de gully sometime. When us started together, look like us would git parted 'fo we reach de gully all together. One of us see som'tin and take to runnin'. Maybe de other darkies in de drove, de wouldn't see nothin' jes den. Dats zactly how it is wid de spirits. De mout (might) sho de'self to you and not to me. De acts raal queer all de way round. Dey can take a notion to scare de daylights outtin you when you is wid a gang; or dey kin scare de whole gang; den, on de other hand, dey kin sho de'self off to jes two or three. It ain't never no knowin' as to how and when dem things is gwine to come in your path right fo your very eyes; specially when you is partakin' in some raal dark secret whar you is planned to act raal sof' and quiet like all de way through.

"Dem things bees light on dark nights; de shines de'self jes like dese 'lectric lights does out dar in dat street ever' night, 'cept dey is a scaird waary light dat dey shines wid. On light nights, I is seed dem look, furs dark like a tree shad'er; den dey gits raal scairy white. T'aint no use fer white folks to low dat it ain't no haints, an' grievements dat follows ye all around, kaise I is done had to many 'spriences wid dem. Den dare is dese young niggers what ain't fit to be called darkies, dat tries to ac' eddicated, and says dat it ain't any spe'rits dat walks de earth. When dey lows dat to me, I rolls my old eyes at dem an' axes dem how comes dey runs so fas' through de woods at night. Yes sirree, dem fool niggers sees dem jes as I does. Raaly de white folks doesn't have eyes fer sech as we darkies does; but dey bees dare jes de same.

"Never mindin' all o' dat, we n'used to steal our hog ever' sa'day night and take off to de gully whar us'd git him dressed and barbecued. Niggers has de mos'es fun at a barbecue dat dare is to be had. As none o' our gang didn't have no 'ligion, us never felt no scruples bout not gettin de 'cue' ready fo' Sunday. Us'd git back to de big house along in de evenin' o' Sunday. Den Marse, he come out in de yard an' low whar wuz you niggers dis mornin'. How come de chilluns had to do de work round here. Us would tell some lie bout gwine to a church 'siety meetin'. But we got raal scairt and mose 'cided dat de best plan wuz to do away wid de barbecue in de holler. Conjin 'Doc.' say dat he done put a spell on ole Marse so dat he wuz 'blevin ev'y think dat us tole him bout Sa'day night and Sunday morning. Dat give our minds 'lief; but it turned out dat in a few weeks de Marse come out from under de spell. Doc never even knowed nothin' bout it. Marse had done got to countin' his hogs ever' week. When he cotch us, us wuz all punished wid a hard long task. Dat cured me o' believing in any conjuring an' charmin' but I still kno's dat dare is haints; kaise ever time you goes to dat gully at night, up to dis very day, you ken hear hogs still gruntin' in it, but you can't see nothing.

"After Marse Glenn tuck and died, all o' de white folks went off and lef' de plantation. Some mo' folks dat wuz not o' quality, come to live dare an' run de plantation. It wuz done freedom den. Wo'nt long fo dem folks pull up and lef' raal onexpected like. I doesn't recollect what dey went by, fat is done slipped my mind; but I must 'av knowed. But dey lowed dat de house wuz to draffy and dat dey couldn't keep de smoke in de chimney an' dat de doo's would not stay shet. Also dey lowed dat folks prowled aroun' in de yard in de night time a keepin' dem awake.

"Den Marse Glenn's boys put Mammy in de house to keep it fer 'em. But Lawd God! Mammy said dat de furs night she stayed dare de haints nebber let her git not narr'y mite o' sleep. Us all had lowed dat wuz de raal reason dem white folks lef out so fas'. When Mammy could not live in dat big house whar she had stayed fer years, it won't no use fer nobody else to try. Mammy low dat it de Marse a lookin' fer his money what he done tuck and burried and de boys couldn't find no sign o' it. Atter dat, de sons tuck an' tacked a sign on de front gate, offering $200.00 to de man, white or black, dat would stay dar and fin' out whar dat money wuz burried. Our preacher, the Rev. Wallace, lowed dat he would stay dar and find out whar dat money wuz from de spirits. He knowed dat dey wuz tryin to sho de spot what dat money wuz.

"He went to bed. A dog began running down dem steps; and a black cat run across de room dat turned to white befo' it run into de wall. Den a pair of white horses come down de stairway a rattling chains fer harness. Next a woman dressed in white come in dat room. Brother Wallace up and lit out dat house and he never went back no mo'.

"Another preacher tried stayin' dar. He said he gwine to keep his head kivered plum up. Some'tin unkivered it and he seed a white goat a grinnin' at him. But as he wuz a brave man and trus' de Lawd, he lowed, 'What you want wid me nohow?' The goat said, 'what is you doin' here. Raise, I knows dat you ain't sleep.' De preacher say, 'I wants you to tell me what ole Marse don tuck and hid dat money?' De goat grin and low, 'How come you don' look under your pillar, sometime?' Den he run away. De preacher hopped up and looked under de pillar, and dar wuz de money sho nuf. Peers like it wuz de one on de lef' end o' de back porch, but I jes remembers 'bout dat."

Source: Mrs. M. E. Abrams, Whitmire, S. C.; told her by old "uncle" "Mad" Griffin, Whitmire, (Col. 82 yrs.)
Interviewer: Caldwell Sims, Union, S. C. 2/25/37.

United States

Project #1655
Henry Grant
Columbia, S. C.

# EZRA ADAMS

## Ex-Slave 83 Years Old

Ezra Adams is incapable of self-support, owing to ill health. He is very well taken care of by a niece, who lives on the Caughman land just off S. C. #6, and near Swansea, S. C.

"My mammy and pappy b'long to Marster Lawrence Adams, who had a big plantation in de eastern part of Lancaster County. He died four years after de Civil War and is buried right dere on de old plantation, in de Adams family burying grounds. I was de oldest of de five chillun in our family. I 'members I was a right smart size plowboy, when freedom come. I think I must of been 'bout ten or eleven years old, then. Dere's one thing I does know; de Yankees didn't tech our plantation, when they come through South Carolina. Up in de northern part of de county they sho' did destroy most all what folks had.

"You ain't gwine to believe dat de slaves on our plantation didn't stop workin' for old marster, even when they was told dat they was free. Us didn't want no more freedom than us was gittin' on our plantation already. Us knowed too well dat us was well took care of, wid a plenty of vittles to eat and tight log and board houses to live in. De slaves, where I lived, knowed after de war dat they had abundance of dat somethin' called freedom, what they could not wat, wear, and sleep in. Yes, sir, they soon found out dat freedom ain't nothin', 'less you is got somethin' to live on and a place to call home. Dis livin' on liberty is lak young folks livin' on love after they gits married. It just don't work. No, sir, it las' so long and not a bit longer. Don't tell me! It sho' don't hold good when you has to work, or when you gits hongry. You knows dat poor white folks and niggers has got to work to live, regardless of liberty, love, and all them things. I believes a person loves more better, when they feels good. I knows from experience dat poor folks feels better when they has food in deir frame and a few dimes to jingle in deir pockets. I knows what it means to be a nigger, wid nothin'. Many times I had to turn every way I knowed to git a bite to eat. I didn't care much 'bout clothes. What I needed in sich times was food to keep my blood warm and gwine 'long.

"Boss, I don't want to think, and I knows I ain't gwine to say a word, not a word of evil against deir dust lyin' over yonder in deir graves. I was old enough to know what de passin' 'way of old marster and missus meant to me. De very stream of lifeblood in me was dryin' up, it 'peared lak. When marster died, dat was my fust real sorrow. Three years later, missus passed 'way, dat was de time of my second sorrow. Then, I 'minded myself of a little tree out dere in de woods in November. Wid every sharp and cold wind of trouble dat blowed, more leaves of dat tree turnt loose and went to de ground, just lak they was tryin' to follow her. It seem lak, when she was gone,

I was just lak dat tree wid all de leaves gone, naked and friendless. It took me a long time to git over all dat; same way wid de little tree, it had to pass through winter and wait on spring to see life again.

"I has farmed 'most all my life and, if I was not so old, I would be doin' dat same thing now. If a poor man wants to enjoy a little freedom, let him go on de farm and work for hisself. It is sho' worth somethin' to be boss, and, on de farm you can be boss all you want to, 'less de man 'low his wife to hold dat 'portant post. A man wid a good wife, one dat pulls wid him, can see and feel some pleasure and experience some independence. But, bless your soul, if he gits a woman what wants to be both husband and wife, fare-you-well and good-bye, too, to all love, pleasure, and independence; 'cause you sho' is gwine to ketch hell here and no mild climate whenever you goes 'way. A bad man is worse, but a bad woman is almost terrible.

"White man, dere is too many peoples in dese big towns and cities. Dere is more of them than dere is jobs to make a livin' wid. When some of them find out dat they can't make a livin', they turns to mischief, de easy way they thinks, takin' widout pay or work, dat which b'longs to other people. If I understands right, de fust sin dat was committed in de world was de takin' of somethin' dat didn't b'long to de one what took it. De gentleman what done dis was dat man Adam, back yonder in de garden. If what Adam done back yonder would happen now, he would be guilty of crime. Dat's how 'ciety names sin. Well, what I got to say is dis: If de courts, now, would give out justice and punishment as quick as dat what de Good Master give to Adam, dere would be less crime in de land I believes. But I 'spose de courts would be better if they had de same jurisdiction as de Master has. Yes, sir, they would be gwine some then.

"I tells you, dis gittin' what don't b'long to you is de main cause of dese wars and troubles 'bout over dis world now. I hears de white folks say dat them Japanese is doin' dis very thing today in fightin' them Chinamens. Japan say dat China has done a terrible crime against them and de rest of de world, when it ain't nothin' but dat they wants somethin' what don't belong to them, and dat somethin' is to git more country. I may be wrong, anyhow, dat is what I has heard.

"What does I think de colored people need most? If you please sir, I want to say dis. I ain't got much learnin', 'cause dere was no schools hardly 'round where I was brung up, but I thinks dat good teachers and work is what de colored race needs worser than anything else. If they has learnin', they will be more ashame to commit crime, most of them will be; and, if they has work to do, they ain't gwine to have time to do so much wrong. Course dere is gwine to be black sheeps in most flocks, and it is gwine to take patience to git them out, but they will come out, just as sho' as you is born.

"Is de colored people superstitious? Listen at dat. You makes me laugh. All dat foolishness fust started wid de black man. De reason they is superstitious comes from nothin' but stomp-down ignorance. De white chillun has been nursed by colored women and they has told them stories 'bout hants and sich lak. So de white chillun has growed up believin' some of dat stuff 'til they natchally pass it on from generation to generation. Here we is, both white and colored, still believin' some of them lies started back when de whites fust come to have de blacks 'round them.

"If you wants to know what I thinks is de best vittles, I's gwine to be obliged to omit (admit) dat it is cabbage sprouts in de spring, and it is collard greens after frost has struck them. After de best vittles, dere come some more what is mighty tasty, and they is hoghead and chittlings wid 'tatoes and turnips. Did you see dat? Here I is talkin' 'bout de joys of de appetite and water drapping from my mouth. I sho' must be gittin' hongry. I lak to eat. I has been a good eater all my life, but now I is gittin' so old dat 'cordin' to de scriptures, 'De grinders cease 'cause they are few', and too, 'Those dat look out de windows be darkened'. My old eyes and teeth is 'bout gone, and if they does go soon, they ain't gwine to beat dis old frame long, 'cause I is gwine to soon follow, I feels. I hope when I does go, I can be able to say what dat great General Stonewall Jackson say when he got kilt in de Civil War, 'I is gwine to cross de river and rest under de shade of de trees'."

[HW: Ezra Adams, Swansea (about 10m. south of Columbia)]

United States

Project 1885-1.
Folk Lore
District No. 4.
May 27, 1937.
Edited by: J. J. Murray.

# MARY ADAMS
## Ex-Slave Stories

"Aunt" Mary Adams was swinging easily back and forth in the porch swing as the writer stopped to speak to her. When questioned, she replied that she and her mother were ex-slaves and had belonged to Dr. C. E. Fleming. She was born in Columbia, but they were moved to Glenn Springs where her mother cooked for Dr. Fleming.

She remembers going with a white woman whose husband was in jail, to carry him something to eat. She said that Mr. Jim Milster was in that jail, but he lived to get out, and later kept a tin shop in Spartanburg.

"Yes sir, Dr. Fleming always kept enough for us Niggers to eat during the war. He was good to us. You know he married Miss Dean. Do you know Mrs. Lyles, Mrs. Simpson, Mr. Ed Fleming? Well, dey are my chilluns.

"Some man here told me one day that I was ninety years old, but I do not believe I am quite that old. I don't know how old I am, but I was walking during slavery times. I can't work now, for my feet hurt me and my fingers ain't straight."

She said all of her children were dead but two, that she knew of. She said that she had a room in that house and white people gave her different things. As the writer told her good-bye, she said, "Good-bye, and may the Lord bless you".

Source: "Aunt" Mary Adams, 363 S. Liberty Street, Spartanburg, S. C.
Interviewer: F. S. DuPre, Spartanburg, S. C.

Project #1655
Everett R. Pierce
Columbia, S. C.

## VICTORIA ADAMS
### Ex-Slave 90 Years Old.

"You ask me to tell you something 'bout myself and de slaves in slavery times? Well Missy, I was borned a slave, nigh on to ninety years ago, right down here at Cedar Creek, in Fairfield County.

"My massa's name was Samuel Black and missus was named Martha. She used to be Martha Kirkland befo' she married. There was five chillun in de family; they was: Alice, Manning, Sally, Kirkland, and de baby, Eugene. De white folks live in a great big house up on a hill; it was right pretty, too.

"You wants to know how large de plantation was I lived on? Well, I don't know 'zackly but it was mighty large. There was forty of us slaves in all and it took all of us to keep de plantation goin'. De most of de niggers work in de field. They went to work as soon as it git light enough to see how to git 'round; then when twelve o'clock come, they all stops for dinner and don't go back to work 'til two. All of them work on 'til it git almost dark.

No ma'am, they ain't do much work at night after they gits home.

"Massa Samuel ain't had no overseer, he look after his own plantation. My old granddaddy help him a whole heap though. He was a good nigger and massa trust him.

"After de crops was all gathered, de slaves still had plenty of work to do. I stayed in de house wid de white folks. De most I had to do was to keep de house clean up and nurse de chillun. I had a heap of pretty clothes to wear, 'cause my missus give me de old clothes and shoes dat Missy Sally throw 'way.

"De massa and missus was good to me but sometime I was so bad they had to whip me. I 'members she used to whip me every time she tell me to do something and I take too long to move 'long and do it. One time my missus went off on a visit and left me at home. When she come back, Sally told her that I put on a pair of Bubber's pants and scrub de floor wid them on. Missus told me it was a sin for me to put on a man's pants, and she whip me pretty bad. She say it's in de Bible dat: 'A man shall not put on a woman's clothes, nor a woman put on a man's clothes'. I ain't never see that in de Bible though, but from then 'til now, I ain't put on no more pants.

"De grown-up slaves was punished sometime too. When they didn't feel like taking a whippin' they went off in de woods and stay 'til massa's hounds track them down; then they'd bring them out and whip them. They might as well not run away. Some of them never come back a-tall, don't know what become of them. We ain't had no jail for slaves; never ain't see none in chains neither. There was a guard-house right in de town but us niggers never was carried to it. You ask me if I ever see a slave auctioned off? Yes ma'am, one time. I see a little girl 'bout ten years old sold to a soldier man. Dis soldier man was married and didn't had no chillun and he buy dis little girl to be company for his wife and to help her wid de house work.

"White folks never teach us to read nor write much. They learned us our A, B, C's, and teach us to read some in de testament. De reason they wouldn't teach us to read and write, was 'cause they was afraid de slaves would write their own pass and go over to a free county. One old nigger did learn enough to write his pass and got 'way wid it and went up North.

"Missus Martha sho' did look after de slaves good when they was sick. Us had medicine made from herbs, leaves and roots; some of them was cat-nip, garlic root, tansy, and roots of burdock. De roots of burdock soaked in whiskey was mighty good medicine. We dipped asafetida in turpentine and hung it 'round our necks to keep off disease.

"Befo' de Yankees come thru, our peoples had let loose a lot of our hosses and de hosses strayed over to de Yankee side, and de Yankee men rode de hosses back over to our plantation. De Yankees asked us if we want to be free. I never say I did; I tell them I want to stay wid my missus and they went on and let me alone. They 'stroyed most everything we had 'cept a little vittles; took all de stock and take them wid them. They burned all de buildings 'cept de one de massa and missus was livin' in.

"It wasn't long after de Yankees went thru dat our missus told us dat we don't b'long to her and de massa no more. None of us left dat season. I got married de next year and left her. I like being free more better. Any niggers what like slavery time better, is lazy people dat don't want to do nothing.

"I married Fredrick Adams; he used to b'long to Miss Tenny Graddick but after he was freed he had to take another name. Mr. Jess Adams, a good fiddler dat my husband like to hang 'round, told him he could take his name if he wanted to and dats how he got de name of Adams. Us had four chillun; only one livin', dat Lula. She married John Entzminger and got several chillun. My gran'chillun a heap of comfort to me."

    Home Address:
    Colonial Heights,
    Columbia, S. C.

Project #1655
W. W. Dixon
Winnsboro, S. C.

# FRANK ADAMSON
## Ex-Slave 82 Years Old.

"I 'members when you was barefoot at de bottom; now I see you a settin' dere, gittin' bare at de top, as bare as de palm of my hand.

"I's been 'possum huntin' wid your pappy, when he lived on de Wateree, just after de war. One night us got into tribulation, I tells you! 'Twas 'bout midnight when de dogs make a tree. Your pappy climb up de tree, git 'bout halfway up, heard sumpin' dat once you hears it you never forgits, and dats de rattlin' of de rattles on a rattle snake's tail. Us both 'stinctly hear dat sound! What us do? Me on de ground, him up de tree, but where de snake? Dat was de misery, us didn't know. Dat snake give us fair warnin' though! Marster Sam (dats your pa) 'low: 'Frank, ease down on de ground; I'll just stay up here for a while.' I lay on them leaves, skeered to make a russle. Your pa up de tree skeered to go up or down! Broad daylight didn't move us. Sun come up, he look all 'round from his vantage up de tree, then come down, not 'til then, do I gits on my foots.

"Then I laugh and laugh and laugh, and ask Marster Sam how he felt. Marster Sam kinda frown and say: 'Damn I feels like hell! Git up dat tree! Don't you see dat 'possum up dere?' I say: 'But where de snake, Marster?' He say: 'Dat rattler done gone home, where me and you and dat 'possum gonna be pretty soon!'

"I b'longs to de Peays. De father of them all was, Korshaw Peay. My marster was his son, Nicholas; he was a fine man to just look at. My mistress was always tellin' him 'bout how fine and handsome-like he was. He must of got use to it; howsomever, marster grin every time she talk like dat.

"My pappy was bought from de Adamson peoples; they say they got him off de ship from Africa. He sho' was a man; he run all de other niggers 'way from my mammy and took up wid her widout askin' de marster. Her name was Lavinia. When us got free, he 'sisted on Adamson was de name us would go by. He name was William Adamson. Yes sir! my brothers was: Justus, Hillyard, and Donald, and my sisters was, Martha and Lizzettie.

"'Deed I did work befo' freedom. What I do? Hoed cotton, pick cotton, 'tend to calves and slop de pigs, under de 'vision of de overseer. Who he was? First one name Mr. Cary, he a good man. Another one Mr. Tim Gladden, burn you up whenever he just take a notion to pop his whip. Us boys run 'round in our shirt tails. He lak to see if he could lift de shirt tail widout techin' de skin. Just as often as not, though, he tech de skin. Little boy holler and Marster Tim laugh.

"Us live in quarters. Our beds was nailed to de sides of

de house. Most of de chillun slept on pallets on de floor. Got water from a big spring.

"De white folks 'tend to you all right. Us had two doctors, Doctor Carlisle and Doctor James.

"I see some money, but never own any then. Had plenty to eat: Meat, bread, milk, lye hominy, horse apples, turnips, collards, pumpkins, and dat kind of truck.

"Was marster rich? How come he wasn't? He brag his land was ten miles square and he had a thousand slaves. Them poor white folks looked up to him lak God Almighty; they sho' did. They would have stuck their hands in de fire if he had of asked them to do it. He had a fish pond on top of de house and terraces wid strawberries, all over de place. See them big rock columns down dere now? Dats all dats left of his grandness and greatness. They done move de whippin' post dat was in de backyard. Yes sah, it was a 'cessity wid them niggers. It stood up and out to 'mind them dat if they didn't please de master and de overseer, they'd hug dat post, and de lend of dat whip lash gwine to flip to de hide of dat back of their's.

"I ain't a complainin'. He was a good master, bestest in de land, but he just have to have a whippin' post, 'cause you'll find a whole passle of bad niggers when you gits a thousand of them in one flock.

"Screech owl holler? Women and men turn socks and stockings wrong side out quick, dat they did, do it now, myself. I's black as a crow but I's got a white folks heart. Didn't ketch me foolin' 'round wid niggers in radical times. I's as close to white folks then as peas in a pod. Wore de red shirt and drunk a heap of brandy in Columbia, dat time us went down to General Hampton into power. I 'clare I hollered so loud goin' 'long in de procession, dat a nice white lady run out one of de houses down dere in Columbia, give me two biscuits and a drum stick of chicken, patted me on de shoulder, and say: 'Thank God for all de big black men dat can holler for Governor Hampton as loud as dis one does.' Then I hollers some more for to please dat lady, though I had to take de half chawed chicken out dis old mouth, and she laugh 'bout dat 'til she cried. She did!

"Well, I'll be rockin' 'long balance of dese days, a hollerin' for Mr. Roosevelt, just as loud as I holler then for Hampton.

"My young marsters was: Austin, Tom, and Nicholas; they was all right 'cept they tease you too hard maybe some time, and want to mix in wid de 'fairs of slave 'musements.

"Now what make you ask dat? Did me ever do any courtin'? You knows I did. Every he thing from a he king down to a bunty rooster gits cited 'bout she things. I's lay wake many nights 'bout sich things. It's de nature of a he, to take after de she. They do say dat a he angel ain't got dis to worry 'bout.

"I fust courted Martha Harrison. Us marry and jine de church. Us had nine chillun; seven of them livin'. A woman can't stand havin' chillun, lak a man. Carryin', sucklin', and 'tending to them wore her down, dat, wid de malaria of de Wateree brung her to her grave.

"I sorrow over her for weeks, maybe five months, then I got to thinking how I'd pair up wid dis one and dat one and de other one. Took to shavin' again and gwine to Winnsboro every Saturday, and different churches every Sunday. I hear a voice from de choir, one Sunday, dat makes me sit up and take notice of de gal on de off side in front. Well sir! a spasm of fright fust hit me dat I might not git her, dat I was too old for de likes of her, and dat some no 'count nigger might be in de way. In a few minutes I come to myself. I rise right up, walked into dat choir, stand by her side, and wid dis voice of mine, dat always 'tracts 'tention, jined in de hymn and out sung them all. It was easy from dat time on.

"I marry Kate at de close of dat revival. De day after de weddin', what you reckon? Don't know? Well, after gittin' breakfas' she went to de field, poke 'round her neck, basket on her head and picked two hundred pounds of cotton. Dats de kind of woman she is."

Project 1815-1
FOLKLORE
Spartanburg Dist. 4
June 10, 1937
Edited by: Elmer Turnage

# FRANCES ANDREWS

## Stories From Ex-Slaves

"I was born in Newberry County, S. C., near Belfast, about 1854. I was a slave of John Wallace. I was the only child, and when a small child, my mother was sold to Joe Liggins by my old master, Bob Adams. It is said that the old brick house where the Wallaces lived was built by a Eichleberger, but Dr. John Simpson lived there and sold it to Mr. Wallace. In the attic was an old skeleton which the children thought bewitched the house. None of them would go upstairs by themselves. I suppose old Dr. Simpson left it there. Sometimes later, it was taken out and buried. Marse Wallace had many slaves and kept them working, but he was not a strict master.

"I married Allen Andrews after the war. He went to the war with his master. He was at Columbia with the Confederate troops when Sherman burnt the place. Some of them, my husband included, was captured and taken to Richmond Va. They escaped and walked back home, but all but five or six fell out or died.

"My young master, Editor Bill Wallace, a son of Marse John, was a soldier. When he was sick at home, I fanned the flies from him with a home-made fan of peacock feathers, sewed to a long cane.

"After the war, the 'bush-whackers', called Ku Klux, rode there. Preacher Pitts' brother was one. They went to negro houses and killed the people. They wore caps over the head and eyes, but no long white gowns. An old muster ground was above there about three miles, near what is now Wadsworth school."

Source: Frances Andrews (col. 83), Newberry, S. C
Interviewer: G. Leland Summer, Newberry, S. C.

Project 1885-1
FOLKLORE
Spartanburg Dist. 4
Sept. 22, 1937
Edited by: Elmer Turnage

# FRANCES ANDREWS
## Stories From Ex-Slaves

"I live in a comfortable two-room cottage which my son owns. I can't do much work except a little washing and ironing. My grandchildren live with me. My other children help me a little when I need it. I heard about the 40 acres of land and a mule the ex-slaves would get after the war, but I didn't pay any attention to it. They never got anything. I think this was put out by the Yankees who didn't care about much 'cept getting money for themselves.

"I come from the Indian Creek section of Newberry County. After about 1880 when things got natural, some of the slaves from this section rented small one-horse farms and made their own money and living. Some would rent small tracts of land on shares, giving the landlord one-half the crop for use of the land.

"Everything is changed so much. I never learned to read and write and all I know is what I heard in old times.

But I think the younger generation of negroes is different from what they used to be. They go where they want to and do what they want to and don't pay much attention to old folks anymore.

"My mother's mother come from Virginia and my mother's father was born and raised in this county. I don't remember anything about the Nat Turner Rebellion, and never heard anything about it. We never had any slave up-risings in our neighborhood."

Source: Frances Andrews (83), Newberry, S. C.
Interviewer: G. L. Summer, Newberry, S. C. 8/11/37.

Project 1885-(1)
Folklore
Spartanburg, S. C.
District No. 4
May 27, 1937.
Edited by
R. V. Williams

[HW: Lambright]

## UNCLE PETER
### Folk Lore: Folk Tales (negro)

"I was 'bout nine year ole when de big war broke loose. My pa and ma 'longed to de Scotts what libbed in Jonesville Township. When I got big 'nough to work, I was gib to de youngest Scott boy. Soon atter dis, Sherman come through Union County. No ma'm, I nebber seed Sherman but I seed some of his soldiers. Dat's de time I run off in de wood and not narry a soul knowed whar I was till de dus' had done settled in de big road.

"Every Sunday, Marse Scott sent us to church in one of his waggins. White folks rid to church in de buggy and Marse went on de big saddle hoss. 'Bout dis time, Marse Scott went to Columbia to git coffee and sugar. He stay mos' two weeks, kaize he drive two fine hosses to de buggy 'long wid a long hind end to fetch things to and fro in. De roads was real muddy and de hosses haf to res' ever night. Den in Columbia, he would have a little 'joyment befo' he come back home."

Source: Miss Dorothy Lambright, W. Main St., Union, S. C. (Story told her by "Uncle Peter" Arthur.) Information by Caldwell Sims, Union, S. C.

Code No.
Project, 1885-(1)
Prepared by Annie Ruth Davis
Place, Marion, S. C.
Date, January 4, 1938
No. of Words --
Reduced from -- words
Rewritten by --

## JOSEPHINE BACCHUS
### Ex-Slave, 75-80 Years

"No, my mercy God, I don' know not one thought to speak to you bout. Seems like, I does know your face, but I been so sick all de year dat I can' hardly remember nothin. Yes, sweetheart, I sho caught on to what you want. Oh, I wishes I did know somethin bout dat old time war cause I tell you, if I been know anything, I would sho pour it out to you. I got burn out here de other day en I ain' got near a thing left me, but a pair of stockings en dat old coat dere on de bed. Dat how-come I stayin here wid Miss Celia. My husband, he dead en she took me in over here for de present. No'um, I haven't never had a nine months child. Reckon dat what ailin me now. Bein dat I never had no mother to care for me en give me a good attention like, I caught so much of cold dat I ain' never been safe in de family way. Yes, mam, I had my leg broke plenty times, but I ain' never been able to jump de time. Lord, I got a misery in my back dere. I hope it ain' de pneumonias."

"Well, you see, I couldn' tell you nothin bout my mother cause I never didn' know nothin bout my mother. My Jesus, my brother tell bout when dey had my mother layin out on de coolin board, I went in de room whe' she was en axed her for somethin to eat en pushed her head dat way. You know, I wouldn' touch my hand to do nothin like dat, but I never know. Dat it, de coolin board, dat what dey used to have to lay all de dead people on, but dis day en time, de undertaker takes dem en fixes dem up right nice, I say. I tellin you, I ain' had no sense since I lost my people. Sometimes, I axes de Lord what he keepin me here for anyhow. Yes, mam, dat does come to me often times in de night. Oh, it don' look like I gwine ever get no better in dis life en if I don', I just prays to God to be saved. Yes, Lord, I prays to be lifted to a restful home."

"Just like as I been hear talk, some of de people fare good in slavery time en some of dem fare rough. Dat been accordin to de kind of task boss dey come up under. Now de poor colored people in slavery time, dey give dem very little rest en would whip some of dem most to death. Wouldn' none of dem daresen to go from one plantation to another widout dey had a furlough from dey boss. Yes, mam, if dey been catch you comin back widout dat walkin paper de boss had give you, great Jeruseleum, you would sho catch de devil next mornin. My blessed a mercy, hear talk dey spill de poor nigger's blood awful much in slavery time. Hear heap of dem was free long time fore dey been know it cause de white folks, dey wanted to keep dem in bondage. Oh, my Lord, dey would cut dem so hard till dey just slash de flesh right off dem. Yes, mam, dey call dat thing dey been whip dem wid de cat o' nine tail. No, darlin, I hear talk it been made out of pretty leather plaited most all de way en den all dat part down to de bottom, dey just left it loose to do de cuttin wid. Yes, honey, dem kind of whips was made out of pretty leather like one of dese horse whips. Yes, mam, dat been how it was in slavery time."

"Yankees! Oh, I hear folks speak bout de Yankees plunderin through de country plenty times. Hear bout de Yankees gwine all bout stealin white people silver. Say, everywhe' dey went en found white folks wid silver, dey would just clean de place up. Dat de blessed truth, too, cause dat exactly what I hear bout dem."

"Lord, pray Jesus, de white people sho been mighty proud to see dey niggers spreadin out in dem days, so dey tell me. Yes, mam, dey was glad to have a heap of colored people bout dem cause white folks couldn' work den no more den dey can work dese days like de colored people can. Reckon dey love to have dey niggers back yonder just like dey loves to have dem dese days to do what dey ain' been cut out to do. You see, dey would have two or three women on de plantation dat was good breeders en dey would have chillun pretty regular fore freedom come here. You know, some people does be right fast in catchin chillun. Yes'um, dey must been bless wid a pile of dem, I say, en every colored person used to follow up de same name as dey white folks been hear to."

"No'um, I never didn' go to none of dem cornshuckin en fodder pullin en all dem kind of thing. Reckon while dey was at de cornshuckin, I must been somewhe' huntin somethin to eat. Den dem kind of task was left to de men folks de most of de time cause it been so hot, dey was force to strip to do dat sort of a job."

"Lord, I sho remembers dat earth shake good as anything. When it come on me, I was settin down wid my foots in a tub of water. Yes, my Lord, I been had a age on me in de shake. I remember, dere been such a shakin dat evenin, it made all de people feel mighty queer like. It just come in a tremble en first thing I know, I felt de difference in de crack of de house. I run to my sister Jessie cause she had been live in New York en she was well acquainted wid dat kind of gwine on. She say, 'Josie, dis ain' nothin but dem shake I been tellin you bout, but dis de first time it come here en you better be a prayin.' En, honey, everything white en colored was emptied out of doors dat night. Lord, dey was scared. Great Jeruseleum! De people was scared everywhe'. Didn' nobody know what to make of it. I tellin you, I betcha I was 30 years old in de shake."

"Now, I guess time you get done gettin up all dem memorandums, you gwine have a pile. I tell you, if you keep on, you sho gwine have a bale cause dere a lot of slavery people is spring up till now. I ought to could fetch back more to speak to you bout, but just like I been tell you, I wasn' never cared for by a mother en I is caught on to a heap of roughness just on account dat I ain' never had a mother to have a care for me."

"Oh, de people never didn' put much faith to de doctors in dem days. Mostly, dey would use de herbs in de fields for dey medicine. Dere two herbs, I hear talk of. Dey was black snake root en Sampson snake root. Say, if a person never had a good appetite, dey would boil some of dat stuff en mix it wid a little whiskey en rock candy en dat would sho give dem a sharp appetite. See, it natural cause if you take a tablespoon of dat bitter medicine three times a day like a person tell you, it bound to swell your appetite. Yes, mam, I know dat a mighty good mixture."

"Oh, my Lord, child, de people was sho wiser in olden times den what dey be now. Dey been have all kind of signs to forecast de times wid en dey been mighty true to de word, too. Say, when you hear a cow low en cry so mournful like, it ain' gwine be long fore you hear tell of a death."

"Den dere one bout de rain. Say, sometimes de old rain crow stays in de air en hollers en if you don' look right sharp, it gwine rain soon. Call him de rain crow. He hollers mostly like dis, 'Goo-oop, goo-oop.' Like dat."

"De people used to have a bird for cold weather, too. Folks say, 'Don' you hear dat cold bird? Look out, it gwine be cold tomorrow.' De cold bird, he a brown bird. If you can see him, he a fine lookin bird, too. Yes'um, right large en strong lookin, but don' nobody hardly ever see him dese days."

"En I reckon you hear talk bout dis one. Say, not to wash on de first day of de New Year cause if you do, you will wash some of your family out de pot. Say, somebody will sho die. Dat right, too. Den if possible, must boil some old peas on de first day of de New Year en must cook some hog jowl in de pot wid dem. Must eat some of it, but don' be obliged to eat it all. En ought to have everything clean up nicely so as to keep clean all de year. Say, must always put de wash out on de line to be sure de day fore New Years en have all your garments clean."

"What my ideas bout de young folks dese days? Well,

dey young folks en dey ain' young folks, I say. Cose I don' bother up wid dem none, but I think wid my own weak judgment, dey quite different from when I come along. Folks is awful funny dis day en time to my notion. Don' care what people see dem do no time. I sho think dey worser den what dey used to be. De way I say dey worser, I used to have to be back at such en such a time, if I went off, but now dey go anytime dey want to en dey comes back anytime dey want to. I sho think dey worser. De fact of it, I know dey worser."

Source: Josephine Bacchus, colored, age 75-80, Marion, S. C.
Personal interview by Annie Ruth Davis, Dec., 1937.

Project 1885-1
Folklore
Spartanburg Dist. 4
June 14, 1937
Edited by: Elmer Turnage

# WILLIAM BALLARD
## Stories From Ex-Slaves

"I was born near Winnsboro, S. C., Fairfield County. I was twelve years old the year the Confederate war started. My father was John Ballard and my mother was Sallie Ballard. I had several brothers and sisters. We belonged to Jim Aiken, a large landowner at Winnsboro. He owned land on which the town was built. He had seven plantations. He was good to us and give us plenty to eat, and good quarters to live in. His mistress was good, too; but one of his sons, Dr. Aiken, whipped some of de niggers, lots. One time he whipped a slave for stealing. Some of his land was around four churches in Winnsboro.

"We was allowed three pounds o' meat, one quart o' molasses, grits and other things each week—plenty for us to eat.

"When freedom come, he told us we was free, and if we wanted to stay on with him, he would do the best he could for us. Most of us stayed, and after a few months, he paid wages. After eight months, some went to other places to work.

"The master's wife died and he married a daughter of Robert Gillam and moved to Greenville, S. C.

"The master always had a very big garden with plenty of vegetables. He had fifty hogs, and I helped mind the hogs. He didn't raise much cotton, but raised lots of wheat and corn. He made his own meal and flour from the mill on the creek; made home-made clothes with cards and spinning wheels.

"They cooked in wide chimneys in a kitchen which was away off from the big house. They used pots and skillets to cook with. The hands got their rations every Monday night. They got their clothes to wear which they made on old spinning wheels, and wove them themselves.

"The master had his own tanyard and tanned his leather and made shoes for his hands.

"He had several overseers, white men, and some Negro foremen. They sometimes whipped the slaves, that is the overseers. Once a nigger whipped the overseer and had to run away in the woods and live so he wouldn't get caught. The nigger foremen looked after a set of slaves on any special work. They never worked at night unless it was to bring in fodder or hay when it looked like rain was coming. On rainy days, we shucked corn and cleaned up around the place.

"We had old brick ovens, lots of 'em. Some was used to make molasses from our own sugar cane we raised.

"The master had a 'sick-house' where he took sick slaves for treatment, and kept a drug store there. They didn't use old-time cures much, like herbs and barks, except sassafras root tea for the blood.

"We didn't learn to read and write, but some learned after the war.

"My father run the blacksmith shop for the master on the place. I worked around the place. The patrollers were there and we had to have a pass to get out any. The nigger children sometimes played out in the road and were chased by patrollers. The children would run into the master's place and the patrollers couldn't get them 'cause the master wouldn't let them. We had no churches for slaves, but went to the white church and set in the gallery. After freedom, niggers built 'brush harbors' on the place.

"Slaves carried news from one plantation to another by riding mules or horses. They had to be in quarters at night. I remember my mother rode side-saddle one Saturday night. I reckon she had a pass to go; she come back without being bothered.

"Some games children played was, hiding switches, marbles, and maybe others. Later on, some of de nigger boys started playing cards and got to gambling; some went to de woods to gamble.

"The old cotton gins on de farms were made of wooden screws, and it took all day to gin four bales o' cotton.

"I was one of the first trustees that helped build the first colored folks' church in the town of Greenwood. I am the only one now living. I married Alice Robinson, and had five sons and one daughter, and have five or six grandchildren.

"Abraham Lincoln, I think, was a good man; had a big reputation. Couldn't tell much about Jefferson Davis. Booker T. Washington—Everybody thinks he is a great man for the colored race.

"Of course I think slavery was bad. We is free now and better off to work. I think anybody who is any count can work and live by himself.

"I joined de church when I was 17 years old, because a big preaching was going on after freedom for the colored people.

"I think everybody should join the church and do right; can't get anywhere without it, and do good."

Source: William Ballard (88), Greenwood, S. C.
Interviewed by: G. L. Summer, Newberry, S. C. (6/10/37)

Project #1655
W. W. Dixon
Winnsboro, S. C.

# CHARLEY BARBER

## EX-SLAVE 81 YEARS OLD.

Charley Barber lives in a shanty kind of house, situated on a plot of ground containing two acres all his own. It is a mile and a half southeast of Winnsboro, S. C. He lives with an anaemic daughter, Maggie, whose chief interests are a number of cats, about the premises, and a brindled, crumple-horned cow that she ties out to graze every morning and milks at evening.

Charley is squat of figure, short neck, popeyed, and has white hair. He tills the two acres and produces garden truck that he finds a sale for among the employees of the Winnsboro mills, just across the railroad from his home. He likes to talk, and pricks up his ears,(so to speak), whenever anything is related as having occurred in the past. He will importune those present to hear his version of the event unusual.

"Well sah, dis is a pleasure to have you call 'pon me, howsomever it be unexpected dis mornin'. Shoo! (driving the chickens out of the house) Shoo! Git out of here and go scratch a livin' for them chickens, dat's followin' you yet, and you won't wean and git to layin' again. Fust thing you know you'll be spoilin' de floor, when us is got company dis very minute. Scat! Maggie; git them cats out de chairs long 'nough for Mr. Wood to set in one whilst he's come to see me dis mornin'.

"And dat's it? You wants me to talk over de days dat am gone? How dis come 'bout and how dat come 'bout, from de day I was born, to dis very hour? Let's light, up our smokestacks befo' us begin. Maybe you wants a drink of, water. Maggie, fetch de water here!

"How old you think I is, sixty-five? My goodness! Do you hear dat Maggie? (Rubbing his hands; his eyes shining with pleasure) Take another look and make another guess. Seventy-five? You is growin' warm but you'll have to come again!

"Bless your soul Marse Wood, you know what old Mudder Shifton say? She 'low dat: 'In de year 1881, de world to an end will surely come'. I was twenty-five years old when all de niggers and most of de white folks was believin' dat old lady and lookin' for de world to come to an end in 1881. Dat was de year dat I jined de church, 'cause I wanted to make sure dat if de end did come, I'd be caught up in dat rapture dat de white Methodist preacher was preachin' 'bout and explainin' to my marster and mistress at deir house on de piazza dat year.

"I is eighty-one years old. I was born up on de Wateree River, close to Great Falls. My marster was Ozmond Barber. My mistress was name Miss Elizabeth; her de wife of Marse Ozmond. My pappy was name Jacob. My mammy went by de name of Jemima. They both come from Africa where they was born. They was 'ticed on a ship, fetch 'cross de ocean to Virginny, fetch to Winnsboro by a slave drover, and sold to my marster's father. Dat what they tell me. When they was sailin' over, dere was five or six hundred others all together down under de first deck of de ship, where they was locked in. They never did talk lak de other slaves, could just' say a few words, use deir hands, and make signs. They want deir collards, turnips, and deir 'tators, raw. They lak sweet milk so much they steal it.

"Pappy care-nothin' 'bout clothes and wouldn't wear shoes in de winter time or any time. It was 'ginst de law to bring them over here when they did, I learn since. But what is de law now and what was de law then, when bright shiny money was in sight? Money make de automobile go. Money make de train go. Money make de mare go, and at dat time I 'spect money make de ships go. Yes sir, they, my pappy and mammy, was just smuggled in dis part of de world, I bet you!

"War come on, my marster went out as a captain of de Horse Marines. A tune was much sung by de white folks on de place and took wid de niggers. It went lak dis:

> 'I'm Captain Jenks of de Horse Marines
> I feed my horse on corn and beans.
> Oh! I'm Captain Jenks of de Horse Marines
> And captain in de army!'"

"When de Yankees come they seem to have special vengeance for my white folks. They took everything they could carry off and burnt everything they couldn't carry off.

"Mistress and de chillun have to go to Chester to git

a place to sleep and eat, wid kinfolks. De niggers just lay 'round de place 'til master rode in, after de war, on a horse; him have money and friends and git things goin' agin. I stay on dere 'til '76. Then I come to Winnsboro and git a job as section hand laborer on de railroad. Out of de fust money,—(I git paid off de pay train then; company run a special pay train out of Columbia to Charlotte. They stop at every station and pay de hands off at de rear end of de train in cash). Well, as I was a sayin': Out de fust money, I buys me a red shirt and dat November I votes and de fust vote I put in de box was for Governor Wade Hampton. Dat was de fust big thing I done.

"De nex' big thing I done was fall in love wid Mary Wylie. Dat come 'bout on de second pay day. De other nigger gals say her marry me for my money but I never have believed it. White ladies do dat 'kalkilating' trick sometime but you take a blue-gum nigger gal, all wool on de top of her head and lak to dance and jig wid her foots, to pattin' and fiddle music, her ain't gonna have money in de back of her head when her pick out a man to marry. Her gonna want a man wid muscles on his arms and back and I had them. Usin' dat pick and shovel on de railroad just give me what it took to git Mary. Us had ten chillun. Some dead, some marry and leave. My wife die year befo' last. Maggie is puny, as you see, and us gits 'long wid de goodness of de Lord and de white folks.

"I b'longs to de St. John Methodist Church in Middlesix, part of Winnsboro. They was havin' a rival (revival) meetin' de night of de earthquake, last day of August, in 1886. Folks had hardly got over de scare of 1881, 'bout de world comin' to an end. It was on Tuesday night, if I don't disremember, 'bout 9 o'clock. De preacher was prayin', just after de fust sermon, but him never got to de amen part of dat prayer. Dere come a noise or rumblin', lak far off thunder, seem lak it come from de northwest, then de church begin to rock lak a baby's cradle. Dere was great excitement. Old Aunt Melvina holler: 'De world comin' to de end'. De preacher say: 'Oh, Lordy', and run out of de pulpit. Everbody run out de church in de moonlight. When de second quake come, 'bout a minute after de fust, somebody started up de cry: 'De devil under de church! De devil under de church! De devil gwine to take de church on his back and run away wid de church!' People never stop runnin' 'til they got to de court house in town. Dere they 'clare de devil done take St. John's Church on his back and fly away to hell wid it. Marse Henry Galliard make a speech and tell them what it was and beg them to go home. Dat Mr. Skinner, de telegraph man at de depot, say de main part of it was way down 'bout Charleston, too far away for anybody to git hurt here, 'less a brick from a chimney fall on somebody's head. De niggers mostly believes what a fine man, lak Marse Henry, tell them. De crowd git quiet. Some of them go home but many of them, down in de low part of town, set on de railroad track in de moonlight, all night. I was mighty sleepy de nex' mornin' but I work on de railroad track just de same. Dat night folks come back to St. John's Church, find it still dere, and such a outpourin' of de spirit was had as never was had befo' or since.

"Just think! Dat has been fifty-one years ago. Them was de glorious horse and buggy days. Dere was no air-ships, no autos and no radios. White folks had horses to drive. Niggers had mules to ride to a baseball game, to see white folks run lak de patarollers (patrollers) was after them and they holler lak de world was on fire."

United States

Project #1655
W. W. Dixon
Winnsboro, S. C.

# ED BARBER
## Ex-Slave 77 Years Old

Ed Barber lives in a small one-room house in the midst of a cotton field on the plantation of Mr. A. M. Owens, ten miles southeast of Winnsboro, S. C. He lives alone and does his own cooking and housekeeping. He is a bright mulatto, has an erect carriage and posture, appears younger than his age, is intelligent and enjoys recounting the tales of his lifetime. His own race doesn't give him much countenance. His friends in the old days of reconstruction were white people. He presumes on such past affiliation and considers himself better than the full-blooded Negro.

"It's been a long time since I see you. Maybe you has forgot but I ain't forgot de fust time I put dese lookers on you, in '76. Does you 'members dat day? It was in a piece of pines beyond de Presbyterian Church, in Winnsboro, S. C. Us both had red shirts. You was a ridin' a gray pony and I was a ridin' a red mule, sorrel like. You say dat wasn't '76? Well, how come it wasn't? Ouillah Harrison, another nigger, was dere, though he was a man. Both of us got to arguin'. He 'low he could vote for Hampton and

I couldn't, 'cause I wasn't 21. You say it was '78 'stead of '76, dat day in de pines when you was dere? Well! Well! I sho' been thinkin' all dis time it was '76.

"'Member de fight dat day when Mr. Pole Barnadore knock Mr. Blanchard down, while de speakin' was a gwine on? You does? Well, us come to common 'greement on dat, bless God!

"Them was scary times! Me bein' just half nigger and half white man, I knowed which side de butter was on de bread. Who I see dere? Well, dere was a string of red shirts a mile long, dat come into Winnsboro from White Oak. And another from Flint Hill, over de Pea Ferry road, a mile long. De bar-rooms of de town did a big business dat day. Seem lak it was de fashion to git drunk all 'long them days.

"Them red shirts was de monkey wrench in de cotton-gin of de carpet bag party. I's here to tell you. If a nigger git hungry, all he have to do is go to de white folk's house, beg for a red shirt, and explain hisself a democrat. He might not git de shirt right then but he git his belly full of everything de white folks got, and de privilege of comin' to dat trough sometime agin.

"You wants me to tell you 'bout who I is, where I born, and how old I is? Well, just cross examine me and I'll tell you de facts as best I knows how.

"I was born twelve miles east of Winnsboro, S. C. My marster say it was de 18th of January, 1860.

"My mother name Ann. Her b'long to my marster, James Barber. Dat's not a fair question when you ask me who my daddy was. Well, just say he was a white man and dat my mother never did marry nobody, while he lived. I was de onliest child my mother ever had.

"After freedom my mother raised me on de Marse Adam Barber place, up by Rocky Mount and Mitford. I stayed dere 'til all de 'citement of politics die down. My help was not wanted so much at de 'lection boxes, so I got to roamin' 'round to fust one place and then another. But wheresomever I go, I kept a thinkin' 'bout Rosa and de ripe may-pops in de field in cotton pickin' time. I landed back to de Barber place and after a skirmish or two wid de old folks, marry de gal de Lord always 'tended for me to marry. Her name was Rosa Ford. You ask me if she was pretty? Dat's a strange thing. Do you ever hear a white person say a colored woman is pretty? I never have but befo' God when I was trampin' 'round Charleston, dere was a church dere called St. Mark, dat all de society folks of my color went to. No black nigger welcome dere, they told me. Thinkin' as how I was bright 'nough to git in, I up and goes dere one Sunday. Ah, how they did carry on, bow and scrape and ape de white folks. I see some pretty feathers, pretty fans, and pretty women dere! I was uncomfortable all de time though, 'cause they was too 'hifalootin' in de ways, in de singin', and all sorts of carryin' ons.

"Glad you fetch me back to Rosa. Us marry and had ten chillun. Francis, Thompkins, William, Jim, Levi, Ab and Oz is dead. Katie marry a Boykin and is livin' in New York. My wife, Rosa, die on dis place of Mr. Owens.

"I lives in a house by myself. I hoes a little cotton, picks plums and blackberries but dewberries 'bout played out.

"My marster, James Barber, went through de Civil

War and died. I begs you, in de name of de good white folks of '76 and Wade Hampton, not to forget me in dis old age pension business.

"What I think of Abe Lincoln? I think he was a poor buckra white man, to de likes of me. Although, I 'spects Mr. Lincoln meant well but I can't help but wish him had continued splittin' them fence rails, which they say he knowed all 'bout, and never took a hand in runnin' de government of which he knowed nothin' 'bout. Marse Jeff Davis was all right, but him oughta got out and fought some, lak General Lee, General Jackson and 'Poleon Bonaparte. Us might have won de war if he had turned up at some of de big battles lak Gettysburg, 'Chickenmaroger', and 'Applemattox'. What you think 'bout dat?

"Yes sah, I has knowed a whole lot of good white men. Marse General Bratton, Marse Ed P. Mobley, Marse Will Durham, dat owned dis house us now settin' in, and Dr. Henry Gibson. Does I know any good colored men? I sho' does! Dere's Professor Benjamin Russell at Blackstock. You knows him. Then dere was Ouillah Harrison, dat own a four-hoss team and a saddle hoss, in red shirt days. One time de brass band at Winnsboro, S. C. wanted to go to Camden, S. C. to play at de speakin' of Hampton. He took de whole band from Winnsboro to Camden, dat day, free of charge. Ah! De way dat band did play all de way to Ridgeway, down de road to Longtown, cross de Camden Ferry, and right into de town. Dere was horns a blowin', drums a beatin', and people a shoutin': 'Hurrah for Hampton!' Some was a singin': 'Hang Dan Chamberlain on a Sour Apple Tree'. Ouillah come home and found his wife had done had a boy baby. What you reckon? He name dat boy baby, Wade Hampton. When he come home to die, he lay his hand on dat boy's head and say: 'Wade, 'member who you name for and always vote a straight out democrat ticket'. Which dat boy did!"

United States

Project #1655
W. W. Dixon
Winnsboro, S. C.

## MILLIE BARBER
### Ex-Slave 82 Years Old

"Hope you find yourself well dis mornin', white folks. I's just common; 'spect I eats too much yesterday. You know us celebrated yesterday, 'cause it was de Fourth of July. Us had a good dinner on dis 2,000 acre farm of Mr. Owens. God bless dat white boss man! What would us old no 'count niggers do widout him? Dere's six or seven, maybe eight of us out here over eighty years old. 'Most of them is like me, not able to hit a lick of work, yet he take care of us; he sho' does.

"Mr. Owens not a member of de church but he allowed dat he done found out dat it more blessed to give than to receive, in case like us.

"You wants to know all 'bout de slavery time, de war, de Ku Kluxes and everything? My tongue too short to tell you all dat I knows. However, if it was as long as my stockin's, I could tell you a trunk full of good and easy, bad and hard, dat dis old life-stream have run over in eighty-two years. I's hoping to reach at last them green fields of Eden of de Promise Land. 'Scuse me ramblin' 'round, now just ask me questions; I bet I can answer all you ask.

"My pa name, Tom McCullough; him was a slave of old Marster John McCullough, whose big two-story house is de oldest in Fairfield County. It stands today on a high hill, just above de banks of Dutchman Creek. Big road run right by dat house. My mammy name, Nicie. Her b'long to de Weir family; de head of de family die durin' de war of freedom. I's not supposed to know all he done, so I'll pass over dat. My mistress name, Eliza; good mistress. Have you got down dere dat old marster just took sick and die, 'cause he wasn't touched wid a bullet nor de life slashed out of him wid a sword?

"Well, my pa b'longin' to one man and my mammy b'longin' to another, four or five miles apart, caused some confusion, mix-up, and heartaches. My pa have to git a pass to come to see my mammy. He come sometimes widout de pass. Patrollers catch him way up de chimney hidin' one night; they stripped him right befo' mammy and give him thirty-nine lashes, wid her cryin' and a hollerin' louder than he did.

"Us lived in a log house; handmade bedstead, wheat straw mattress, cotton pillows, plenty coverin' and plenty to eat, sich as it was. Us never git butter or sweet milk or coffee. Dat was for de white folks but in de summer time, I minds de flies off de table wid the peafowl feather brush and eat in de kitchen just what de white folks eat; them was very good eatin's I's here for to tell you. All de old slaves and them dat worked in de field, got rations and de chillun were fed at de kitchen out-house. What did they git? I 'members they got peas, hog meat, corn bread, 'lasses, and buttermilk on Sunday, then they got greens, turnips, taters, shallots, collards, and beans through de week. They were kept fat on them kind of rations.

"De fact is I can't 'member us ever had a doctor on de place; just a granny was enough at child birth. Slave women have a baby one day, up and gwine 'round de next day, singin' at her work lak nothin' unusual had happened.

"Did I ever git a whippin'? Dat I did. How many times? More than I can count on fingers and toes. What I git a whippin' for? Oh, just one thing, then another. One time I break a plate while washin' dishes and another time I spilt de milk on de dinin' room floor. It was always for somethin', sir. I needed de whippin'.

"Yes sir, I had two brothers older than me; one sister older than me and one brother younger than me.

"My young marster was killed in de war. Their names was Robert, Smith, and Jimmie. My young mistress, Sarah, married a Sutton and moved to Texas. Nancy marry Mr. Wade Rawls. Miss Janie marry Mr. Hugh Melving. At this marriage my mammy was give to Miss Janie and she was took to Texas wid her young baby, Isaiah, in her arms. I have never seen or heard tell of them from dat day to dis.

"De Yankees come and burn de gin-house and barns. Open de smokehouse, take de meat, give de slaves some, shoot de chickens, and as de mistress and girls beg so hard, they left widout burnin' de dwellin' house.

"My oldest child, Alice, is livin' and is fifty-one years old de 10th of dis last May gone. My first husband was Levi Young; us lived wid Mr. Knox Picket some years after freedom. We moved to Mr. Rubin Lumpkin's plantation, then to George Boulwares. Well, my husband die and I took a fool notion, lak most widows, and got into slavery again. I marry Prince Barber; Mr. John Hollis, Trial Justice, tied de knot. I loved dat young nigger more than you can put down dere on paper, I did. He was black and shiny as a crow's wing. Him was white as snow to dese old eyes. Ah, the joy, de fusses, de ructions, de beatin's, and de makin' ups us had on de Ed Shannon place where us lived. Us stay dere seven long years.

"Then de Klu Kluxes comed and lak to scared de life out of me. They ask where Prince was, searched de house and go away. Prince come home 'bout daylight. Us took fright, went to Marster Will Durham's and asked for advice and protection. Marster Will Durham fixed it up. Next year us moved to dis place, he own it then but Marster Arthur Owens owns it now. Dere is 2,000 acres in dis place and another 1,000 acres in de Rubin Lumpkin place 'joinin' it.

"Prince die on dis place and I is left on de mercy of Marster Arthur, livin' in a house wid two grandchillun, James twelve years, and John Roosevelt Barber, eight years old. Dese boys can work a little. They can pick cotton and tote water in de field for de hands and marster say: 'Every little help'.

"My livin' chillun ain't no help to me. Dere's Willie, I don't know where he is. Prince is wid Mr. Freeman on de river. Maggie is here on de place but she no good to me.

"I 'spect when I gits to drawin' down dat pension de white folks say is comin', then dere will be more folks playin' in my backyard than dere is today."

Project 1655
W. W. Dixon
Winnsboro, S. C.

# ANDERSON BATES
## Ex-Slave 87 Years Old

Anderson Bates lives with his son-in-law and daughter, Ed and Dora Owens, in a three-room frame house, on lands of Mr. Dan Heyward, near the Winnsboro Granite Company, Winnsboro, S. C. Anderson and his wife occupy one of the rooms and his rent is free. His son-in-law has regular employment at the Winnsboro Cotton Mills. His wife, Carrie, looks after the house. Anderson and his daughter, Dora, are day laborers on the neighborhood farms, but he is able to do very little work.

"I was born on de old Dr. Furman place, near Jenkinsville, S. C., in de year, 1850. My pappy was name Nat and mammy name Winnie. They was slaves of old Dr. Furman, dat have a big plantation, one hundred slaves, and a whole lot of little slave chillun, dat him wouldn't let work. They run 'round in de plum thickets, blackberry bushes, hunt wild strawberries, blow cane whistles, and have a good time.

"De old Dr. Furman house is ramshackle but it is still

standin' out dere and is used as a shelter for sawmill hands dat is cuttin' down de big pines and sawin' them on de place.

"Where did my pappy and mammy come from? Mammy was born a slave in de Furman family in Charleston, but pappy was bought out of a drove dat a Baltimore speculator fetch from Maryland long befo' de war. Doctor practice all 'round and 'bout Monticello, happen 'long one day, see my pappy and give a thousand dollars for him, to dat speculator. I thank God for dat!

"Dr. Furman, my old marster, have a brudder called Jim, dat run de Furman School, fust near Winnsboro, then it move to Greenville, S. C.

"My mistress name Nancy. Her was of de quality. Her voice was soft and quiet to de slaves. Her teach us to sing:

> 'Dere is a happy land, far, far 'way,
> Where bright angels stand, far, far 'way,
> Oh! How them angels sing!
> Oh! How them bells ring!
> In dat happy land, far, far 'way!'

"Dere was over a thousand acres, maybe two thousand in dat old Furman place. Them sawmill folks give $30,000.00 for it, last year.

"My pappy and mammy was field hands. My brudders and sisters was: Liddie, Millie, Ria, Ella, Harriet, Thomas, Smith, and Marshall. All dead but me and Marshall.

"I was fifteen when de Yankees come thru. They took off everything, hosses, mules, cows, sheep, goats, turkeys, geese, and chickens. Hogs? Yes sah, they kill hogs and take off what parts they want and leave other parts bleedin' on de yard. When they left, old marster have to go up into Union County for rations.

"Dat's funny, you wants to set down dere 'bout my courtship and weddin'? Well, sir, I stay on de old plantation, work for my old marster, de doctor, and fell head over heels in love wid Carrie. Dere was seven more niggers a flyin' 'round dat sugar lump of a gal in de night time when I breezes in and takes charge of de fireside cheer. I knocks one down one night, kick another out de nex' night, and choke de stuffin' out of one de nex' night. I landed de three-leg stool on de head of de fourth one, de last time. Then de others carry deir 'fections to some other place than Carrie's house. Us have some hard words 'bout my bad manners, but I told her dat I couldn't 'trol my feelin's wid them fools a settin' 'round dere gigglin' wid her. I go clean crazy!

"Then us git married and go to de ten-acre quarry wid Mr. Anderson. I work dere a while and then go to Captain Macfie, then to his son, Wade, and then to Marse Rice Macfie. Then I go back to de quarry, drill and git out stone. They pay me $3.50 a day 'til de Parr Shoals Power come in wid 'lectric power drills and I was cut down to eighty cents a day. Then I say: 'Old grey hoss! Damn 'lectric toolin', I's gwine to leave.' I went to Hopewell, Virginia, and work wid de DuPonts for five years. War come on and they ask me to work on de acid area. De atmosphere dere tear all de skin off my face and arms, but I stuck it out to de end of de big war, for $7.20 a day. I drunk a good deal of liquor then, but I sent money to Carrie all de time and fetch her a roll every fourth of July and on Christmas. After de war they dismantle de plant and I come back to work for Mr. Eleazer, on de Saluda River for $2.00 a day, for five years.

"Carrie have chillun by me. Dere was Anderson, my son, ain't see him in forty years. Essie, my daughter, marry Herbert Perrin. Dora, another daughter, marry Ed Owens. Ed makes good money workin' at de factory in Winnsboro. They have seven chillun. Us tries to keep them chillun in school but they don't have de good times I had when a child, a eatin' cracklin' bread and buttermilk, liver, pig-tails, hog-ears and turnip greens.

"Does I 'member anything 'bout de Klu Kluxes? Jesus, yes! My old marster, de doctor, in goin' 'round, say out loud to people dat Klu Kluxes was doin' some things they ought not to do, by 'stortin' money out of niggers just 'cause they could.

"When he was gone to Union one day, a low-down pair of white men come, wid false faces, to de house and ask where Dick Bell was. Miss Nancy say her don't know. They go hunt for him. Dick made a bee-line for de house. They pull out hoss pistols, fust time, 'pow'. Dick run on, secon' time, 'pow'. Dick run on, third time, 'pow' and as Dick reach de front yard de ball from de third shot keel him over lak a hit rabbit. Old miss run out but they git him. Her say: 'I give you five dollars to let him 'lone.' They say: 'Not 'nough.' Her say: 'I give you ten dollars.' They say: 'Not 'nough.' Her say: 'I give you fifteen dollars.' They say: 'Not 'nough.' Her say: 'I give you twenty-five dollars.' They take de money and say: 'Us'll be back tomorrow for de other Dick.' They mean Dick James.

"Nex' day, us see them a comin' again. Dick James done load up de shotgun wid buckshot. When they was comin' up de front steps, Uncle Dick say to us all in de big house: 'Git out de way!' De names of de men us find out afterwards was Bishop and Fitzgerald. They come up de steps, wid Bishop in de front. Uncle Dick open de door, slap dat gun to his shoulder, and pull de trigger. Dat man Bishop hollers: 'Oh Lordy.' He drop dead and lay dere 'til de coroner come. Fitzgerald leap 'way. They bring Dick to jail, try him right in dat court house over yonder. What did they do wid him? Well, when Marse Bill Stanton, Marse Elisha Ragsdale and Miss Nancy tell 'bout it all from de beginnin' to de end, de judge tell de jury men dat Dick had a right to protect his home, and hisself, and to kill dat white man and to turn him loose. Dat was de end of de Klu Kluxes in Fairfield."

Project 1885-1
From Field Notes
Spartanburg, Dist. 4
April 28. 1937
Edited by:
Elmer Turnage

## MILLIE BATES

### Folk Lore: Folk Tales (Negro)

"I sho members when de soldiers come home from de war. All de women folks, both black as well as white wuz so glad to see 'em back dat we jus jumped up and hollered 'Oh, Lawdy, God bless you.' When you would look around a little, you would see some widout an arm or maybe dey would be a walkin' wid a cruch or a stick. Den you would cry some widout lettin your white folks see you. But Jane, de worsest time of all fer us darkies wuz when de Ku Klux killed Dan Black. We wuz little chilluns a playin' in Dans house. We didn't know he had done nothin' ginst de white folks. Us wuz a playin by de fire jus as nice when something hit on de wall. Dan, he jump up and try to git outten de winder. A white spooky thing had done come in de doo' right by me. I was so scairt dat I could not git up. I had done fell straight out on de flo'. When Dan stick his head outten dat winder something say bang and he fell right down in de flo'. I crawles under de bed. When I got dar, all de other chilluns wuz dar to, lookin' as white as ashed dough from hickory wood. Us peeped out and den us duck under de bed agin. Ain't no bed ebber done as much good as dat one. Den a whole lot of dem come in de house. De wuz all white and scairy lookin'. It still makes de shivvers run down my spine and here I is ole and you all a settin' around wid me and two mo' wars done gone since dat awful time. Dan Black, he wo'nt no mo' kaise dey took dat nigger and hung him to a simmon tree. Dey would not let his folks take him down either. He jus stayed dar till he fell to pieces.

"After dat when us chilluns seed de Ku Klux a comin', us would take an' run breakneck speed to de nearest wood. Dar we would stay till dey wuz plum out o' sight and you could not even hear de horses feet. Dem days wuz worse'n de war. Yes Lawd, dey wuz worse'n any war I is ebber heard of.

"Was not long after dat fore de spooks wuz a gwine round ebber whar. When you would go out atter dark, somethin' would start to a haintin' ye. You would git so scairt dat you would mighty ni run every time you went out atter dark; even iffin you didn't see nothin'. Chile, don't axe me what I seed. Atter all dat killin' and a burnin' you know you wuz bliged to see things wid all dem spirits in distress a gwine all over de land. You see, it is like dis, when a man gits killed befo he is done what de good Lawd intended fer him to do, he comes back here and tries to find who done him wrong. I mean he don' come back hisself, but de spirit, it is what comes and wanders around. Course, it can't do nothin', so it jus scares folks and haints dem."

Source: "Aunt" Millie Bates, 25 Hamlet street, Union, S. C.
Interviewer: Caldwell Sims, Union, S. C.

United States

Project #1655
Mrs. Genevieve W. Chandler
Murrells Inlet, S. C.
Georgetown County

# UNCLE WELCOME BEES

## Visit With Uncle Welcome Bees—Age 104 Years

The road is perfectly camouflaged from the King's Highway by wild plums that lap overhead. Only those who have traveled this way before could locate the 'turn in' to Uncle Welcome's house. When you have turned in and come suddenly out from the plum thicket you find your road winding along with cultivated patches on the left—corn and peas—a fenced-in garden, the palings riven out by hand, and thick dark woods on the left. A lonesome, untenanted cabin is seemingly in the way but your car swings to the left instead of climbing the door-step and suddenly you find you are facing a bog. The car may get through; it may not. So you switch off and just sit a minute, seeing how the land lies. A great singing and chopping of wood off to the left have kept the inmates from hearing the approach of a car. When you rap therefore you hear, 'Come in'.

A narrow hall runs through to the back porch and off this hall on your right opens a door from beyond which comes a very musical squeaking—you know a rocking chair is going hard—even before you see it in motion with a fuzzy little head that rests on someone's shoulder sticking over the top. And the fuzzy head which in size is like a small five-cent cocoanut, belongs to Uncle Welcome's great-grand. On seeing a visitor the grand, the mother of the infant, rises and smiles greeting, and, learning your errand, points back to the kitchen to show where Uncle Welcome sits. You step down one step and ask him if you may come in and he pats a chair by his side. The old man isn't so spry as he was when you saw him in the fall; the winter has been hard. But here it is warm again and at most four in the April afternoon, he sits over his plate of hopping John—he and innumerable flies. At his feet, fairly under the front of a small iron stove, sits another great-grand with a plate of peas between her legs. Peas and rice, 'hopping John'. (Someone says peas and hominy cooked together makes "limping Lizzie in the Low-Country." But that is another story.)

"Uncle Welcome, isn't Uncle Jeemes Stuart the oldest liver on Sandy Island?" Welcome: "Jeemes Stuart? I was married man when he born. Jeemes rice-field. (Worker in rice-field) posed himself. In all kinds of weather. Cut you down, down, down. Jeemes second wife gal been married before but her husband dead.

"I couldn't tell the date or time I born. Your Maussa (Master) take it down. When I been marry, Dr. Ward Fadder (Father) aint been marry yet. My mother had twelve head born Oatland. He bought my mother from Virginia. Dolly. Sam her husband name. Sam come from same course. When my mother been bought, her been young woman. Work in rice. Plow right now (Meaning April is time to plow rice fields). I do carpenter work and mind horse for plantation. Come from Georgetown in boat. Have you own carriage. Go anywhere you want to go. Oatland church build for colored people and po-buckra. I helped build that church. The boss man, Mr. Bettman. My son Isaac sixty-nine. If him sixty-nine, I one hundred four. That's my record. Maussa didn't low you to marry till you twenty-two. Ben Allston own Turkey Hill. When him dead, I was twelve years old. Me! (Knocking his chest)"

    Welcome Bees—
    Parkersville, S. C.
    (Near Waverly Mills, S. C.)
    Age 104.

Project #1655
W. W. Dixon
Winnsboro, S. C.

# ANNE BELL

## Ex-Slave 83 Years Old.
## [Hw: (Near Winnsboro, S. C.)]

Anne Bell lives with her niece, in a one-room annex to a two-room frame house, on the plantation of Mr. Lake Howze, six miles west of Winnsboro, S. C. Her niece's husband, Golden Byrd, is a share-cropper on Mr. Howze's place. The old lady is still spry and energetic about the cares of housekeeping and attention to the small children of her niece. She is a delightful old lady and well worth her keep in the small chores she undertakes and performs in the household.

"My marster was John Glazier Rabb; us call him Marse Glazier. My mistress was Nancy Kincaid Watts; us call her Miss Nancy. They lived on a big plantation in Fairfield County and dere I come into dis world, eighty-three years ago, 10th day of April past.

"My pappy name just Andy but after de freedom, he took de name of Andrew Watts. My old mammy was Harriett but she come to you if you calls her Hattie. My brudders was Jake and Rafe. My sister name Charity.

They all dead and gone to glory long time ago; left me here 'lone by myself and I's settin' here tellin' you 'bout them.

"My mammy was de cook at de 'Big House' for marster, Miss Nancy, and de chillun. Let me see if I can call them over in my mind. Dere was Marse John, went off to de war, color bearer at Seven Pines. Yes sir, him was killed wid de colors a flyin' in his hand. Heard tell of it many times. He lies right now in de old Buck Church graveyard. De pine trees, seven of them, cry and sob 'round him every August 6th; dat's de day he was killed. Oh, my God!

"Marse James went wid old Colonel Rion. They say he got shot but bullets couldn't kill him. No, bless God! Him comed back. Then come Marse Clarence. He went wid Captain Jim Macfie, went through it all and didn't get a scratch. Next was Miss Jesse. Then come Marse Horace, and Miss Nina. Us chillun all played together. Marse Horace is livin' yet and is a fine A. R.P. preacher of de Word. Miss Nina a rich lady, got plantation but live 'mong de big bugs in Winnsboro. She married Mr. Castles; she is a widow now. He was a good man, but he dead now.

"De one I minds next, is Charlie. I nussed him. He married Colonel Province's daughter. Dat's all I can call to mind, right now.

"Course de white folks I b'longs to, had more slaves than I got fingers and toes; whole families of them. De carpenter and de blacksmith on de place made de bedsteads. Us had good wheat straw mattresses to sleep on; cotton quilts, spreads, and cotton pillows. No trouble to sleep but it was hard to hear dat white overseer say at day break: 'Let me hear them foots hit de floor and dat befo' I go! Be lively! Hear me?' And you had to answer, 'Yas sah', befo' he'd move on to de nex' house. I does 'member de parts of de bed, was held together by wooden pins. I sho' 'members dat!

"Mammy Harriett was de cook. I didn't done no work but 'tend to de chillun and tote water.

"Money? Go 'way from here, boss! Lord, no sir, I never saw no money. What I want wid it anyhow?

"How did they feed us? Had better things to eat then, than now and more different kind of somethin's. Us had pears, 'lasses, shorts, middlings of de wheat, corn bread, and all kinds of milk and vegetables.

"Got a whuppin' once. They wanted me to go after de turkeys and I didn't want to go past de graveyard, where de turkeys was. I sho' didn't want to go by them graves. I's scared now to go by a graveyard in de dark. I took de whuppin' and somebody else must have got de turkeys. Sho' I didn't drive them up!

"Slaves spun de thread, loomed de cloth, and made de clothes for de plantation. Don't believe I had any shoes. I was just a small gal anyhow then, didn't need them and didn't want them.

"Yes, I's seen nigger women plow. Church? I wouldn't fool you, all de slaves big enough and not sick, had to go to church on de Sabbath.

"They give us a half Saturday, to do as we like.

"I was 'bout ten years old when de Yankees come. They was full to de brim wid mischief. They took de frocks out de presses and put them on and laugh and carry on powerful. Befo' they went they took everything. They took de meat and 'visions out de smoke-house, and de 'lasses, sugar, flour, and meal out de house. Killed de pigs and cows, burnt de gin-house and cotton, and took off de live stock, geese, chickens and turkeys.

"After de freedom, I stayed on wid mammy right dere, 'til I married Levi Bell. I's had two chillun. Dis my grand-daughter, I visitin'. I never 'spects to have as good a home as I had in slavery time, 'til I gits my title to dat mansion in de sky. Dats de reason I likes to sing dat old plantation spiritual, 'Swing Low Sweet Chariot, Jesus Gwinter Carry me Home'. Does I believe in 'ligion? What else good for colored folks? I ask you if dere ain't a heaven, what's colored folks got to look forward to? They can't git anywhere down here. De only joy they can have here, is servin' and lovin'; us can git dat in 'ligion but dere is a limit to de nigger in everything else. Course I knows my place in dis world; I 'umbles myself here to be 'zalted up yonder."

Project 1885-1
FOLKLORE
Spartanburg, Dist. 4
July 26, 1937
Edited by:
Elmer Turnage

# MISS CAROLINE BEVIS
## SLAVERY REMINISCENCES

"I was raised in the wood across the road about 200 yards from here. I was very mischievous. My parents were honest and were Christians. I loved them very much. My father was William Bevis, who died at the age of eighty. Miss Zelia Hames of Pea Ridge was my mother. My parents are buried at Bethlehem Methodist Church. I was brought up in Methodism and I do not know anything else. I had two brothers and four sisters. My twin sister died last April 1937. She was Fannie Holcombe. I was in bed with pneumonia at the time of her death and of course I could not go to the funeral. For a month, I was unconscious.

"When I was a little girl I played 'Andy-over' with a ball, in the moonlight. Later I went to parties and dances. Calico, chambric and gingham were the materials which our party dresses were made of.

"My grandmother, Mrs. Phoebe Bevis used to tell Revolutionary stories and sing songs that were sung during that period. Grandmother knew some Tories. She always told me that old Nat Gist was a Tory ... that is the way he got rich.

"Hampton was elected governor the morning my mother died. Father went in his carriage to Jonesville to vote for Hampton. We all thought that Hampton was fine.

"When I was a school girl I used the blue back speller. My sweetheart's name was Ben Harris. We went to Bethlehem to school. Jeff and Bill Harris were our teachers. I was thirteen. We went together for six years. The Confederate War commenced. He was very handsome. He had black eyes and black hair. I had seven curls on one side of my head and seven on the other. He was twenty-four when he joined the 'Boys of Sixteen'.

"He wanted to marry me then, but father would not let us marry. He kissed me good bye and went off to Virginia. He was a picket and was killed while on duty at Mars Hill. Bill Harris was in a tent nearby and heard the shot. He brought Ben home. I went to the funeral. I have never been much in-love since then.

"I hardly ever feel sad. I did not feel especially sad during the war. I made socks, gloves and sweaters for the Confederate soldiers and also knitted for the World War soldiers. During the war, there were three looms and three shuttles in our house.

"I went often to the muster grounds at Kelton to see the soldiers drill and to flirt my curls at them. Pa always went with me to the muster field. Once he invited four recruits to dine with us. We had a delicious supper. That was before the Confederacy was paralyzed. Two darkies waited on our table that night, Dorcas and Charlotte. A fire burned in our big fireplace and a lamp hung over the table. After supper was over, we all sat around the fire in its flickering light.

"My next lover was Jess Holt and he was drowned in the Mississippi River. He was a carpenter and was building a warf on the river. He fell in and was drowned in a whirlpool."

> Source: Miss Caroline Bevis (W. 96), County Home, Union, S. C.
> Interviewer: Caldwell Sims, Union, S. C. (7/13/37)

Prepared by Annie Ruth Davis
Place, Marion, S. C.
Date, June 21, 1937

# MAGGIE BLACK
## Ex-Slave, 79 Years

"Honey, I don' know wha' to tell yuh 'bout dem times back dere. Yuh see I wus jes uh young child when de free war close en I ain' know much to tell yuh. I born o'er de river dere to Massa Jim Wilkerson plantation. Don' know wha' 'come uv my ole Massa chillun a'ter dey head been gone. Yuh see, honey, Massa Jim Wilkerson hab uh heap uv slave en he hire my mudder out to Colonel Durant place right down de road dere whey Miss Durant lib now. Coase I been back o'er de river to visit 'mongest de peoples dere a'ter freedom wuz 'clare, but I ain' ne'er lib dere no more."

"Gawd been good to me, honey. I been heah uh long ole time en I can' see mucha dese days, but I gettin' 'long sorta so-so. I wuz train up to be uh nu'se 'oman en I betcha I got chillun more den any 60 year ole 'bout heah now dat I nu'se when dey wuz fust come heah. No, honey, ain' got no chillun uv me own. Aw my chillun white lak yuh."

"No, no'mam, dey wear long ole frock den en uh girl

comin' on dere when dey ge' to be any kind uv uh girl, dey put dat frock down. Oh, my child, dey can' ge' em short 'nough dese days. Ain' hab nuthin but uh string on dese day en time. Dey use'er wear dem big ole hoop skirt dat sit out broad lak from de ankle en den dey wear little panty dat show down twixt dey skirt en dey ankle. Jes tie em 'round dey knees wid some sorta string en le' em show dat way 'bout dey ankle. I 'member we black chillun'ud go in de woods en ge' wild grape vine en bend em round en put em under us skirt en make it stand out big lak. Hadder hab uh big ole ring fa de bottom uv de skirt en den one uh little bit smaller eve'y time dey ge' closer to de waist. Ne'er hab none tall in de waist cause dat wuz s'ppose to be little bitty t'ing."

"Dey weave aw de cloth dey use den right dere on de plantation. Wear cotton en woolens aw de time den. Coase de Madam, she could go en ge' de finest kind uv silk cause mos' uv her t'ing come from 'broad. Child, I c'n see my ole mammy how she look workin' dat spinning wheel jes us good uz ef dat day wuz dis day right heah. She set dere at dat ole spinning wheel en take one shettle en t'row it one way en den annuder de udder way en pull dat t'ing en make it tighter en tighter. Sumptin say zum, zum, zum, en den yuh hadder work yuh feet dere too. Dat wuz de way dey make dey cloth dat day en time."

"Honey, peoples hadder work dey hand fa eve'yt'ing dey hab mos' den. Dey grew dey own rice right dere on de plantation in dem days. Hadder plant it on some uv de land wha' wuz weter den de udder land wuz. Dey hadder le' de rice ge' good en ripe en den dey'ud cut it en hab one uv dem big rice whipping days. Heap uv people come from plantation aw 'bout en help whip dat rice. Dey jes take de rice en beat it 'cross some hoes dat dey hab fix up somewhey dere on de plantation. Honey, dey hab hoss jes lak dese hoss yuh see carpenter use 'boat heah dese days. Dey'ud hab hundreds uv bushels uv dat rice dere. Den when dey ge' t'rough, dey hab big supper dere fa aw dem wha' whip rice. Gi'e em aw de rice en hog head dey is e'er wan'. Man, dey'ud hab de nicest kind uv music dere. Knock dem bones togedder en slap en pat dey hands to aw kind uv pretty tune."

"Dem dey hab rice mortars right dere on de plantation wha' dey fix de rice in jes uz nice. Now dey hab to take it to de mill. Yuh see dey hab uh big block outer in de yard wid uh big hole in it dat dey put de rice in en take dese t'ing call pestles en beat down on it en dat wha' knock de shaft offen it. Coase dey ne'er hab no nice pretty rice lak yuh see dese days cause it wusn't uz white uz de rice dat dey hab 'boat heah dis day en time, but it wuz mighty sweet rice, honey, mighty sweet rice."

"No'mam, didn't hab no schools tall den. Ne'er gi'e de colored peoples no l'arnin' no whey 'fore freedom 'clare. Wha' little l'arnin' come my way wuz wha' I ge' when I stay wid Miss Martha Leggett down dere to Leggett's Mill Pond. A'ter freedom 'clare, uh lady from de north come dere en Miss Leggett send we chillun to school to dat lady up on de hill dere in de woods. No, honey, yah ain' ne'er see no bresh tent 'bout heah dis day en time. Dis jes de way it waz make. Dey dig four big holes en put postes in aw four corner 'bout lak uh room. Den dey lay log 'cross de top uv dat en kiver it aw o'er wid bresh (brush) dat dey break outer de woods. Ne'er hab none uv de side shet up. En dey haul log dere en roll em under dat bresh tent fa we chillun to set on. Oh, de teacher'ud hab uh big box fa her stand jes lak uh preacher. Eve'ybody dat go to school dere hab one uv dem t'ing call slate dat yah ne'er hadder do nuthin but jes wash it offen. En dey hab dese ole l'arnin' book wha' yuh call Websters."

"My white folks al'ays waz good to me, honey. Ne'er didn't nab to do no field work in aw me life. When I stay dere wid Miss Leggett, I hadder pick up little chip 'bout de yard when I fust come home from school en den I hadder go 'way up in de big field en drib de turkeys up. We didn't find dat no hard t'ing to do lak de peoples talk lak it sumptin hard to do dese days. We wuz l'arnt to work en didn't mind it neither. Al'ays minded to us own business."

"Oh, gourds waz de t'ing in dem days. Dey waz wha' de peoples hab to drink outer en wash dey hominy en rice in aw de time. Dey was de bestest kind uv bowl fa we chillun to eat corn bread en clabber outer. Peoples dis day en time don' hab no sech crockery lak de people use'er hab. Honey, day hab de prettiest little clay bowls den."

"Annuder t'ing de peoples do den dat yuh ain' ne'er hear 'bout nobody doing dese days, dey al'ays boil sumptin fa dey cows to eat lak peas en corn in uh big ole black pot somewhey dere in de back lot. Coase it wuz jes half cooked, but day sho' done dat. Nobody ne'er t'ought 'bout not cookin' fa dey cow den."

"Dat was sho' uh different day from dis, honey. De little chillun wus jes uz foolish den cause de peoples ne'er tell dem 'bout nuthin tall in dat day en time. Aw dese little chillun 'bout heah dese days don' hab no shame 'bout em no whey. Dey hab head full uv eve'yt'ing, honey, aw sorta grown people knowings."

Source: Maggie Black, ex-slave, age 79, Marion, S. C. Personal interview, June 1937

United States

Project 1885 -1-
District #4
Spartanburg, S. C.
June 7, 1937

# GORDON BLUFORD

## Folklore: Ex-Slaves

"I was born in Laurens County, S. C., at the 'brick house', which is close to Newberry County line, and my master was Dr. Felix Calmes. The old brick house is still there. My daddy was Joe Grazier and my mammy, Nellie Grazier.

"We had a pretty good house to live in in slavery time, and some fair things to eat, but never was paid any money. We had plenty to eat like fat meat, turnips, cabbages, cornbread, milk and pot-liquor. Master sent his corn and apples, and his peaches to old man Scruggs at Helena, near Newberry, to have him make his whiskey, brandy, and wine for him. Old man Scruggs was good at that business. The men hunted some, squirrels, rabbits, possums, and birds.

"In the winter time I didn't have much clothes, and no shoes. At nights I carded and spinned on the mistress's wheels, helping my mammy. Then we got old woman Wilson to weave for us.

"Master had a big plantation of several farms, near about 1,000 acres or more. It was said he had once 250 slaves on his places, counting children and all. His overseers had to whip the slaves, master told them to, and told them to whip them hard. Master Calmes was most always mean to us. He got mad spells and whip like the mischief. He all the time whipping me 'cause I wouldn't work like he wanted. I worked in the big house, washed, ironed, cleaned up, and was nurse in the house when war was going on.

"We didn't have a chance to learn to read and write, and master said if he caught any of his slaves trying to learn he would 'skin them alive'.

"There was a church in the neighborhood on Dr. Blackburn's place, but we didn't get to go to it much. I was 17 years old when I joined the church. I joined because the rest of the girls joined. I think everybody ought to join the church.

"On Saturday afternoons the slaves had to work, and all day Sunday, too, if master wanted them. On Christmas Day we was give liquor to get drunk on, but didn't have no dinner.

"When I was sick old Dr. P. B. Ruff attended me. Old Dr. Calmes, I 'member, traveled on a horse, with saddle-bag behind him, and made his own medicines. He made pills from cornbread.

"I saw many slaves sold on the block—saw mammy with little infant taken away from her baby and sent away. I saw families separated from each other, some going to one white master and some to another.

"I married at 14 years old to Arthur Bluford. We had 10 children. I now have about 8 grandchildren and about 7 or 8 great-grandchildren. I was married in the town of Newberry at the white folk's Methodist church, by a colored preacher named Rev. Geo. De Walt.

"When freedom come, they left and hired out to other people, but I stayed and was hired out to a man who tried to whip me, but I ran away. Dat was after I married and had little baby. I told my mammy to look after my little baby 'cause I was gone. I stayed away two years 'till after Dr. Calmes and his family moved to Mississippi."

    Source: Gordon Bluford (92), Newberry, S. C.
    Interviewer: G. Leland Summer, 1707 Lindsey St., Newberry, S. C.

Project #1655
Henry Grant
Columbia, S. C.

# SAMUEL BOULWARE
## Ex-Slave 82 Years Old

Samuel Boulware's only home is one basement room, in the home of colored friends, for which no rent charges are made. He is old and feeble and has poor eyesight, yet, he is self-supporting by doing light odd jobs, mostly for white people. He has never married, hence no dependents whatever. One of the members of the house, in which Samuel lives, told him someone on the front porch wanted to talk with him.

From his dingy basement room he slowly mounted the steps and came toward the front door with an irregular shamble. One seeing his approach would naturally be of the opinion, that this old darkey was certainly nearing the hundred year mark. Apparently Father Time had almost caught up with him; he had been caught in the winds of affliction and now he was tottering along with a bent and twisted frame, which for many years in the past, housed a veritable physical giant. The winds of 82 years had blown over him and now he was calmly and humbly approaching the end of his days. Humility was his attitude, a characteristic purely attributable to the genuine and old-fashion southern Negro. He slid into a nearby chair and began talking in a plain conversational way.

"Dis is a mighty hot day white folks but you knows dis is July and us gits de hot days in dis month. De older I gits de more I feels de hot and de cold. I has been a strong, hard working man most all my life and if it wasn't for dis rheumatism I has in my right leg, I could work hard every day now.

"Does I 'member much 'bout slavery times? Well, dere is no way for me to disremember, unless I die. My mammy and me b'long to Doctor Hunter, some called him Major Hunter. When I was a small boy, I lived wid my mammy on de Hunter plantation. After freedom, I took de name of my daddy, who was a Boulware. He b'long to Reuben Boulware, who had a plantation two and one-half miles from Ridgeway, S. C., on de road dat leads to Longtown. My mistress' name was Effie. She and marster had four sons, no girls a-tall. George, Abram, Willie, and Henry, was their names. They was fine boys, 'cause they was raised by Mistress Effie's own hands. She was a good woman and done things 'zackly right 'round de plantation. Us slaves loved her, 'cause she said kind and soft words to us. Many times I's seen her pat de little niggers on de head, smile and say nice words to them. Boss, kind treatment done good then and it sho' does good dis present day; don't you think I's right 'bout dat? Marster had a bad temper. When he git mad, he walk fast, dis way and dat way, and when he stop, would say terrible cuss words. When de mistress heard them bad words, she would bow her pretty head and walk 'way kinda sad lak. It hurt us slaves to see de mistress sad, 'cause us wanted to see her smilin' and happy all de time.

"My mammy worked hard in de field every day and as I was just a small boy, I toted water to de hands in de field and fetched wood into de kitchen to cook wid. Mammy was de mother of twelve chillun; three of them die when they was babies. I's de oldest of de twelve and has done more hard work than de rest. I had five brothers and all of them is dead, 'cept one dat lives in Savannah, Georgia. I has four sisters, one living in Charleston, one in New York City, one in Ithaca, N. Y., and one in Fairfield County, dis State.

"Does my folks help me along any? No sir, they sho' don't. I gits nothin' from them, and I don't expect nothin' neither. Boss, a nigger's kinfolks is worse than a stranger to them; they thinks and acts for theirselves and no one else. I knows I's a nigger and I tries to know my place. If white folks had drapped us long time ago, us would now be next to de rovin' beasts of de woods. Slavery was hard I knows but it had to be, it seem lak. They tells me they eats each other in Africa. Us don't do dat and you knows dat is a heap to us.

"Us had plenty to eat in slavery time. It wasn't de best but it filled us up and give us strength 'nough to work. Marster would buy a years rations on de first of every year and when he git it, he would have some cooked and would set down and eat a meal of it. IIe would tell us it didn't hurt him, so it won't hurt us. Dats de kind of food us slaves had to eat all de year. Of course, us got a heap of vegetables and fruits in de summer season, but sich as dat didn't do to work on, in de long summer days.

"Marster was good, in a way, to his slaves but dat overseer of his name John Parker, was mean to us sometimes. He was good to some and bad to others. He strung us up when he done de whippin'. My mammy got many whippin's on 'count of her short temper. When she got mad, she would talk back to de overseer, and dat would make him madder than anything else she could do.

"Marster had over twenty grown slaves all de time. He bought and sold them whenever he wanted to. It was sad times to see mother and chillun separated. I's seen de slave speculator cut de little nigger chillun with keen leather whips, 'cause they'd cry and run after de wagon dat was takin' their mammies away after they was sold.

"De overseer was poor white folks, if dats what you is askin' 'bout, and dat is one thing dat made him so hard on de slaves of de plantation. All de overseers I knowed 'bout was poor white folks; they was white folks in de neighborhood dat wasn't able to own slaves. All dis class of people was called by us niggers, poor white folks.

"Us slaves had no schoolin', 'cause dere was no teacher and school nigh our plantation. I has learnt to read a little since I got grown. Spelling come to me natural. I can spell 'most any word I hears, old as I is.

"Marster and mistress was Baptist in 'ligious faith, and b'long to Concord Baptist Church. Us slaves was allowed to 'tend dat church, too. Us set up in de gallery and jined in de singin' every Sunday. Us slaves could jine Concord Church but Doctor Durham, who was de preacher, would take de slaves in another room from de white folks, and git their 'fessions, then he would jine them to de church.

"My daddy was a slave on Reuben Boulware's plantation, 'bout two miles from Marster Hunter's place. He would git a pass to come to see mammy once every week. If he come more than dat he would have to skeedaddle through de woods and fields from de patrollers. If they ketched him widout a pass, he was sho' in for a skin crackin' whippin'. He knowed all dat but he would slip to see mammy anyhow, whippin' or not.

"Most them there patrollers was poor white folks, I believes. Rich folks stay in their house at night, 'less they has some sort of big frolic amongst theirselves. Poor white folks had to hustle 'round to make a living, so, they hired out theirselves to slave owners and rode de roads at night and whipped niggers if they ketched any off their plantation widout a pass. I has found dat if you gives to some poor folks, white or black, something a little better than they is used to, they is sho' gwine to think too high of theirselves soon, dats right. I sho' believes dat, as much as I believes I's setting in dis chair talkin' to you.

"I 'members lak yesterday, de Yankees comin' 'long. Marster tried to hide the best stuff on de plantation but some of de slaves dat helped him hide it, showed de Yankee soldiers just where it was, when they come dere. They say: 'Here is de stuff, hid here, 'cause us put it dere.' Then de soldiers went straight to de place where de valuables was hid and dug them out and took them, it sho' set old marster down. Us slaves was sorry dat day for marster and mistress. They was gittin' old, and now they had lost all they had, and more that dat, they knowed their slaves was set free. De soldiers took all de good hosses, fat cattle, chickens, de meat in de smoke house, and then burnt all empty houses. They left de ones dat folks lived in. De Yankees 'pear to me, to be lookin' for things to eat, more than anything else.

"Does I believe in 'ligion? Dat is all us has in dis world to live by and it's gwine to be de onliest thing to die wid. Belief in God and a 'umble spirit is how I's tryin' to live these days. I was christened fust a Methodist, but when I growed up, I jine de Presbyterian Church and has 'mained a member of dat church every since.

"Thank God I's had 'nough sense not to believe in haunts and sich things. I has 'possum hunt at night by myself in graveyards and I ain't seen one yet. My mammy say she see haunts pass her wid no heads but these old eyes has never seen anything lak dat. If you has done somebody a terrible wrong, then I believes dat person when they die, will 'pear to you on 'count of dat."

Project 1885-1
Folklore
Spartanburg, Dist. 4
Feb. 7, 1938
Edited by:
Elmer Turnage

# MR. JOHN BOYD

## Reminiscences: The Red Shirts
[Hw: Boyd]

"The Red Shirts had a big parade and barbecue in Spartanburg. They met at the courthouse. There were about 500 Red Shirts, besides others who made up a big crowd. I remember four leaders who came from Union County. One of the companies was led by Squire Gilliam Jeter, and one by Squire Bill Lyles. The company from the city was led by Capt. James Douglass and 'Buck' Kelley from Pea Ridge was there with his company.

"Everything drilled in Spartanburg that day. The speakers of the day from Union were Squire Jeter and Capt. Douglass. While they were speaking, old Squire George Tucker from lower Fish Dam came with his company. Mr. Harrison Sartor, father of Will Sartor, was one of the captains. We saw Gen. Wade Hampton and old man Ben Tillman there.

"About this time I was bound out to Mr. Jim Gregory, a blacksmith. The wealthy landlords bought negroes. Mr. Jim Gregory was the blacksmith for old Johnny Meador and Aunt Polly, his wife. He told me that Uncle Johnny bought a man, Heath, for $3,500. He also bought Heath's wife, Morrow, for Aunt Polly, but I don't know what he paid. The Meador house is just this side of Simstown. Aunt Polly's father, Triplett Meador, built that mansion. The brick were made in a home kiln which was near the house. Aunt Polly was a little girl when the house was built. While the brick for the sitting-room fireplace were still wet, he made little Polly step on each one of them to make the impression of her feet. So those foot prints in that fireplace are Aunt Polly's when she was five years old. She grew up there and married, and lived there until her death.

"Miss Ida Knight's house (formerly the Sims house) was built not later than 1840. Dr. Thompson lived there first. Dr. Billy Sims married Dr. Thompson's sister, Miss Patsy, and that is how the house got into the Sims family. The old post office was known as Simstown, and I believe it was up near the Nat Gist mansion. Simstown was the name for the river community for years, because the Sims settled there and they were equally or more prominent than the Thompsons and Gists in that community. All the Sims men were country doctors.

"To this community at the close of the Confederate War, came old man Ogle Tate, his wife, and Ben Shell, as refugees, fleeing from the Yankees. When they came into the community, Nat Gist gave them a nice house to live in on his plantation.

"Mr. Gregory got all the sheet iron used on the Meador

and Gist plantations, and also on the Sims and Thompson plantations. Plows were made in his blacksmith shop from 10 inch sheet iron. The sheet was heated and beaten into shape with his hammer. After cooling, the tools could be sharpened. Horse and mule shoes were made from slender iron rods, bought for that purpose. They were called 'slats', and this grade of iron was known as 'slat iron'. The shoe was moulded while hot, and beaten into the correct shape to fit the animal's foot. Those old shoes fit much better than the store-bought ones of more recent days. The horseshoe nails were made there, too. In fact, every farm implement of iron was made from flat or sheet iron.

"I spun the first pants that I wore. Ma sewed them for me, and wove and finished them with her hands. She made the thread that they were sewed with by hand on the loom. I made cloth for all my shirts. I wore home-made cotton underwear in summer and winter, for we were poor. Of course my winter clothes were heavier.

"We raised some sheep, and the winter woolens were made from the wool sheared from the sheep every May. Wool was taken to the factory at Bivensville and there made into yarn. Often, cotton was swapped for yarn to warp at home. Then ma ran it off on spools for her loom. 'Sleigh hammers' were made from cane gotten off the creek banks and bottoms.

"Aunt Polly Meador had no patrollers on her place. She would not allow one there, for she did her own patrolling with her own whip and two bull dogs. She never had an overseer on her place, either. Neither did she let Uncle Johnny do the whipping. Those two dogs held them and she did her own whipping. One night she went to the quarter and found old 'Bill Pea Legs' there after one of her negro women. He crawled under the bed when he heard Aunt Polly coming. Those dogs pulled old 'Pea Legs' out and she gave him a whipping that he never forgot. She whipped the woman, also.

"Morg was Morrow's nickname. Morg used to sit on the meat block and cut the meat for Aunt Polly to give out. Morg would eat her three pounds of raw meat right there. Uncle Johnny asked her what she would do all the week without any meat, she said that she would take the skin and grease her mouth every morning; then go on to the field or house and do her work, and wait until the next Saturday for more.

"I do not know how old I am, but I well remember when Wheeler's men came to the plantation. They tore up everything. We heard that they were coming, so we dug holes and buried the meat and everything we could. We hid them so well that we could never find some of them ourselves. Wheeler and 36 men stopped on the Dick Jeter place. I think that was in 1864. The Jeter place touched Miss Polly's plantation. The Jeter place was right near Neal Shoals on Broad River. Mr. Jeter had the biggest gin house in the entire township. Old Mr. Dick was at home because he was too old to go to the war. Pa was still in the war then, of course. Ma and I and one of the other children and a few darkies were at our home.

"We saw Wheeler and his men when they stopped at that gin house. They began to ransack immediately. Wheeler gave some orders to his men and galloped off towards our house. The negroes ran but ma and I stayed in the house. Wheeler rode up in front of the door and spoke to my mother. He said that he had to feed his men and horses and asked her where the corn was. She told him that the gin house and the crib which contained the corn did not belong to her, so she could not give him the keys. At that he ordered his men to remove a log from the crib. By this means they broke into the crib and got all the corn. They then ransacked the house and took everything there was to eat. They tore out the big cog wheel in the gin and camped in it for the night. Next morning they set fire to the gin and then galloped away. Soon Mr. Jeter's big gin had gone up in flames. They took all of our corn and all of the fodder, 200 bundles that we had in the barn, away with them."

Source: Mr. John Boyd, County Home, Union, R. F. D.
Interviewer: Caldwell Sims, Union, S. C. 1/26/38

United States

Project 1885-1
FOLKLORE
Spartanburg Dist. 4
May 24, 1937
Edited by: Elmer Turnage

# JANE BRADLEY
## Stories From Ex-Slaves

"I was born in Newberry County, near the Laurens County line, above Little River. Me and my mother belonged to the Workman family. Afterwards, I belonged to Madison Workman. He was a good man to his slaves. My work was around the house and home. I was too young to work in the fields until after the war.

"I can't remember much about them times. I married there and soon after come to town and lived, where I have worked ever since. I do washing and other work.

"On the farm, the old folks had to cook outdoors, or in a kitchen away off from the house. They had wide fireplaces where they put their pots to cook the meals.

"I remember the old Little River Presbyterian Church where people would go on Sundays. They would go in the mornings, and again in the afternoons and have preaching."

United States

Source: Jane Bradley (80), Newberry, S. C.
Interviewer: G. L. Summer, Newberry, S. C. May 17, 1937

Project #1655
W. W. Dixon
Winnsboro, S. C.

## ANDY BRICE
### Ex-Slave 81 Years Old.

Andy Brice lives with his wife and two small children, about twelve miles east of Ridgeway, S. C., in a two-room frame building, chimney in the center. The house is set in a little cluster of pines one hundred and fifty yards north of state highway #34. Andy, since the amputation of his right leg five years ago, has done no work and is too old to learn a trade. He has a regular beggar's route including the towns of Ridgeway, Winnsboro, Woodward, and Blackstock. His amiability and good nature enable him to go home after each trip with a little money and a pack of miscellaneous gifts from white friends.

"Howdy Cap'n! I come to Winnsboro dis mornin' from way 'cross Wateree, where I live now 'mongst de bull-frogs and skeeters. Seem lak they just sing de whole night thru: 'De bull-frog on de bank, and de skeeter in de pool.' Then de skeeter sail 'round my face wid de tra la, la la la, la la la part of dat old song you is heard, maybe many times.

"I see a spit-box over dere. By chance, have you got any 'bacco? Make me more glib if I can chew and spit; then I 'members more and better de things done past and gone.

"I was a slave of Mistress Jane. Her was a daughter of old Marster William Brice. Her marry Henry Younge and mammy was give to Marse Henry and Miss Jane.

"My pappy name Tony. Mammy name Sallie. You is seen her a many a day. Marse Henry got kilt in de war. His tombstone and Mistress Jane's tombstone am in Concord Cemetery. They left two chillun, Miss Kittie and Miss Maggie. They both marry a Caldwell; same name but no kin. Miss Kittie marry Marse Joe Caldwell and move to Texas. Miss Maggie marry Marse Camel Caldwell and move to North Carolina.

"My pappy die durin' de war. After freedom, mammy marry a ugly, no 'count nigger name Mills Douglas. She had one child by him, name Janie. My mammy name her dat out of memory and love for old mistress, in slavery time. I run away from de home of my step-pappy and got work wid Major Thomas Brice. I work for him 'til I become a full grown man and come to be de driver of de four-hoss wagon.

"One day I see Marse Thomas a twistin' de ears on a fiddle and rosinin' de bow. Then he pull dat bow 'cross de belly of dat fiddle. Sumpin' bust loose in me and sing all thru my head and tingle in my fingers. I make up my mind, right then and dere, to save and buy me a fiddle. I got one dat Christmas, bless God! I learn and been playin' de fiddle ever since. I pat one foot while I playin'. I kept on playin' and pattin' dat foot for thirty years. I lose dat foot in a smash up wid a highway accident but I play de old tunes on dat fiddle at night, dat foot seem to be dere at de end of dat leg (indicating) and pats just de same. Sometime I ketch myself lookin' down to see if it have come back and jined itself up to dat leg, from de very charm of de music I makin' wid de fiddle and de bow.

"I never was very popular wid my own color. They say behind my back, in '76, dat I's a white folks nigger. I wear a red shirt then, drink red liquor, play de fiddle at de 'lection box, and vote de white folks ticket. Who I marry? I marry Ellen Watson, as pretty a ginger cake nigger as ever fried a batter cake or rolled her arms up in a wash tub. How I git her? I never git her; dat fiddle got her. I play for all de white folks dances down at Cedar Shades, up at Blackstock. De money roll in when someone pass 'round de hat and say: 'De fiddler?' Ellen had more beaux 'round her than her could shake a stick at but de beau she lak best was de bow dat could draw music out of them five strings, and draw money into dat hat, dat jingle in my pocket de nex' day when I go to see her.

"I 'members very little 'bout de war, tho' I was a good size boy when de Yankees come. By instint, a nigger can make up his mind pretty quick 'bout de creed of white folks, whether they am buckra or whether they am not. Every Yankee I see had de stamp of poor white trash on them. They strutted 'round, big Ike fashion, a bustin' in rooms widout knockin', talkin' free to de white ladies, and familiar to de slave gals, ransackin' drawers, and runnin' deir bayonets into feather beds, and into de flower beds in de yards.

"What church I b'long to? None. Dat fiddle draws

down from hebben all de sermons dat I understan'. I sings de hymns in de way I praise and glorify de Lord.

"Cotton pickin' was de biggest work I ever did, outside of drivin' a wagon and playin' de fiddle. Look at them fingers; they is supple. I carry two rows of cotton at a time. One week I pick, in a race wid others, over 300 pounds a day. Commencin' Monday, thru Friday night, I pick 1,562 pounds cotton seed. Dat make a bale weighin' 500 pounds, in de lint.

"Ellen and me have one child, Sallie Ann. Ellen 'joy herself; have a good time nussin' white folks chillun. Nussed you; she tell me 'bout it many time. 'Spect she mind you of it very often. I knows you couldn't git 'round dat woman; nobody could. De Lord took her home fifteen years ago and I marry a widow, Ida Belton, down on de Kershaw County side.

"You wants me to tell 'bout dat 'lection day at Woodward, in 1878? You wants to know de beginnin' and de end of it? Yes? Well, you couldn't wet dis old man's whistle wid a swallow of red liquor now? Couldn't you or could you? Dis was de way of it: It was set for Tuesday. Monday I drive de four-hoss wagon down to dis very town. Marse John McCrory and Marse Ed Woodward come wid me. They was in a buggy. When us got here, us got twenty, sixteen shooters and put them under de hay us have in de wagon. Bar rooms was here. I had fetched my fiddle 'long and played in Marse Fred Habernick's bar 'til dinner time. Us leave town 'bout four o'clock. Roads was bad but us got home 'bout dark. Us put de guns in Marse Andy Mobley's store. Marse Ed and me leave Marse John to sleep in de store and to take care of de guns.

"De nex' mornin', polls open in de little school house by de brick church. I was dere on time, help to fix de table by de window and set de ballot boxes on it. Voters could come to de window, put deir arms thru and tuck de vote in a slit in de boxes. Dere was two supervisors, Marse Thomas for de Democrats and Uncle Jordan for de Radicals. Marse Thomas had a book and a pencil, Uncle Jordan had de same.

"Joe Foster, big buckra nigger, want to vote a stranger. Marse Thomas challenge dis vote. In them times colored preachers so 'furiate de women, dat they would put on breeches and vote de 'Publican radical ticket. De stranger look lak a woman. Joe Foster 'spute Marse Thomas' word and Marse Thomas knock him down wid de naked fist. Marse Irish Billy Brice, when him see four or five hindred blacks crowdin' 'round Marse Thomas, he jump thru de window from de inside. When he lit on de ground, pistol went off pow! One nigger drop in his tracks. Sixteen men come from nowhere and sixteen, sixteen shooters. Marse Thomas hold up his hand to them and say: 'Wait!' Him point to de niggers and say: 'Git.' They start to runnin' 'cross de railroad, over de hillside and never quit runnin' 'til they git half a mile away. De only niggers left on dat ground was me, old Uncle Kantz, (you know de old mulatto, club-foot nigger) well, me and him and Albert Gladney, de hurt nigger dat was shot thru de neck was de only niggers left. Dr. Tom Douglas took de ball out Albert's neck and de white folks put him in a wagon and sent him home. I drive de wagon. When I got back, de white boys was in de graveyard gittin' names off de tombstones to fill out de talley sheets, dere was so many votes in de box for de Hampton ticket, they had to vote de dead. I 'spect dat was one resurrection day all over South Carolina."

Project 1885-1
Folklore
Spartanburg, Dist. 4
Nov. 10, 1937
Edited by: Elmer Turnage

# GEORGE BRIGGS

## Stories From Ex-Slaves

"I is gwine over to Tosch to see Maria. Everybody know Maria. She go by Rice—Maria Rice. She sont fer me to cure her misery. First, I went from my home in lower Cross Keys, across de Enoree, to see Maria. When I reached dar whar she stay, dey tell me dat her daughter over to Tosch. Done come and got her.

"A kind friend dat de Lawd put in my path fetched me back across de Enoree and over to Tosch to Maria's gal's house. I is gwine straight over dar and lay my hand on Maria and rid her of dat misery dat she sont word was ailing her all dis spring. Don't make no diff'uns whar you hurts—woman, man or suckling babe—if you believes in de holler of my hand, it'll ease you, allus do it. De Bible say so, dat's why it be true. Ain't gwine to tell you nothing but de truth and de whole truth, so help me Jesus. Gone 65 years, I is been born agin dat long; right over in Padgett's Creek church, de white folks' church, dat's what de Lawd tuck my sins away and washed me clean agin wid His blood. Dat's why I allus sticks to de truth, I does.

"Dey all 'lows dat I is gwine on 89, and I has facts to believe it am true. I 'longed to Marse Jesse Briggs. Did you know dat it was two Jesse Briggs? Yes sir, sho was two Jesse Briggses.

"What I gwine to relate to you is true, but in respect to my old Marse, and in de case dat dem what reads dat book won't understand, you needs not to write dis statement down. My marster was called 'Black Jesse', but de reason fer dat was to keep him from gitting mixed up wid de other Jesse. Dat is de secret of de thing. Now dat's jes' fer your own light and knowledge, and not to be wrote down. He was de blacksmith fer all de Cross Keys section, and fer dat very thing he got de name by everybody, 'Black Jesse'. I allus 'longed to dat man and he was de kindest man what de countryside had knowledge of.

"In Union County is whar I was born and raised, and it's whar I is gwine to be buried. Ain't never left de county but once in my life, and if de Lawd see fitten, I ain't gwine to leave it no mo', 'cept to reach de Promise Land. Lawd! Lawd! De Promise Land, dat's whar I is gwine when I leaves Union County. Dey carried me a hundred miles to cure a sick woman, onliest time I ever left Union County. I loves it and I is fit throughout and enduring de time dem Yankees tried to git de county, to save it. What is I gwine to leave it fer? Mr. Perrin and all de white folks is good to me since my marse done gone and left his earthly home. And he is waiting up dar wid Missie to see me agin. Dat I is sho of.

"Listen brother, de Lawd is setting on His throne in

Glory. He hear every word dat I gwine to tell you. Folks fergits dat when dey talks real often sometimes, don't dey? I put my hand on any 'flux' man or woman and removes de pain, if dey have faith in my hand. I don't tell nothing but de truth. I was born on Gist Briggs' plantation in Union County, in de lower section of Cross Keys. Marse Sexton and all dem good folks in lower Keys says dat I sho is 88. Give my name right flat, it's George Briggs; giving it round, it like dis, George McDuffie Briggs. My papa's name was Ike Wilburn, and my mother's name was Margaret Briggs. Pa 'longed to Marse Lige Wilburn. Mama 'longed to Jesse (Black Jesse) Briggs. Dey both born and raised in Union County. Dese was my brothers and sisters, coming in de order dey was born to my parents in: Charlie, Dave, Aaron, Tom, Noah, Charlotte, Polly, Fannie, Mattie, Horace, Cassie. I'm de oldest, and Cassie and me lives in Union County. Fannie and Mattie lives in Asheville, and de rest is done journeyed to de Promise Land. Yes Lawd, to de Promise Land.

"Marse and Missus was good to us all. Missus name was Nancy. She die early and her grave is in Cross Keys at de Briggs graveyard. Be still! Lemme git my mind together so dat I don't git mixed up and can git you de Briggses together. Here 'tis: Chency and Lucindy, Lucindy married a Floyd from Spartanburg, and de Floyds lived at de Burn't factory. Cheney Briggs had a son, Henry Briggs.

"Not so fast, fer I'se gwine to start way back, dat time when us was lil' darky boys way back in slavery. We started to work wid de marster's mules and hosses. When us was real little, we played hoss. Befo' Cheney Briggs went to Arkansas he was our play hoss. His brother, Henry, was de wagoner and I was de mule. Henry was little and he rid our backs sometimes. Henry rid old man Sam, sometimes, and old man Sam jes' holler and haw haw at us chilluns. Dis was in sech early childhood dat it is not so I can 'zactly map out de exact age us was den; anyway, from dis we rid de gentle hosses and mules and larn't how to feed dem. Every word dat I tells you is de truth, and I is got to meet dat word somewhars else; and fer dat reason, de truth is all dat dis old man ever tells.

"In dat day we lived in a log cabin or house. Sometimes us never had nothing to do. Our house had only one room, but some of de houses had two rooms. Our'n had a winder, a do', and a common fireplace. Now dey makes a fireplace to scare de wood away. In old days dey made fireplaces to take care of de chilluns in de cold weather. It warm de whole house, 'cause it was so big and dar was plenty wood. Wood wasn't no problem den, and it ain't no problem yet out in de lower Keys. In town it is, and I ain't guessing. I done seed so.

"I sho can histronize de Confederates. I come along wid de Secession flag and de musterings. I careful to live at home and please de Marse. In de war, I'se mo' dan careful and I stick close to him and please him, and he mo' dan good. Us did not git mobbed up like lots of dem did.

"When Tice Myers' chilluns was born, he had a house built wid a up-stairs. But never no stage coach stopped dar as I ever heard tell about, and I done saw 75 years at Padgett's Creek.

"Way 'tis, from de bundle of de heart, de tongue speaketh. Been in service reg'lar since Monday. I went to Neal Greege's house but she wasn't dar. I is speaking 'bout Ria (Maria Rice). She done gone to town. At de highway, de Lawd prepared a friend to carry me to Union, and when I got dar I take and lay hands on Ria Rice, she laying down and suffering, and I sot down and laid my hand on her. We never say nothing, jes' pray. She be real quiet, and atter while, she riz up and take a breath. She kept on a setting up fer so long dat her husband make her lay back down fer fear dat she git worser. I stay dar all through de night and she sleep sound and wake up dis morning feeling like a new woman.

"Befo' breakfast, here is de words of praise I lifted to de Lawd, over dar on Tosch. You set down de coser (chorus): 'First to de graveyard; den to de Jedgement bar!' Is you got dat verser (verses)? Den git dis: 'All de deacons got to go; all de members got to go; all de sinners got to go.' Mo' 'longs to it, but dat's all I takes when I is praising Him fer relieving pain through me. (He sings each line five times. He takes off his hat; bows; holds his hands over his head, and closes his eyes while singing. His hair is snow white.)

"Lawd, help me dis morning! Here's another first line to one of our songs: 'All dem preachers got to go'.

"Nehemiah, when he wid de king, de king axed him to reveal de wall whar his father was buried. Nehemiah did what de king had done axed him. I 'tends Galilee Baptist church in lower Cross Keys; and at Sedalia, I goes to New Hope Methodist church, but I don't know nothing else but Baptist. We peoples is barrence (barren of the Holy Spirit), but not God; He, Hisself, is born of God, and all is of de same source and by dat I means de Spirit. All has to be born of de Spirit to become chilluns of God. Romans, Chap. 6, 'lows something like dis: 'He dat is dead in sin, how is it dat he can continue in sin?' Dat tell us dat every man, white or black, is de child of God. And it is Christ dat is buried in baptism, and we shall be buried in like manner. If Christ did not rise, den our preaching is in vain. And if we is not born agin, why den we is lost and our preaching is in vain.

"In picking up de New Testament, consider all dat you hear me arguing and saying is from a gift and not from edication. Romans 6, 'lows: 'Speak plain words, not round words, kaise all de round words is fer dem dat is edicated.' Jacob had twelve sons. Dey went and bundled up deir wheat, and eleven bundles bowed to de one. Dat Joseph's bundle what he done up. Other brothers up and got and sold Joseph into captivity to de Egyptians. Dat throw'd Jacob to send Reuben to Egypt. Den dey bowed to Jacob and his sons. It run on and on till dey all had to go to Egypt, and all of dem had to live under Joseph.

"When I was a little shaver and come to myself. I was sleeping in a corded bed. (He scratched his head) I jes' studying fer a minute; can't 'zactly identify my grandpa, but I can identify my grandma. We all raised on de same place together. She name Cindy Briggs, but dey call her Cina kaise dar was so many Cindys 'round dar. One thing I does 'member 'bout her, if she tote me, she sho to whip me. I was raised strict.

"All my life I is stayed in de fur (far) end of Union County whar it borders Laurens, wid de Enoree dividing de two counties. It is right dar dat I is plowed and hoed and raised my craps fer de past 75 years, I reckons. Lawd have mercy! No, I doesn't recalls de names of none of dem mules. Dat's so fur back dat I is jes' done forgot, dat's all. But I does recall 'fur back' things de best, sometimes.

Listen good now. When I got big and couldn't play 'round at chillun's doings, I started to platting cornshucks and things fer making hoss and mule collars, and scouring-brooms and shoulder-mats. I cut hickory poles and make handles out of dem fer de brooms. Marse had hides tanned, and us make buggy whips, wagon whips, shoe strings, saddle strings and sech as dat out of our home-tanned leather. All de galluses dat was wo' in dem days was made by de darkies.

"White oak and hickory was split to cure, and we made fish baskets, feed baskets, wood baskets, sewing baskets and all kinds of baskets fer de Missus. All de chair bottoms of straight chairs was made from white oak splits, and de straight chairs was made in de shop. You made a scouring brush like dis: (He put his hands together to show how the splits were held) By splitting a width of narrow splits, keep on till you lay a entire layer of splits; turn dis way; den dat way, and den bind together and dat hold dem like you want dem to stay. Last, you work in a pole as long as you want it fer de handle, and bind it tight and tie wid de purtiest knots.

"I git money fer platting galluses and making boot strings and other little things. Allus first, I desires to be well qualified wid what I does. I is gwine to be qualified wid everything dat I does, iffen I does it fer money or no. Dat's de reason white people has allus give me words of encouragement.

"Now I gwine to sing a song fer Miss Polly, kaise she de grand-daughter of de late Sheriff Long, and I goes to see her grandma at de Keys (Cross Keys House). Dar she come now.

"How is you dis morning, Miss Polly? De Lawd sho does shower you, Miss Polly, and dat's de reason I is gwine to sing fer you dis morning. You'll be able to tell Mr. Jimmie (her father) dat Uncle George sing fer you, 'Jesus Listening All De Day Long'.

> "Jesus listening all de day long to hear some sinner pray.
> De winding sheet to wrop (wrap) dis body in,
> De coffin to hold you fast;
> Pass through death's iron do'.
> Come ye dat love de Lawd and let your joy be know'd;
> Dis iron gate you must pass through, if you gwine to be Born agin."

He sang these lines over three times and then bowing, said: "Ain't it glory dat we can live whar de Lawd can use us? Dat's power. A strong man entereth in; a weak man cometh out. Dat represent Christ gwine into your heart.

"Sho I can remember when dey had de mustering grounds at de Keys. Dar day mustered and den dey turn't in and practiced drilling dem soldiers till dey larn't how to march and to shoot de Yankees. Drilling, dat's de proper word, not practice, I knows, if I ain't ed'icated. Dey signed me to go to de 16th regiment, but I never reached de North. When us got to Charleston, us turn't around and de bosses fetched us right back to Union through Columbia. Us heard dat Sherman was coming, fetching fire along 'hind him.

"Don't know nothing 'bout no militia to make no statement, but it went on and turn't back. Another regiment had a barbecue somewhars in Union County befo' it went off to war; might a been de 18th regiment, but I does not feel dat I can state on dat.

"My soul reaches from God's foot-stool up to his heavenly home. I can histronize de poor white folks' wives and chilluns enduring de time of de Civil War fer you. When dese poor white men went to de war, dey left deir little chillun and deir wives in de hands of de darkies dat was kind and de rich wives of our marsters to care fer. Us took de best care of dem poor white dat us could under de circumstances dat prevailed.

"We was sont to Sullivan's Island, but befo' we reached it, de Yankees done got it and we won't 'lowed to cross in '64. But jes' de same, we was in service till dey give Capt. Franklin Bailey 'mission to fetch us home. Dar we had to git 'mission fer everything, jes' as us niggers had to git 'mission to leave our marster's place at home in Union County. Capt. Bailey come on back to Cross Keys wid us under his protection, and we was under it fer de longest time atter we done got home.

"Fer 65 years I been licensed as a preacher, and fer longer dan dat I been a member of Padgett's Creek Baptist church. Mo' work I does, mo' work I has to do. You know how to pray. Well, you does not know how to make polish out of pinders.

"I ain't ed'icated yet, but even Lige what teaches school out to de Keys (de big black school), dat big black buck dat teaches de chilluns deir 'rithmetic; even he couldn't do dis here one. A heap of ed'icated folks can't give it. Here it is: 'What's de biggest figger in de figger ten?'"

With his old black, rough and gnarled forefinger he drew on the table the figure 1. "Now you see dat? Dat's de figger 1. A naught ain't nothing by itself or multiplied by other naughts; but set it down in front of de figger 1, and it takes on de value 9. Dar you is got ten—one and nine is ten. Dat naught becomes something. I is old, and I ain't had narry bit of schooling, but I likes to be close to de orchard, and I knows it's dar by de smell of it. Dat's de way I is when I gits along side ed'icated folks—I knows dat dey is.

"It's like dat sum dem scholars couldn't git; standing alone dat naught ain't worth nothing, but set it up against dat which is of value and it takes on value. Set a naught ag'inst dat which is one and you has ten; set up another naught dar and you has a hundred. Now if somebody was to give me a note worth $10, and I found room to add another naught along side of de first; den dem two naughts what ain't worth nothing by deirselves gives de note de value of $99 if dey is sot along wid de one. Ed'icated folks calls dat raising de note. I is ig'nant and I calls dat robbery. And dat's like you and me. We is naughts and Christ is de *One*, and we ain't nothing till we carries de Spirit of de Lawd along wid us.

"On de pathway of life, may you allus keep Christ in front of you and you will never go wrong. De Lawd will den see fit to give you a soul dat will reach from His foot-stool here on earth to His dwelling place on high." He ended with a deep sob and good-bye.

Source: George Briggs (88), Union, S. C. RFD 2.
Interviewer: Caldwell Sims, Union, S. C. 6/9/37

Project 1885-1
FOLKLORE
Spartanburg Dist. 4
July 20, 1937
Edited by:
Elmer Turnage

# GEORGE BRIGGS

## Stories From Ex-Slaves

"Some white men called in question today about de reigning governor enduring time of de Civil War. I knowed dat, and 'cides dat, I knowed him well. It was Governor 'Bill' as us called him.

"What you want to git, is history about muster grounds. Yes, it was on Jones Ferry Road, jest south of Cross Keys whar dey had what dey allus called de muster field. Now, Jones Ferry Road leads across Enoree River into Laurens County. Enoree River is de thing dat devides Union County from Laurens County, dat it is.

"Well as I remember, Mr. Bill Ray was in de mustering of de 18th Regiment. Billy, Robert, Sara and Miss Nancy was Mr. Alex's chilluns. Understand me, don't think dat Bob and Sam was in de Regiment ... satisfied Billy was, kaise he used to pass our house on horse back, coming from de Laurens side where he lived.

"Sixteen-year-old boys come in de same time dat I did. Course I ain't told all dat I knows, kaise dat wouldn't be proper. All I tell you, I wants it to be recognized. De better it's done, de better it'll help you.

"I goes from home and stays five days or more, and don't nothing happen to a thing at my home. I does fer de sick and de Lawd blesses me. He looks atter my things while I am away. He soon shows his presence atter I gits dar. He calls fer me and I feeds Him.

"Once had 26 biles (boils). Dat make me consider my disobedience against de Lawd. Den I went to Him in prayer. He told me Satan done got ahead of Him. Dat show me dat I done forgot to be particular. I got mo' 'ticular and pray mo' often, and in six weeks my biles had done all gone.

"Dar is times when I gits lost fer not knowing. I can't keep up, kaise I cannot read. Man in Sunday school reads and I hears. He read de olden Testament; den he read de new Testament. Dat my schooling. I 'clar unto you, I got by all my life by praying and thinking. I sho does think a lot. ('Uncle' George's facial and scalp muscles work so when he thinks, that his straw hat moves up and down.)

"When good man prays fer bad man, de Holy Ghost works on bad man's consciousness, and afo' he knows it, he's a-saying 'Lawd have Mercy' 'stead of 'G'dam', like all wicked folks says every day. He—dat de Holy Ghost dat I still is speaking of—jest penetrates de wicked man's consciousness widout him a-knowing it. Dat penetrating make de bad man say, 'Lawd have Mercy.' I hoes and I cuts sprouts, and den I plows. When you plows, mules is allus so aggravating dat dey gits you all ruffled up. Dat de devil a-working at you. Dat's all old mules is anyhow. I does not cuss, nohow, kaise it sho am wicked and I is had de Holy Spirit in my soul, now gone sixty-five years, since I jined Padgett Creek Church. When my old mule gits to de row's end, and he act mulish—kaise dat's in him and he don't know nothing else to do—I means to say either 'ha' or 'gee', and often since I jined Padgett Creek Church I finds myself saying 'Lawd have Mercy' 'stead of 'gee' or 'ha'. So you see dat de Lawd has command, whar-so-ever if I was wicked, Satan would.

"A child fo God allus will agree wid de Word of God. We mens dat claim to be leaders in de Kingdom, got to step up and sho folks what dey must do. Man learns right smart from Exodus 'bout how to lead. A male child was born to rule de world. Moses still de strongest impression dat we has as rulers. God gits Hisself into de heads of men dat he wants to rule and He don't tell nobody else nothing 'bout it neither.

"Mr. Roosevelt de president and he sho looks atter de po' folks. He ain't no ig'nant man neither, kaise he got de light. Folks ain't a-gwine to drown him out neither wid dere wicked words 'gainst him, kaise he strive in de Lawd's name to do His will. Mr. Roosevelt got learning like I is from de throne of God. He may have education also, but if he is, he sho knows how to keep dem both jined together. Folks reads to me how he got crippled and how he washed in dem springs in Georgia, and dat keep him a-gwine right on anyhow. It ain't dem springs by deself, but it's God a dipping his hand down dar fer de President to git well. Oh yes, suh, I knows dat he twan't de president when he was a-washing, but dem de plans dat de Lawd had done already planned and you and me never know'd nothing 'bout all dat. You and me does not know what is planned up in sto' fer us in de future neither.

"I is a Baptist, and at Padgett's Creek we does not believe in no back-sliding. 'Once in de Spirit, allus in de Spirit'. A child of your'n is allus a child of your'n. Dat de way de Baptist teach—once a child of God, allus God's child. T'ain't no sech thing as drapping back. If you draps back, you ain't never been no child of de Lawd, and you never had no business being baptized. Christ was baptized in de waters of Jordan, won't (weren't) He? Well, He never drapped back, did He? He say we must follow in His footsteps, didn't He? Well, dar you is, and dat's all dar is to it.

"God gits in de heads of men to help de aged and de po' also. I never axes fer nothing, but when I sets around de courthouse and informs men as I been doing dis evening, de Lawd has dem to drap a nickle or a dime or a quarter in my hand but He never gits dem to a half of a dollar."

Source: George Briggs, (88) Rt. 2, Union, S. C.
Interviewer: Caldwell Sims, Union, S. C. (7/12/37)

Project 1885-1
FOLKLORE
Spartanburg Dist. 4
July 12, 1937
Edited by:
Elmer Turnage

# GEORGE BRIGGS
## Stories From Ex-Slaves

"What-so-ever I can find! I traveling dat way over 73 years. If he ax de Lawd and have faith, he ken do; and iffen he don't have no faith, by den he can't. When a man comes along dat wants his own way, and he won't pay no attention to de Lawd, by den de Lawd don't pay him no mind; and so dat man jest keeps a-gwine on wid his way and he don't never reach de Cross. Jesus say, 'deny yourself, pick up de Cross and follow Me.'

"I see a man in de courthouse dis morning, and he was like Nicodemus. Why dat man want to be resto'd back like he was when he was jest 21 years old. I seed him setting down dar in Mr. Perrin's office, and I knowed his troubles when he 'low dat he done been to every doctor in town. De trouble was, he never had no faith in de doctors and nobody else. How could he have faith in Jesus when he never had none in nothing else? Brother, you has to have faith in your fellowman befo' you has faith in de Lawd. I don't know how come, but dat's de way it is. My plan is working by faith. Jesus say, 'Work widout faith ain't nothing; but work wid faith'll move mountains'.

"Dat man told me he gwine give me a hundred dollars if I rid him of misery. Dat show he never know nothing 'bout faith.

"If Mr. Emslie Nicholson ax me to rid him of a misery, I couldn't take no money from him, and he de richest man in all Union County. Mr. Nicholson would know better dan to offer me money, kaise he has faith. You know he's a good 'Presmuterian' (Presbyterian).

"Dey looks at de back of my head, and de hair on it ain't rubbed against no college and fer dat reason dese young negroes don't want me to preach. Dey wants to hear dat man preach dat can read. Man dat can read can't understand less'n some divine man guide him. I speak as my Teacher gives it to me, dat's de Lawd. In so doing, I testify de word dat no man can condemn. Dat is my plan of Salvation: to work by faith widout price or purse, as de Lawd, my Teacher has taught me.

"Dar was no church on our plantation when I was a boy. All de Baptists went to Padgett's Creek, and all de Methodist went to Quaker Church and Belmont. Padgett's Creek had a section in de back of de church fer de slaves to sit. Quaker Church and Belmont both had slaves' galleries. Dar is a big book at Padgetts wid three pages of slaves' names that was members. Mr. Claude Sparks read it to me last year. All de darky members dead, but one, dat's me.

"Nobody never read de Bible to me when I was little. It jest a gift of God dat teached to me through de Holy Ghost. It's de Spirit of de One in Three dat gits into you, and dat's de Holy Ghost or de Holy Spirit dat gives me my enlightment.

"If I can git to de do' of Padgett's Creek Church, I can jest feel de Power of God. ('Uncle' George pats his foot and softly cries at this point, and his face takes on a calm and peaceful expression.)

"If you eats befo' you gits hongry, you never will feast on dead air. I makes it a practice to feed my soul and body befo' dey gits hongry. Even I does eat by myself, dis old man take off his hat and ax de Lawd to bless his soul and body in nourishment fer de future.

"I ain't never seed Mr. Lincoln, but from what I learn't dey said dat God had placed in him de revelation to give de plan dat he had fer every man. Dat plan fer every man to worship under his own vine and fig tree. From dat, we should of liked Mr. Lincoln.

"Dis here 'Dick Look-Up'. No sir, I don't know him, kaise I caught his name since I come on dis side of de river. Mr. Perrin knows him, and I heard him say dat every time anybody ax him how old he is, he add on ten years. Dat's how come dey got in de paper he a hundred and twenty-five years old. Now me and Mr. Perrin doesn't speak unless we is obleeged to know dat what we is gwine to say is de truth. Us is careful, kaise us knows dat de Lawd am looking down from his throne, and dat He is checking every word dat we says. Some folks does not recall dat fact when dey speaks, or dey would be careful.

"I'll say it slow so dat you can catch it; I start in time of de Confederate War. Wid dirt dug up out of de smokehouse, water was run through it so us could get salt fer bread. Hickory wood ashes was used fer soda. If we didn't have no hickory wood, we burnt red corn cobs; and de ashes from dem was used fer cooking soda.

"Molasses was made from watermelons in time of de war. Dey was also made from May-apples or may-pops as some call dem, and sometimes dey was made from persimmons and from wheat brand. In Confederate days, Irish potato tops was cooked fer vegetables. Blackberry leaves was ocassionally used fer greens or fer seasoning lambs quarters.

"Dis way watermelon was done: Soak watermelon twenty and four hours to de'self; strain off all juice and put on fire to bile. When dey thickens dey bees good. Yes sir, good, good.

"Wid may-pops: peel de outside green off, den bust 'em open and mash up together; strain juice off and cook thick.

"'Simmons and wheat bran are mashed up together and baked in water. Let set twenty and four hours and cook down to molasses. Dat winds up dat part of it.

"Git plums and blackberries and de like of dat and make up in Jelly, or can fer scarce times, dat's de way we done den and folks does dat yet. Dese is some of de particularest things of de Confederate times dat I come back from Sedalia to give you, dat's right. (This old negro, who had already been interviewed by the writer, came a long way and looked-up the author to tell him some incidents which he had forgotten to tell in the first interview.) Some customs is done went by now, but dey was practiced in Sedalia, and as to whar dem was done fer off as Spartanburg, I cannot say.

"In Confederate time, all wimmens stayed close home and carded and spun all de day long. Dey wove all dere own clothes. Men at home, old men, made leather shoes and shoe strings and belts and galloses.

"Our darkies tried hard to be obedient to our master so dat we might obtain (keep) our pleasant home. Obedience makes it better dan sacrifice. I restes my mind dar."

Source: George Briggs (88), Rt. 2, Union, S. C.
Interviewed by: Caldwell Sims, Union, S. C. (7/7/37)

Code No.
Project, 1885-(1)
Prepared by Annie Ruth Davis
Place, Marion, S. C.
Date, January 27, 1938
No. Words --
Reduced from -- words
Rewritten by --

# JOSEPHINE BRISTOW
## Ex-Slave, 73 Years

"Remembers de Confederate War, Miss. Yes, mam, I'm supposed to be, if I can live to see February, bout 73 year old. What age Hester say she was? Dat what I had thought from me en her conversation. Miss, I don' remember a thing more bout de war den de soldiers comin through old Massa's plantation en we chillun was 'fraid of dem en ran. Knew dey was dressed in a different direction from us white folks. All was in blue, you know, wid dem curious lookin hats en dem brass buttons on dey bodies. No, mam, dey didn' stop nowhe' bout us. Dey was ridin on horses en it seem like dey was in a hurry gwine somewhe'. En dey didn' stop to old Massa's house neither. No, mam, not to my knowin, dey didn'. Well, we was livin out to de plantation, we calls it, en Massa en Missus was livin up here to Marion. Mr. Ferdinand Gibson, dat who been us

Massa in slavery time en Miss Connie, dat what we used to call her, was us Missus. To my knowin, dey didn' have no chillun dey own, but dey sho had plenty colored people. Yes, mam, seems like to my remembrance, my Massa ran bout 30 plantations en 'sides dat, he had a lot of servants right up here to de big house, men en women."

"I was real small in dem days en far as I can remember, we lived on de quarter dere to old Massa's plantation in de country. Us little tots would go every mornin to a place up on de hill, called de milk house, en get our milk 'tween meals while de old folks was off workin. Oh, dey had a old woman to see after we chillun en tend to us in de daytime. De old lady dat looked after us, her name was Mary Novlin. Lord, Mr. Gibson, he had big farms en my mother en father, dey worked on de farms. Yes'um, my mother en father, I used to never wouldn' know when dey come home in de evenin, it would be so late. De old lady, she looked after every blessed thing for us all day long en cooked for us right along wid de mindin. Well, she would boil us corn meal hominy en give us dat mostly wid milk for breakfast. Den dey would have a big garden en she would boil peas en give us a lot of soup like dat wid dis here oven bread. Oh, dem what worked in de field, dey would catch dey meals when dey could. Would have to cook way in de night or sometimes fore day. Cose dey would take dey dinner rations wid dem to de field. More or less, dey would cook it in de field. Yes'um, dey would carry dey pots wid dem en cook right dere in de field whe' dey was workin. Would boil pots en make bread, too. I don' know how long dey had to work, mam, but I hear dem say dat dey worked hard, cold or hot, rain or shine. Had to hoe cotton en pick cotton en all such as dat. I don' know, mam, but de white folks, I guess dey took it dat dey had plenty colored people en de Lord never meant for dem to do no work. You know, white folks in dem days, dey made de colored people do."

"De people used to spin en weave, my Lord! Like today, it cloudy en rainy, dey couldn' work in de field en would have to spin dat day. Man, you would hear dat thing windin en I remember, I would stand dere en want to spin so bad, I never know what to do. Won' long fore I got to whe' I could use de shuttle en weave, too. I bad a grandmother en when she would get to dat wheel, she sho know what she been doin. White folks used to give de colored people task to spin en I mean she could do dat spinnin. Yes'um, I here to tell you, dey would make de prettiest cloth in dat day en time. Old time people used to have a kind of dye dey called indigo en dey would color de cloth just as pretty as you ever did see."

"Den I recollects dat dey would have to shuck corn some of de days en wouldn' nobody work in de field dat day. Oh, my Lord, dey would have de big eats on dem days. Would have a big pot right out to de barn whe' dey was shuckin corn en would boil it full as it could hold wid such as peas en rice en collards. Would cook big bread, too, en would save a hog's head for dat purpose often times."

"Colored people didn' have no schools nowhe' in dat day en time. No'um, us didn' go to no church neither cause we was way off dere on de plantation en wasn' any church nowhe' bout dere, Miss. I likes to be truthful en I tellin you, when we was comin up, we never didn' know nothin 'cept what we catch from de old folks."

"Old Massa, he used to come to de plantation drivin

his rockaway en my Lord a mercy, we chillun did love to run en meet him. Dey used to have a great big gate to de lane of de plantation en when we been hear him comin, we would go a runnin en holler, 'Massa comin! Massa comin!' En he would come ridin through de big gate en say, 'Yonder my little niggers! How my little niggers? Come here en tell me how you all.' Den we would go a runnin to him en try to tell him what he ax us. Yes'um, we was sho pleased to see old Massa cause we had to stay right dere on dat plantation all de time round bout dat old woman what tended to us. Used to hear my mother en my father speak bout dey had to get a ticket from dey boss to go anywhe' dey wanted to go off de place. Pataroller catch dem off de plantation somewhe' widout dat walkin ticket, dey would whip dem most to death. Never didn' hear bout old Massa whippin none of dem, but he was very tight on dem, my father say. Cose he give dem abundance of rations en somethin to eat all de time, but colored people sho been work for what dey would get in dem days. Didn' get nothin dey never pay for. It been like dis, what rations us parents would get, dat would be to dey house en what we chillun been get would be to de old woman's house what took care of us."

"Well, Miss, some people stays here wid me, but dey works out en I tries to help dem out somehow. No, mam, we all stays right here together en while dey on de job, I tries to look out for de chillun. I just thinkin bout when we come to a certain age, honey, it tough. Chillun is a heap of trouble, I say. Well, I was de mother of five, but dey all dead 'cept one. My husband, he been dead seven years. Yes'um, dis a bad little girl settin here in my lap en dat one over dere in de bed, he a boy what a right smart larger den dis one." (Little girl just can stand alone).

(Little boy wakes up). "Son, dere you wantin to get up en I don' know whe' near a rag to put on you is. Dere, you want a piece of bread fore you is dress. Who undressed you last night nohow? Boy, you got to stand dere en wait till your mamma come home cause I can' find none your rags. What de matter wid you? You so hungry, you just standin dere wid your mouth droolin dat way. Dere your bread en tea on de bureau. Gwine on en get it." (Little boy's breakfast consisted of a cold biscuit and a little cold coffee poured in an empty coffee can. The little girl sat with a clump of cold hominy in her hand on which she nibbled.)

"Lord, I think what a blessin it would be if chillun dese days was raise like dey used to be, Miss. Yes, mam, we had what you call strict fathers en mothers den, but chillun ain' got dem dese days. Oh, dey would whip you en put de lash to you in dat day en time. Yes'um, Miss, if we never do right, my father would put it to us. Sho meant what he say. Wouldn' never whip you on Sunday though. Say dat he would get you tomorrow. Den when Monday come, he would knock all bout like he had forget, but toreckly he would call you up en he would sho work on you. Pa say, 'I'm not gwine let you catch me in no lie. When I tell you I gwine cut you, I gwine do it.' Miss, I is had my mother to hurt me so bad till I would just fall down en roll in de sand. Hurt! Dey hurt, dat dey did. Wouldn' whip you wid no clothes on neither. Would make you pull off. Yes, mam, I could sniffle a week, dey been cut me such licks. Thought dey had done me wrong, but dey know dey ain' been doin me wrong en I mean dey didn' play wid me."

"Miss, I think folks is livin too fast in de world today. Seems to me like all de young people is worser, I say.

Well, I tell you, dey be ridin out all times of night en girls meetin up wid Miss Fortune. At least, our colored girls does. En don' care what dey do neither. Don' seem to care what dey do nor how dey do. De girls nowadays, dey gets dey livin. Girls settin higher den what dey makes demselves dese days."

    Source: Josephine Bristow, colored, 73 years, Marion, S. C.
    Personal interview by Annie Ruth Davis, Jan., 1938

Project #1655
W. W. Dixon
Winnsboro, S. C.

# ANNE BROOME
## Ex-Slave 87 Years Old.

"Does you recollect de Galloway place just dis side of White Oak? Well dere's where I was born. When? Can't name de 'zact year but my ma say, no stork bird never fetch me but de fust railroad train dat come up de railroad track, when they built de line, fetched me. She say I was a baby, settin' on de cow-ketcher, and she see me and say to pa: 'Reubin, run out dere and get our baby befo' her falls off and gets hurt under them wheels! Do you know I believed dat tale 'til I was a big girl? Sure did, 'til white folks laugh me out of it!

"My ma was name Louisa. My marster was Billie Brice, but 'spect God done write sumpin' else on he forehead by dis time. He was a cruel marster; he whip me just for runnin' to de gate for to see de train run by. My missus was a pretty woman, flaxen hair, blue eyes, name Mary Simonton, 'til she marry.

"Us live in a two-room plank house. Plenty to eat and enough to wear 'cept de boys run 'round in their shirt tails and de girls just a one-piece homespun slip on in de summer time. Dat was not a hardship then. Us didn't know and didn't care nothin' 'bout a 'spectable 'pearance in those days. Dats de truth, us didn't.

"Gran'pa name Obe; gran'ma, name Rachel. Shoes? A child never have a shoe. Slaves wore wooden bottom shoes.

"My white folks went to New Hope Church. Deir chillun was mighty good to us all. Dere was Miss Martha, her marry Doctor Madden, right here at Winnsboro. Miss Mary marry Marster John Vinson, a little polite smilin' man, nice man, though. Then Miss Jane marry Marster John Young. He passed out, leavin' two lovely chillun, Kitty and Maggie. Both of them marry Caldwells. Dere was Marster Calvin, he marry Congressman Wallace's daughter, Ellen. Then dere was Marster Jim and Marster William, de last went to Florida.

"It was a big place, I tell you, and heaps and heaps of slaves. Some times they git too many and sell them off. My old mistress cry 'bout dat but tears didn't count wid old marster, as long as de money come a runnin' in and de rations stayed in de smoke house.

"Us had a fine carriage. Sam was de driver. Us go to Concord one Sunday and new Hope de next. Had quality fair neighbors. Dere was de Cockerells, 'Piscopalians, dat 'tend St. John in Winnsboro, de Adgers, big buckra, went to Zion in Winnsboro. Marster Burr Cockerell was de sheriff. 'Members he had to hang a man once, right in de open jailyard. Then dere was a poor buckra family name Marshall. Our white folks was good to them, 'cause they say his pappy was close kin to de biggest Jedge of our country, John Marshall.

"When de slaves got bad off sick, marster send for Dr. Walter Brice, his kin folks. Some times he might send for Dr. Madden, him's son-in-law, as how he was.

"When de Yankees come, all de young marsters was off in de 'Federate side. I see them now, gallopin' to de house, canteen boxes on their hips and de bayonets rattlin' by deir sides. De fust thing they ask, was: 'You got any wine?' They search de house; make us sing: 'Good Old Time 'Ligion'; put us to runnin' after de chickens and a cookin'. When they leave they burnt de gin house and everything in dere. They burn de smoke-house and wind up wid burnin' de big house.

"You through wid me now, boss? I sho' is glad of dat. Help all you kin to git me dat pension befo' I die and de Lord will bless you, honey. De Lord not gwine to hold His hand any longer 'ginst us. Us cleared de forests, built de railroads, cleaned up de swamps, and nursed de white folks. Now in our old ages, I hopes they lets de old slaves like me see de shine of some of dat money I hears so much talk 'bout. They say it's free as de gift of grace from de hand of de Lord. Good mornin' and God bless you, will be my prayer always. Has you got a dime to give dis old nigger, boss?"

Project #-1655
Mrs. Genevieve W. Chandler
Murrells Inlet, S. C.
Georgetown County

# HAGAR BROWN

## (Verbatim Conversation)

Mom Hagar Brown lives in her little weathered cabin on forty odd acres left by her husband, Caleb Brown. Caleb died in Georgia where he had been sent to the penitentiary for stealing a hog that another man stole. Aunt Hagar has grands settled all around her and she and the grands divide up the acreage which is planted in corn, sweet potatoes, cotton, and some highland rice. She ministers to them all when sick, acts as mid-wife when necessary, and divides her all with her kin and friends—white and black. She wages a war on ground-moles, at which she laughs and says she resembles. Ground-mole beans almost a foot long protect and decorate her yard. She has apple and fig trees, and scuppernong grape vines grow rank and try to climb all her trees.

(Monday morning she hobbles up on a stick—limping and looking sick.) Comes in kitchen door.

Lillie: "Aunt Hagar, how you?"

Hagar: "Painful. Doctor tell me I got the tonsil. Want to represent me one time and take them out. I say, 'No Doctor! Get in hospital, can't get out! Let me stay here till my change come.' Yeddy? I ain't wuth! Ain't wuth! Ain't got a piece o' sense. Yeddy? Ellen say she want God to take she tomorrow? When you ready it's 'God take me now! All right son!" (Greeting Zackie who enters kitchen.)

Zackie: "Aunt Hagar, how you feel?"

Hagar: "I ain't wuth son. How's all?"

Zackie: "Need a little more grits!"

Lillie: "Hear Zackie! Mom Hagar, that ain't hinder him ordering another!" (The fact that food is scarce doesn't limit Zackie's family.)

Hagar: "You hear bout this Jeremiah broke in somewhere—get all kinds likker and canned things and different thing?"

Zackie: "Must a broke in that place call 'Stumble Inn!' (Very seriously.) That Revenue man been there."

Hagar: "I yeddy last night! Say he there in news-paper. Mary say, 'see 'em in paper!' Mrs. White gone to child funeral. That been in paper too. Mary see that in paper. Easter say old lady gone dere. Doctor say better go. Child sick. Child seven years old. Fore they get there tell 'em say, 'Child dead!'

"People gone in patch to pick watermillon. Ain't want child to go. You know chillun! Child gone in. Ain't want 'em for go. You know. Child pick watermillon. Ketch up one—I forgotten what pound they say. Roll. Roll duh watermillon. Roll 'em on snake! They say, 'Snake bite 'em?' Child say, 'No. Must a scratch.' See blood run on boy leg. Child get unconscion that minute. Gone right out. Jess so. Ease out so. I cry. I cry!"

Lillie: "You know 'em, Mom Hagar?"

Hagar: "No! No! Lill, fever got me! Cold get me till my rump dead. Got hospital boy rouse one time say, 'Ma, less go home! Red stripe snake bite me.'"

Hagar: "Klu Klux?" (Chin cupped in hand—elbow on knee—looking way off—)

"Reckon that the way them old timey people call 'em. Have to run way, you go church. Going to come in to ketch you or do any mischievous thing—come carry you place they going beat you—in suit of white. Old white man to Wilderness Plantation. Parish old man name. Treat his wife bad. Come to house, ain't crack. Come right in suit of white. Drag him out—right to Woodstock there where Mr. Dan get shoot. Put a beating on that white man there till he mess up! Oman never gone back to him yet!"

"A man wuz name (I forgot what the man name wuz)—wuz a white man mess round wid a colored woman and they didn't do a God thing but gone and put a beating on you, darling! Come in. Grab you and go. Put a beating on you till you can't see. Know they got a good grub to lick you wid. They git done you can't sit down. Ain't going carry you just for play with."

"Mom Hagar, you wanter vote?"

Hagar: "Oh my God!"

"Aunt Hagar are the colored people happier now than the old timey slavery time people?"

Hagar: "Young people now got the world by force. Don't care. Got more trick than law low. Tricky! Can't beat the old people. Can't equal to 'em. Some the young people you say 'AMEN' in church they make fun o' you. Every tub stand on his own bottom. Can't truss 'em.

"Ma say some dem plan to run way. Say, 'Less run! Less run!' Master ketch dem and fetch dem in. Lay 'em cross barrel. Beat dem till they wash in blood. Fetch 'em back. Place 'em cross the barrel—hogsket barrel—Christ! They ramp wash in blood! Beat Ma sister. He sister sickly. Never could clear task—like he want. My Ma have to work he self to death to help Henritta so sickly. Clear task to keep from beat. Some obersheer mean. Oaks labor. (Meaning her Ma and ma's family were laboring on Oaks Plantation—the plantation where Gov. Joseph Allston and Theodosia his wife lived on Waccamaw.) Mother Sally Doctor. Ma got four chillun. One was Emmeline, one Getty, one Katrine one Hagar! I older than Gob (Katrine). Could a call doctor for Gob if I had any sense." (Big nuff to gone for doctor when Gob born.)

"Stay in the field!
Stay in the field!
Stay in the field till the war been end!"

(This is Aunt Hagar's favorite song)

Mom Hagar Brown—age 77
Murrells Inlet, S. C.
July 4th, 1937.

Project #-1655
Mrs. Genevieve W. Chandler
Murrells Inlet, S. C.
Georgetown County

# HAGAR BROWN

## Some recollections of Mom Hagar Brown

Visitor: "Mom Hagar, how old did you say you were?"

Hagar: "Don't take care of my age! Had me gang of chillun when ma die. I had Samuel, I had Elias, I had Arthur, I had Beck. Oh, my God! Man, go way! I had Sally! I had Sally again. I didn't want to give the name 'Sally' again. Say, 'First Sally come carry girl.' Ma say, 'Gin 'em name 'Sally!' I faid (afraid) that other one come back for him. Had to do what Ma say. Had to please 'em. Ma name Sally. Ma chillun Catrine, Hagar, Emmeline, Gettie. I born Columbia. Come Freedom, when we left Columbia, ma finer till we get in Charston. Freedom come, battle till we get 'Oaks.' (Battled till they reached the 'Oaks Plantation—.')Stay there till people gin (begin) move bout. Come Watsaw. Gone 'Collins Creek.' In the 'Reb Time' you know, when they sell you bout—Massa sell you all about. Broke through them briar and branch and thing to go to church. Them patrol get you. Church 'Old Bethel.' You don't know 'em. Been gone!

"I yeddy ma! (heard my mother) Ma say, 'I too glad my chillun aint been here Rebs time! Gin you task you rather drown than not done that task! Ma say Auntie poor we weak creeter, couldn't strain. Ma had to strain to fetch sister up with her task. Dere (there) in rice-field. Ma say they on flat going to islant (island), see cloud, pray God send rain! When rooster crow, say they pray God to stop 'em! Rooster crow, broke up wedder! When rooster crow, scare 'em. Broke up rain! Ma say they drag the pot in the river when the flat going cross. Do this to make it rain. Massa! Don't done you task, driver wave that whip, put you over the barrel, beat you so blood run down! I wouldn't take 'em! Ma say, 'I too glad my chillun aint born then!'

"Any cash money? Where you gwine get 'em? Only cash the gospel! Have to get the gospel. Give you cloth! Give you ration! Jess (just according) many chillun you got. Ma say chillun feed all the corn to the fowl.

> Chillun say,
> 'Papa love he fowl!
> Papa love he fowl!
> Three peck a day!
> Three peck a day!

"Parent come to door. Not a grain of corn leave! Poor people! Come, drop! Not a grain! Everybody on the hill help. One give this; one give that. Handle 'em light! (Very careful with victuals). Gone you till Saddy (Saturday.) (Will last you until Saturday when you are rationed again.)

"When Ma get down, she say, 'I gone leave! I gone leave here now! But, oh, Hagar! Be a mudder and fadder for Katrine!'

"I say, (I call Katrine 'Gob') I say, 'Better tell Gob to look atter me!'

"Ma say, 'When I gone I ax the Master when he take me, to send drop o' rain to let true believer know I gone to Glory!'

"When they lift the body to take 'em to the church, rain, 'Tit! Tit! Tit! Tit!' on the house! At the gate, moon shine out' Going to the church! Bury to the 'Oaks.'

"Gob say, 'Titty, all you chillun bury at Oaks. Ma to Oaks. How come you wanter bury Watsaw?'"

"I say, 'When the trumpet sound, I yeddy!' (When the trumpet sounds, I'll hear it!)

"I marry right to Collins Creek hill. Big dance out the door! I free! I kick up! Ma, old rebs time people!"

    Mom Hagar Brown
    Age—(She says 'Born first o'
    Freedom' but got her age from
    a contemporary and reported 77)
    Murrells Inlet, S. C.

United States

Project #-1655
Mrs. Genevieve W. Chandler
Murrells Inlet, S. C.
Georgetown County

# HAGAR BROWN

## Ex-Slave Story
## (Verbatim)

"My old man can 'member things and tell you things and he word carry. We marry to Turkey Hill Plantation. Hot supper. Cake, wine, and all. Kill cow, hog, chicken and all. That time when you marry, so much to eat! Finance wedding! Now—

"We 'lamp-oil chillun'; they 'lectric light' chillun now! We call our wedding 'lamp-oil wedding'. Hall jam full o' people; out-of-door jam full. Stand before the chimbley.

"When that first war come through, we born. I don't know just when I smell for come in the world.

"Big storm? Yinnah talk big storm hang people up on tree? (Noah!) Shake? I here in house. House gone, 'Rack-a-rack-a-racker!'

"My husband run out—with me and my baby left in bed! Baby just come in time of the shake.

"When I first have sense, I 'member I walk on the frost bare-feet. Cow-belly shoe.

"My husband mother have baby on the flat going to Marion and he Auntie Cinda have a baby on that flat.

"From yout (youth) I been a Brown and marry a Brown; title never change.

"Old timey sing?

1.
"Wish I had a hundred dog
And half wuz hound!
Take it in my fadder field
And we run the rabbit down!

Chorus:
Now he hatch
He hatch!
He hatch!
And I run the rabbit down!

2.
"I wish I had a hundred head o' dog
And half of them wuz hound
I'd take 'em back in my bacco field
And run the rabbit down.

Chorus:
Now he hatch—he hatch!
He hatch—he hatch!
Now he hatch—he hatch!

And I run them rabbit down!"

"That wuz a sing we used to have on the plantation. Then we make up sing—we have sing for chillun. Make 'em go sleep. Every one have his own sing.

"Bye-o-baby!
Go sleepy!
Bye-o-baby!
Go sleepy!
What a big alligator
Coming to catch
This one boy!"
"Diss here the Watson one boy child!
Bye-o-baby go sleepy!
What a big alligator
Coming to catch this one boy!"

Emmie Jordan: "Missus, I too plague with bad heart trouble to give you the sing!"

Song and conversation Given by

Mom Louisa Brown (Born time of 'Reb people War')
Waverly Mills, S. C.
Near Parkersville, S. C.

United States

Project #-1655
Jessie A. Butler
Charleston, S. C.
Approximately 930 words

FOLKLORE

# HENRY BROWN
## Ex-slave Age 79

Henry Brown, negro caretaker of the Gibbes House, at the foot of Grove street, once a part of Rose Farm, is a splendid example of a type once frequently met with in the South. Of a rich brown complexion, aquiline of feature, there is none of the "Gullah" about Henry. He is courteous and kindly in his manner, and speaks more correctly than the average negro.

"My father was Abram Brown, and my mother's name was Lucy Brown," he said. "They were slaves of Dr. Arthur Gordon Rose. My grandfather and grandmother were grown when they came from Africa, and were man and wife in Africa. I was born just about two years before the war so I don't remember anything about slavery days, and very little about war times, except that we were taken to Deer Pond, about half mile from Columbia. Dr. Rose leased the place from Dr. Ray, and took his family there for safety. My mother died while he was at Deer Pond, and was buried there, but all the rest of my people is buried right here at Rose Farm. My two brothers were a lot older than me, and were in the war. After the war my brother Tom was on the police force, he was a sergeant, and they called him Black Sergeant. My brother Middleton drove the police wagon: they used to call it Black Maria.

"My father, Abram Brown, was the driver or head man at Rose plantation. Dr. Rose thought a heap of him, and during the war he put some of his fine furniture and other things he brought from England in my father's house and told him if the Yankees came to say the things belonged to him. Soon after that the soldiers came. They asked my father who the things belonged to and he said they belonged to him. The soldiers asked him who gave them to him, and he said his master gave them to him. The Yankees told him that they thought he was lying, and if he didn't tell the truth they would kill him, but he wouldn't say anything else so they left him alone and went away.

"Work used to start on the plantation at four o'clock in the morning, when the people went in the garden. At eight or nine o'clock they went into the big fields. Everybody was given a task of work. When you finished your task you could quit. If you didn't do your work right you got a whipping.

"The babies were taken to the Negro house and the old women and young colored girls who were big enough to lift them took care of them. At one o'clock the babies were taken to the field to be nursed, then they were brought back to the Negro house until the mothers finished their work, then they would come for them.

"Dr. Rose gave me to his son, Dr. Arthur Barnwell Rose, for a Christmas present. After the war Dr. Rose went back to England. He said he couldn't stay in a country with so many free Negroes. Then his son Dr. Arthur Barnwell Rose had the plantation. Those was good white people, good white people.

"The colored people were given their rations once a week, on Monday, they got corn, and a quart of molasses, and three pounds of bacon, and sometimes meat and peas. They had all the vegetables they wanted; they grew them in the gardens. When the boats first came in from Africa with the slaves, a big pot of peas was cooked and the people ate it with their hands right from the pot. The slaves on the plantation went to meeting two nights a week and on Sunday they went to Church, where they had a white preacher Dr. Rose hired to preach to them.

"After the war when we came back to Charleston I went to work as a chimney-sweep. I was seven years old then. They paid me ten cents a story. If a house had two stories I got twenty cents; if it had three stories I got thirty cents. When I got too big to go up the chimneys I went back to Rose plantation. My father was still overseer or driver. I drove a cart and plowed. Afterwards I worked in the phosphate mines, then came back here to take care of the garden and be caretaker. I planted all these Cherokee roses you see round here, and I had a big lawn of Charleston grass. I aint able to keep it like I used to."

Henry is intensely religious. He says "the people don't notice God now because they're free." "Some people say there aint no hell," he continued, "but I think there must be some kind of place like that, because you got to go some place when you leave this earth, and you got to go to the master that you served when you were here. If you serve God and obey His commandments then you go to Him, but if you don't pay any attention to what he tells you in His Book, just do as you choose and serve the devil, then you got to go to him. And it don't make any difference if you're poor or rich, it don't matter what the milliner (millionaire) man says."

He seemed so proud of his garden, with its broad view across the Ashley River, showing his black walnut, pear and persimmon trees, grape vines and roses, that the writer said, "Henry, you know a poet has said that we are nearer God in the garden than anywhere else on earth." "Well ma'am, you see," he replied, with a winning smile, "that's where God put us in the first place."

**Project #-1655**
**Augustus Ladson**
**Charleston, S. C.**

# HENRY BROWN

## Ex-Slave Born 1857
## Grand Parents Came Directly From Africa

I was nickname' durin' the days of slavery. My name was Henry but they call' me Toby. My sister, Josephine, too was nickname' an' call' Jessee. Our mistress had a cousin by that name. My oldes' bredder was a Sergeant on the Charleston Police Force around 1868. I had two other sister', Louise an' Rebecca.

My firs' owner was Arthur Barnwell Rose. Then Colonel A. G. Rhodes bought the plantation who sol' it to Capen Frederick W. Wagener. James Sottile then got in possession who sol' it to the DeCostas, an' a few weeks ago Mrs. Albert Callitin Simms, who I'm tol' is a former member of Congress, bought it. Now I'm wonderin' if she is goin' to le' me stay. I hope so 'cus I'm ol' now en can't work.

My pa was name' Abraham Brown; he was bo'n on Coals Islan' in Beaufort County. Colonel Rhodes bought him for his driver, then he move here. I didn't know much 'bout him; he didn't live so long afta slavery 'cus he was ol.

Colonel Rhodes had a son an' a daughter. The son went back to England afta his death an' the daughter went to Germany with her husban'. They ain't never come back so the place was sol' for tax.

Durin' the war we was carry to Deer Pond, twelve miles on dis side of Columbia. W'en the war was end' pa brought my sister, Louise, Rebecca, who was too small to work, Josephine an' me, home. All my people is long-lifted. My grand pa an' grand ma on pa side come right from Africa. They was stolen an' brought here. They use to tell us of how white men had pretty cloth on boats which they was to exchange for some of their o'nament'. W'en they take the o'nament' to the boat they was carry way down to the bottom an' was lock' in. They was anchored on or near Sullivan's Islan' w'ere they been feed like dogs. A big pot was use' for cookin'. In that pot peas was cook' an' lef' to cool. Everybody went to the pot with the han's an' all eat frum the pot.

I was bo'n two years before the war an' was seven w'en it end. That was in 1857. I never went to school but five months in my life, but could learn easy. Very seldom I had to be tol' to do the same thing twice.

The slaves had a plenty o' vegetables all the time. Master planted t'ree acres jus' for the slaves which was attended to in the mornin's before tas' time. All provision was made as to the distribution on Monday evenin's afta tas'.

My master had two place: one on Big Islan' an' on

Coals Islan' in Beaufort County. He didn't have any overseer. My pa was his driver.

Pa say this place was given to Mr. Rhodes with a thousand acres of lan' by England. But it dwindled to thirty-five w'en the other was taken back by England.

There wasn't but ten slaves on this plantation. The driver call' the slaves at four so they could git their breakfas'. They always work the garden firs' an' at seven go in the co'n an' cotton fiel'. Some finish their tas' by twelve an' others work' 'til seven but had the tas' to finish. No one was whip' 'less he needed it; no one else could whip master' slaves. He wouldn't stan' for it. We had it better then than now 'cause white men lynch an' burn now an' do other things they couldn't do then. They shoot you down like dogs now, an' nothin' said or done.

No slave was suppose' to be whip' in Charleston except at the Sugar House. There was a jail for whites, but if a slave ran away an' got there he could disown his master an' the state wouldn't le' him take you.

All collud people has to have a pass w'en they went travelin'; free as well as slaves. If one didn't the patrollers, who was hired by rich white men would give you a good whippin' an' sen' you back home. My pa didn't need any one to write his pass 'cause he could write as well as master. How he got his education, I didn't know.

Sat'day was a workin' day but the tas' was much shorter then other days. Men didn't have time to frolic 'cause they had to fin' food for the fambly; master never give 'nough to las' the whole week. A peck o' co'n, t'ree pound o' beacon, quart o' molasses, a quart o' salt, an' a pack o' tobacco was given the men. The wife got the same thing but chillun accordin' to age. Only one holiday slaves had an' that was Christmas.

Co'nshuckin' parties was conducted by a group of fa'mers who take their slaves or sen' them to the neighborin' ones 'til all the co'n was shuck'. Each one would furnish food 'nough for all slaves at his party. Some use to have nothin' but bake potatas an' some kind of vegetable.

An unmarried young man was call' a half-han'. W'en he want to marry he jus' went to master an' say there's a gal he would like to have for wife. Master would say yes an' that night more chicken would be fry an' everything eatable would be prepare at master' expense. The couple went home afta the supper, without any readin' of matrimony, man an' wife.

A man once married his ma en' didn't know it. He was sell from her w'en 'bout eight years old. When he grow to a young men, slavery then was over, he met this woman who he like' an' so they were married. They was married a month w'en one night they started to tell of their experiences an' how many times they was sol'. The husban' tol' how he was sol' from his mother who liked him dearly. He tol' how his ma faint' w'en they took him away an' how his master then use to bran' his baby slaves at a year ol'. W'en he showed her the bran' she faint' 'cause she then realize' that she had married her son.

Slaves didn't have to use their own remedy for sickness for good doctors been hired to look at them. There was, as is, though, some weed use for fever an' headache as: blacksnake root, furrywork, jimpsin weed, one that tie' on the head which bring sweat from you like hail, an' hickory leaf. If the hickory is keep on the head too long it will blister it.

W'en the war was fightin' the white men burn the bridge at the foot of Spring Street so the Yankees couldn't git over but they buil' pontoos while some make the horses swim 'cross. One night while at Deer Pond, I hear something like thunder until 'bout eleven the next day. W'en the thing I t'ought was thunder stop', master tell us that evenin' we was free. I wasn't surprise to know for as little as I was I know the Yankees was goin' to free us with the help of God.

I was married twice, an' had two gals an' a boy with firs' wife. I have t'ree boys with the second; the younges' is jus' eight.

Lincoln did jus' what God inten' him to do, but I think nothin' 'bout Calhoun on 'account of what he say in one of his speech 'bout collud people. He said: "keep the niggers down."

To see collud boys goin' 'round now with paper an' pencil in their han's don't look real to me. Durin' slavery he would be whip' 'til not a skin was lef' on his body.

My pa was a preacher why I become a Christian so early; he preach' on the plantation to the slaves. On Sunday the slaves went to the white church. He use to tell us of hell an' how hot it is. I was so 'fraid of hell 'til I was always tryin' to do the right thing so I couldn't go to that terrible place.

I don't care 'bout this worl' an' its vanities 'cause the Great Day is comin' w'en I shall lay down an' my stammerin' tongue goin' to lie silent in my head. I want a house not made with han's but eternal in the Heavens. That Man up there, is all I need; I'm goin' to still trus' Him. Before the comin' of Chris' men was kill' for His name sake; today they curse Him. It's nearly time for the world to come to en' for He said "bout two thousand years I shall come again" an' that time is fas' approachin'.

Source

Interview with Henry Brown, 637 Grove Street. He is much concerned with
the Scottsboro Case and discusses the invasion of Italy into defenseless
Ethiopia intelligently.

Project #1655
W. W. Dixon,
Winnsboro, S. C.

## JOHN C. BROWN AND ADELINE BROWN

### Ex-Slaves 86 Years And 96 Years Old.

John C. Brown and his wife, Adeline, who is eleven years older than himself, live in a ramshackle four-room frame house in the midst of a cotton field, six miles west of Woodward, S. C. John assisted in laying the foundation and building the house forty-four years ago. A single china-berry tree, gnarled but stately, adds to, rather than detracts from, the loneliness of the dilapidated house. The premises and thereabout are owned by the Federal Land Bank. The occupants pay no rent. Neither of them are able to work. They have been fed by charity and the W. P. A. for the past eighteen months.

(John talking)

"Where and when I born? Well, dat'll take some 'hear say', Mister. I never knowed my mammy. They say she was a white lady dat visited my old marster and mistress. Dat I was found in a basket, dressed in nice baby clothes, on de railroad track at Dawkins, S. C. De engineer stop de train, got out, and found me sumpin' like de princess found Moses, but not in de bulrushes. Him turn me over to de conductor. De conductor carry me to de station at Dawkins, where Marse Tom Dawkins come to meet de train dat mornin' and claim me as found on his land. Him say him had de best right to me. De conductor didn't 'ject to dat. Marse Tom carry me home and give me to Miss Betsy. Dat was his wife and my mistress. Her always say dat Sheton Brown was my father. He was one of de slaves on de place; de carriage driver. After freedom he tell me he was my real pappy. Him took de name of Brown and dat's what I go by.

"My father was a ginger-bread colored man, not a full-blooded nigger. Dat's how I is altogether yallow. See dat lady over dere in dat chair? Dat's my wife. Her brighter skinned than I is. How come dat? Her daddy was a full-blooded Irishman. He come over here from Ireland and was overseer for Marse Bob Clowney. He took a fancy for Adeline's mammy, a bright 'latto gal slave on de place. White women in them days looked down on overseers as poor white trash. Him couldn't git a white wife but made de best of it by puttin' in his spare time a honeyin' 'round Adeline's mammy. Marse Bob stuck to him, and never 'jected to it.

"When de war come on, Marse Richard, de overseer, shoulder his gun as a soldier and, as him was educated more than most of de white folks, him rise to be captain in de Confederate Army. It's a pity him got kilt in dat war.

"My marster, Tom Dawkins, have a fine mansion. He owned all de land 'round Dawkins and had 'bout 200 slaves, dat lived in good houses and was we well fed. My pappy was de man dat run de mill and grind de wheat and corn into flour and meal. Him never work in de field. He was 'bove dat. Him 'tend to de ginnin' of de cotton and drive de carriage.

"De Yankees come and burn de mansion, de gin-house and de mill. They take all de sheep, mules, cows, hogs and even de chickens. Set de slaves free and us niggers have a hard time ever since.

"My black stepmammy was so mean to me dat I run away. I didn't know where to go but landed up, one night, at Adeline's mammy's and steppappy's house, on Marse Bob Clowney's place. They had been slaves of Marse Bob and was livin' and workin' for him. I knock on de door. Mammy Charity, dat's Adeline's mammy, say: 'Who dat?' I say: 'Me'. Her say: 'Who is me?' I say: 'John'. Her say: 'John who?' I say: 'Just John'. Her say: 'Adeline, open de door, dat's just some poor boy dat's cold and hungry. Charity is my fust name. Your pappy ain't come yet but I'll let dat boy in 'til he come and see what he can do 'bout it.'

"When Adeline open dat door, I look her in de eyes. Her eyes melt towards me wid a look I never see befo' nor since. Mind you, I was just a boy fourteen, I 'spects, and her a woman twenty-five then. Her say: 'You darlin' little fellow; come right in to de fire.' Oh, my! She took on over me! Us wait 'til her pappy come in. Then him say: 'What us gonna do wid him?' Adeline say: 'Us gonna keep him.' Pappy say: 'Where he gonna sleep?' Adeline look funny. Mammy say: 'Us'll fix him a pallet by de fire.' Adeline clap her hands and say: 'You don't mind dat, does you boy?' I say: 'No ma'am, I is slept dat way many a time.'

"Well, I work for Marse Bob Clowney and stayed wid

Adeline's folks two years. I sure made myself useful in dat family. Never 'spicioned what Adeline had in her head, 'til one day I climbed up a hickory nut tree, flail de nuts down, come down and was helpin' to pick them up when she bump her head 'ginst mine and say: 'Oh, Lordy!' Then I pat and rub her head and it come over me what was in dat head! Us went to de house and her told de folks dat us gwine to marry.

"Her led me to de altar dat nex' Sunday. Gived her name to de preacher as Adeline Cabean. I give de name of John Clowney Brown. Marse Bob was dere and laugh when de preacher call my name, 'John Clowney Brown'.

"Our chillun come pretty fast. I was workin' for $45.00 a year, wid rations. Us had three pounds of bacon, a peck of meal, two cups of flour, one quart of 'lasses, and one cup of salt, a week.

"Us never left Marse Robert as long as him lived. When us have four chillun, him increase de amount of flour to four cups and de 'lasses to two quarts. Then him built dis house for de old folks and Adeline and de chillun to live in. I help to build it forty-four years ago. Our chillun was Clarice, Jim, John, Charity, Tom, Richard, and Adeline.

"I followed Marse Robert Clowney in politics, wore a red shirt, and voted for him to go to de Legislature. Him was 'lected dat time but never cared for it no more.

"Adeline b'long to de church. Always after me to jine but I can't believe dere is anything to it, though I believes in de law and de Ten Commandments. Preacher calls me a infidel. Can't help it. They is maybe got me figured out wrong. I believes in a Great Spirit but, in my time, I is seen so many good dogs and hosses and so many mean niggers and white folks, dat I 'clare, I is confused on de subject. Then I can't believe in a hell and everlastin' brimstone. I just think dat people is lak grains of corn: dere is some good grains and some rotten grains. De good grains is res'rected, de rotten grains never sprout again. Good people come up again and flourish in de green fields of Eden. Bad people no come up. Deir bodies and bones just make phosphate guano, 'round de roots of de ever bloomin' tree of life. They lie so much in dis world, maybe de Lord will just make 'lie' soap out of them. What you think else they would be fit for?"

Project #1655
Martha S. Pinckney
Charleston, S. C.
FOLKLORE
Approx. 660 words

# MARY FRANCES BROWN

## Interview With Ex-Slave
## Age 88-90

Mary Frances Brown is a typical product of the old school of trained house servants, an unusual delicate type, somewhat of the Indian cast, to which race she is related. She is always clean and neat, a refined old soul, as individuals of that class often are. Her memory, sight and hearing are good for her advanced age.

"Our home Marlboro. Mas Luke Turnage was my master—Marlboro-Factory-Plantation name 'Beauty Spot'. My missis was right particular about neat and clean. She raise me for a house girl. My missis was good to me, teach me ebbery ting, and take the Bible and learn me Christlanified manners, charity, and behaviour and good respect, and it with me still.

"We didn't have any hard times, our owners were good to us—no over share (overseer) and no whippin'—he couldn't stan' that. I live there 'til two year after freedom; how I come to leave, my mother sister been sick, and she ask mother to send one of us, an she send me. My mother been Miss Nancy cook. Miss Nancy was Mas Luke's mother—it take me two years learning to eat the grub they cook down here in Charleston. I had to learn to eat these little piece of meat—we had a dish full of meat; the big smoke house was lined from the top down. (Describing how the meat hung) I nebber accustom to dese little piece of meat, so—what dey got here. Missis, if you know smoke house, didn't you find it hard? My master had 'til he didn't know what to do with. My white people were Gentile." (Her tone implied that she considered them the acme of gentle folks). "I don't know what the other people were name that didn't have as much as we had—but I know my people were Gentile!"

Just here her daughter and son appeared, very unlike their mother in type. The daughter is quite as old looking as her mother; the son, a rough stevedore. When the writer suggested that the son must be a comfort, she looked down sadly and said in a low tone, as if soliloquizing, "He way is he way." Going back to her former thought, she said, "All our people were good. Mas Luke was the worse one." (This she said with an indulgent smile) "Cause he was all the time at the race ground or the fair ground.

"Religion rules Heaven and Earth, an there is no religion now—harricanes an washin-aways is all about. Ebberything is change. Dis new name what they call grip is pleurisy-cold—putrid sore-throat is called somethin'— yes, diptheria. Cuttin (surgery) come out in 1911! They kill an they cure, an they save an they loss.

"My Gran'ma trained with Indians—she bin a Indian, an Daniel C. McCall bought her. She nebber loss a baby." (the first Indian relationship that the writer can prove). "You know Dr. Jennings? Ebberybody mus' know him. After he examine de chile an de mother, an 'ee alright, he hold de nurse responsible for any affection (infection) that took place.

"Oh! I know de spiritual—but Missis, my voice too weak to sing—dey aint in books; if I hear de name I can sing—'The Promise Land', Oh, how Mas Joel Easterling (born 1796) use to love to sing dat!"

> "I am bound for de Promise Land!
> Oh! who will arise an go with me?
> I am bound for the Promise Land!
> I've got a mother in the Promise Land,
> My mother calls me an I mus go,
> To meet her in the Promise Land!"

Source: Mary Frances Brown, Age 88-90, East Bay Street, Charleston, S. C.

Project #-1655
Cassels R. Tiedeman
Charleston, S. C.
FOLKLORE

# MARY FRANCES BROWN
## Interview With An Ex-Slave

Mary Frances Brown, about ninety years of age, born in slavery, on the plantation of Luke Turnage, in Marlboro County, was raised as a house-servant and shows today evidence of most careful training. Her bearing is rather a gentle refined type, seemingly untouched by the squalor in which she lives. She willingly gives freely of her small store of strength to those around her.

Her happiest days seem to have been those of her early youth, for when she was questioned about the present times, and even about those closely associated with her today she bowed her head and said: "Deir way is deir way. O! let me tell you now, de world is in a haad (hard) time, wust (worse) den it eber (ever) been, but religion! It eberywhere in Hebben an' in de ert (earth) too, if you want em. De trouble is you ain't want em; 'e right dere jes de same but de time done pass when dis generation hold wid anyt'ing but de debbul. When I a gal, grown up, I had a tight missus dat raise me, you hab to keep clean round her, she good an' kind an' I lub her yet, but don't you forgit to mind what she say.

"My massa, he 'low no whipping on de plantation, he talk heap an' he scold plenty, but den he hab to. Dere was haad time for two year after de war was ober (over) but after dat it better den it is now. Dis is de wust time eber. I ain't eber git use to de wittle (victual) you hab down here. I lib ober Mount Pleasant twenty five year after I come from de old place up Marlboro, den I come to Charleston.

"Dey were happy time back dere. My massa, he run round ebery way, spend plenty money on horse race, he gib good time to eberybody an' tell us we mus' tek good care of de missus when he ain't dere. An de wittles we hab I ain't nebber see de lak no time. Dem were de times to lib. I old now but I ain't forgit what my missus larn (learn) me. It right here in me."

Mary Frances was asked if she could sing spirituals. The following is one that she sang in a very high pitched wavering voice and then she complained of shortness of breath on account of her heart.

> "We got a home ober dere,
> Come an' let us go,
> Come an' let us go,
> Where pleasure neber (never) die.
>
> Chorus:
> "Oh! let us go where pleasure neber die,
> Neber die,
> Come and let us go,
> Where pleasure neber die, neber die.

"Mother is gone ober dere,
Mother is gone ober dere,
Where pleasure neber die,
Where pleasure neber die.

Chorus:

"Father is gone ober dere,
Father is gone ober dere,
Where pleasure neber die,
Where pleasure neber die.

Chorus:

"Sister is gone ober dere,
Sister is gone ober dere,
Where pleasure neber die,
Where pleasure neber die.

Chorus:

"Brudder is gone ober dere,
Brudder is gone ober dere,
Where pleasure neber die,
Where pleasure neber die."

Chorus:


Source: Interview with Mary Frances Brown, 83 East Bay St.,
Charleston, S. C. (age—90)

United States

Code No. --
Project. 1885-(1)
Prepared by Annie Ruth Davis
Place, Marion, S. C.
Date, July 8, 1937
No. Words --
Reduced From -- words
Rewritten by --

# MOM SARA BROWN

## Ex-Slave, 85 years

"Oh, my God, de doctors have me in slavery time. Been here de startin of de first war. I belong to de Cusaac dat live 15 miles low Florence on de road what take you on to Georgetown. I recollects de Yankees come dere in de month of June en free de colored peoples."

"My white folks give me to de doctors in dem days to try en learn me for a nurse. Don' know exactly how old I was in dat day en time, but I can tell you what I done. My Lord, child, can' tell dat. Couldn' never tell how many baby I bring in dis world, dey come so fast. I betcha I got more den dat big square down dere to de courthouse full of em. I nurse 13 head of chillun in one family right here in dis town. You see dat all I ever did have to do. Was learnt to do dat. De doctor tell me, say, when you call to a 'oman, don' you never hesitate to go en help her en you save dat baby en dat mother both. Dat what I is always try to do. Heap of de time just go en let em pay me by de chance. Oh, my Lord, a 'oman birth one of dem babies here bout two weeks ago wid one of dem veil over it face. De Lord know what make dat, I don', but dem kind of baby sho wiser den de other kind of baby. Dat thing look just like a thin skin dat stretch over da baby face en come down low it's chin. Have to take en pull it back over it's forehead en den de baby can see en holler all it ever want to. My blessed, honey, wish I had many a dollar as I see veil over baby face. Sho know all bout dem kind of things."

"Oh, honey, I tell you de people bless dis day en time. Don' know nothin bout how to be thankful enough for what dey have dese days. I tell de truth de peoples sho had to scratch bout en make what dey had in slavery time. Baby, dey plant patches of okra en parch dat en make what coffee dey have. Den dey couldn' get no shoes like dey hab dese days neither. Just make em out of de hide of dey own cows dat dey butcher right dere on de plantation. Coase de peoples had plenty sometin to eat like meat en turkey en chicken en thing like dat. Oh, my God, couldn' see de top of de smoke house for all de heap of meat dey have in dem times. En milk en butter, honey, dey didn' never be widout plenty of dat. De peoples bout here dese days axes ten cents a quart for sweet milk en five cents a quart for old sour clabber. What you think bout dat? Dat how-come people have to hunt jobs so mucha dese days. Have to do some sorta work cause you know dey got to put sometin in dey mouth somewhe' or another. Oh, my child, slavery days was troublesome times. Sugar en salt never run free wid de peoples den neither. I know de day been here when salt was so scarce dat dey had to go to de seashore en get what salt dey had. I gwine to tell you all bout dat. Dey hitch up two horses to a wagon en den dey make another horse go in front of de wagon to rest de other horses long de way. Dey mostly go bout on a Monday en stay three days. Boil dat salty water down dere en fetch two en three of dem barrel of salt back wid em dey get dat way. It was just like dis, it take heap of salt when dey had dem big hog-killin days. En de sugar, dey make dat too. Made de sugar in lil blocks dat dey freeze just like dey freeze ice dis day en time. I know dey do dat—know it. Dey make molasses en some of it would be lighter den de other en dey freeze dat en make de prettiest lil squares just like de ice you see dese days. Dey have sometin to freeze it in. Dis here old black mammy know heap of things you ain' never hear bout. Oh, baby, de peoples sho bless dese days."

"Oh, my god, de colored peoples worship to de white folks church in slavery time. You know dat Hopewell Church over de river dere, dat a slavery church. Dat whe' I go to church den wid my white folks. I had a lil chair wid a cowhide bottom dat I always take everywhe' I go wid me. If I went to church, dat chair go in de carriage wid me en den I take it in de church en set right by de side of my Miss. Dat how it was in slavery time. Oh, my Lord, dere a big slavery people graveyard dere to dat Hopewell Church."

"Honey, you mind if I smoke my pipe a lil whilst I settin here talkin wid you. I worry so much wid dis high blood dese days en a ringin in my ears dat my pipe de only thing dat does seem to satisfy my soul. I tell you dat high blood a bad thing. It get such a hold on me awhile back dat I couldn' do nothin, couldn' pick cotton, couldn' say my—me, couldn' even say, God a mighty—thing pretty. Oh, I don' know. I start smokin pipe long time ago when I first start nursin babies. Had to do sometin like dat den."

"No, Lord, I never believe nothin bout dat but what God put here. I hear some people say dey was conjure, but I don' pay no attention to dey talk. Dey say somebody poison em for sometin dey do, but dere ain' nobody do dat. God gwine to put you down when he get ready. Ain' nobody else do dat."

"Oh, my Lord, I been here a time. I sho been here a time en I thank de Lord I here dis day en time. I can thread my needle good as ever I could en I ain' have no speck neither. Sew night en day. De chillun have dey lamp dere studyin en I hab my lamp dere sewin. My old Miss learnt me to sew when I stay right in de house wid her all de time. I stay bout white folks all my life en dat how-come I so satisfy when I wid em."

Source: Mom Sara Brown, age 85, ex-slave, Marion, S. C. Personal interview, June 1937.

Code No. --
Project, 1885-(1)
Prepared by Annie Ruth Davis
Place, Marion, S. C.
Date, September 10, 1937
No. Words --
Reduced from -- words
Rewritten by --

## SARA BROWN

### Ex-Slave, 85 Years

"I stay in house over dere cross Catfish Swamp on Miss Addie McIntyre place. Lives wid dis grand-daughter dat been sick in bed for four weeks, but she mendin some now. She been mighty low, child. It start right in here (chest) en run down twixt her shoulder. She had a tear up cold too, but Dr. Dibble treat her en de cough better now. She got three chillun dere dat come just like steps. One bout like dat en another like dat en de other bout like dis."

"De house we stay in a two room house wid one of dese end chimney. All sleep in de same room en cook en eat in de other room. My bed on one side en Sue bed on de other side. Put chillun on quilts down on de floor in de other end of de room. Baby, whe' dem curtains you say you gwine give me? I gwine hang dese up in Sue room. Dey help me fix up de room nice en decent like."

"It all on me to feed en clothe both dem chillun en de baby too. It just too much on me old as I is. Can' do nothin worth to speak bout hardly dese days. Can' hold my head down cause dis high blood worries me so much. It get too hot, can' iron. If ain' too hot, I makes out to press my things somehow en sweep my yard bout. Sometimes I helps little bit wid doctor case, but not often. Can wash de baby en de mother, but can' do no stayin up at night. No, baby, can' do no settin up at night."

"I tries to catch all what little I can to help along cause dat how I was raise up. Government truck brings me little somethin once a month pack up in packages like dry milk en oatmeal en potatoes. Give dat to all dem dat can' work en ain' got nobody to help dem. Dat dry milk a good thing to mix up de bread wid en den it a help to fix little milk en bread for dem two little ones. De potatoes, I stews dem for de chillun too. Dey mighty fond of dem. Now de oatmeal, de chillun don' eat dat so I fixes it for Sue en every now en den I takes a little bit wid my breakfast."

"I don' know much what to tell you bout Abraham Lincoln. I think he was a mighty great man, a mighty great man, what I hear of him."

"I remembers de Yankees come dere to my white folks plantation one day en, child, dere was a time on dat place. All dem niggers was just a kickin up dey heels en shoutin. I was standin dere on de piazza lookin at dem en I say, 'I don' see why dey want to carry on like dat for. I been free all de time.' When dey get through de Yankees tell dem dey was free as dey Massa was en give dem so many bushels of corn en so much meat for dey own. Some take dey pile en go on off en some choose to stay on dere wid dey Missus. She was good to all her colored people en dey stay on dere for part de crop. Give dem so much of de crop accordin to de chillun dey had to feed. I know dis much, dey all know dey gwine get 12 bushels of corn a year, if dey ain' get no more. Dat a bushel every month. Yes, dat how it was."

"O Lord, baby, I don' know a thing bout none of dat thing call conjurin. Don' know nothin bout it. Dat de devil work en I ain' bother wid it. Dey say some people can kill you, but dey ain' bother me. Some put dey trust in it, but not me. I put my trust in de Lord cause I know it just a talk de people have. No, Lord, I can' remember dat neither. I hear dem say Raw Head en Bloody Bones would catch you if you be bad, but how it started, I don' know. I know I don' know nothin bout how dey look en I don' want to see dem neither. No, child, people say dey sho to be, but I ain' see none. How dey look, I don' know."

"I don' know what to think bout de times dese days. De times worse den dey used to be, child. You know dey worse. Dis here a fast time de people livin on cause everybody know de people die out heap faster den dey used to. Don' care how dey kill you up. No, child, dey sho worser. My people en yunnah people. Don' it seem so to you dat dey worser?"

"Baby, I got to get up from here en leave now cause I huntin medicine dis mornin. I ain' got time to tell you nothin else dis time, but I gwine get my mind fix up on it en den your old black mammy comin back fore long en stay all day wid you en your mamma. What time dat clock say it now, honey? I got to hurry en catch de doctor fore he get away from his office en be so scatter bout till nobody can' tell whe' he is. Dr. Dibble a good doctor, a mighty good doctor. When he come, don' never come in no hurry. Takes pains wid you. Dat been my doctor. I is just devoted to him."

    Source: Mom Sara Brown, ex-slave, age 85, Marion, S. C. Second Report.

    Personal interview, September, 1937 by Annie Ruth Davis, Marion, S. C.

Project #-1655
Mrs. Genevieve W. Chandler
Murrells Inlet, S. C.
Georgetown County
FOLKLORE

# AUNT MARGARET BRYANT

## Some recollections of 'The Reb Time day'

Visitor: "How are you Aunt Margaret?"

Margaret: "Missus, I ain't wuth! I ain't wuth!"

Visitor: "Aunt Margaret you've been here a long time. How old are you?"

Margaret: "I can't tell you my age no way in the world! When freedom come, I been here. Not big nuff (enough) for work for the Reb, but I been here Reb time. Been big nuff (enough) to know when Yankee gun-boat come to Watsaw (Wachesaw). Whole gang o' Yankee come to the house and didn't do a thing but ketch (catch) a gang o' fowl and gone on. And tell the people (meaning the slaves) to take the house and go in and get what they want. The obersheer (overseer) hear the Doctor whistle to the gate and wabe (wave) him back. And then the Doctor know the Yankee been there and he gone on to the creek house and get all he gold and ting (thing) out the house and gone— Marion till Freedom then he come back.

"Yankee come in that night. Moon shine lak a day. Stay in the Doctor house that night. Morning come, take a gang o' fowl and gone on!"

Visitor: "Aunt Margaret, what was your name before you were married?"

Margaret: "Margaret One. Brother and sister? I ain't one when I come here. Ain't meet aunty, uncle—none. Me and my brudder Michael wuz twin. I ain't meet none when I come here. All been sell. Me and my Ma One here. Mary One. Husband title, husband nichel (initial) been 'One.' Number one carpenter—give 'em that name Michael One—and he gibe 'em that name. Born Sandy Island. Been to landing to Watsaw when gun-boat come. Just a sneak long! Boat white. Hab (have) a red chimbley (chimney.) Didn't try to carry we off. Tell 'em 'Go and help youself.' Been after the buckra. (The Yankee trying to catch the buckra.)

"I see my Ma dye with some bush they call 'indigo,' and black walnut bark. Big old pen for the sheep-folds.

"My Pa sister, Ritta One had that job. Nuss (nurse) the chillun. Chillun house. One woman nuss (nurse) all the chillun while they ma in the field—rice field. All size chillun. Git the gipsy (gypsum) weed. Beat 'em up for worm. Give 'em when the moon change. Take a bucket and follow dem. And tell the Doctor how much a worm that one make and that one and count dem (them). When the moon change, do that.

"I have one born with caul. Loss he caul. Rat carry 'em. Ain't here; he see nothin. (The custom seems to be, to preserve the caul.)

"Child born feet fore-most see 'um too." (See spirit) "Talk chillun? Put duh switch. Put you 'Bull pen.' Hab 'um (have them) a place can't see you hand before you. Can't turn round good in there. Left you in there till morning. Give you fifty lash and send you to work. You ain't done that task, man and woman lick!

"Couldn't manage my ma. Obersheer (overseer) want to lick ma, Mary One say, 'Going drownded meself! I done my work! Fore I take a lick, rather drownded meself.'" Obersheer gone tell the Doctor. Tie her long rope. Right to Sandy Island. Man hold the rope. Gone on. Jump in river. So Doctor say, 'You too good labor for drown. Take dem (them) to Watsaw.' Me and she and man what paddle the boat. Bring her to weave. Two womans fuh card; two spin. Ma wop 'em off. Sail duh sheckel (shuttle) through there.

"Po-buckra come there and buy cloth from Ma. Buy three and four yard. Ma sell that, have to weave day and night to make up that cloth to please obersheer. Come big day time. 'Little chillun, whey (where) Mama?' Tell 'em Ma to the weaving house. Don't have money fuh pay. Bring hog and such like as that to pay.

"You know Marse Allard age? Me and Marse Allard suck together. Me and Marse Allard and my brudder Michael. My ma fadder mix wid (with) the Injun. Son Larry Aikens. Stay Charston (Charlestown). Just as clean! (Meaning Larry, her Uncle, very bright skin. Mixed with Indian.) See 'em the one time. Come from Charston bring Doctor two horse."

    Given by Aunt Margaret Bryant
    Age—(Born before Freedom)

## Murrells Inlet, S. C.

Project #1655
W. W. Dixon
Winnsboro, S. C.

# SAVILLA BURRELL
## Ex-Slave, 83 Years

"Our preacher, Beaty, told me that you wanted to see me today. I walked three miles dis mornin' before the sun gits hot to dis house. Dis house is my grand daughter's house. Willie Caldwell, her husband, work down to de cotton mill. Him make good money and take good care of her, bless the Lord, I say."

"My Marster in slavery time was Captain Tom Still. He had big plantation down dere on Jackson Crick. My Mistress name was Mary Ann, though she wasn't his fust wife—jest a second wife, and a widow when she captivated him. You know widows is like dat anyhow, 'cause day done had 'sperience wid mens and wraps dem 'round their little finger and git dem under their thumb 'fore the mens knows what gwine on. Young gals have a poor chance against a young widow like Miss Mary Ann was. Her had her troubles with Marse Tom after her git him, I tell you, but maybe best not to tell dat right now anyways."

"Marse Tom had four chillun by his fust wife, dey was John, Sam, Henretta and I can't 'member de name of the other one; least right now. Dey teached me to call chillun three years old, young Marse and say Missie. Dey whip you if dey ever hear you say old Marse or old Missie. Dat riled dem."

"My pappy name Sam. My mother name Mary. My pappy did not live on the same place as mother. He was a slave of de Hamiltons, and he got a pass sometimes to come and be with her; not often. Grandmammy name Ester and she belonged to our Marse Tom Still, too."

"Us lived in a log cabin wid a stick chimney. One time de sticks got afire and burnt a big hole in de back of de chimney in cold winter time wid the wind blowing, and dat house was filled wid fire-sparks, ashes, and smoke for weeks 'fore dey tore dat chimney down and built another jest like the old one. De bed was nailed to de side of de walls. How many rooms? Jest one room."

"Never seen any money. How many slaves? So many you couldn't count dem. Dere was plenty to eat sich as it was, but in the summer time before us git dere to eat de flies would be all over de food and some was swimmin' in de gravy and milk pots. Marse laugh 'bout dat, and say, it made us fat."

"Dey sell one of mother's chillun once, and when she take on and cry 'bout it, Marse say, 'stop dat sniffin' dere if you don't want to git a whippin'.' She grieve and cry at night 'bout it. Clothes? Yes Sir, us half naked all de time. Grown boys went 'round bare footed and in dey shirt tail all de summer."

"Marse was a rich man. 'Fore Christmus dey would kill thirty hogs and after Christmus, thirty more hogs. He had a big gin house and sheep, goats, cows, mules, hosses, turkeys, geese, and a stallion; I members his name, Stockin'-Foot. Us little niggers was skeered to death of dat stallion. Mothers used to say to chillun to quiet dem, 'Better hush, Stockin'-Foot will git you and tramp you down.' Any child would git quiet at dat."

"Old Marse was de daddy of some mulatto chillun. De 'lations wid de mothers of dese chillun is what give so much grief to Mistress. De neighbors would talk 'bout it and he would sell all dem chillun away from dey mothers to a trader. My Mistress would cry 'bout dat.

"Our doctor was old Marse son-in-law, Dr. Martin. I seen him cup a man once. He was a good doctor. He give slaves castor oil, bleed dem some times and make dem take pills."

"Us looked for the Yankees on dat place like us look now for de Savior and de host of angels at de second comin'. Dey come one day in February. Dey took everything carryable off de plantation and burnt de big house, stables, barns, gin house and dey left the slave houses."

"After de war I marry Osborne Burrell and live on de Tom Jordan place. I'se de mother of twelve chillun. Jest three livin' now. I lives wid the Mills family three miles 'bove town. My son Willie got killed at de DuPont Powder Plant at Hopewell, Virginia, during de World War. Dis house you settin' in belongs to Charlie Caldwell. He marry my grand daughter, Willie B. She is twenty-three years old."

"Young Marse Sam Still got killed in de Civil War. Old Marse live on. I went to see him in his last days and I set by him and kept de flies off while dere. I see the lines of sorrow had plowed on dat old face and I 'membered he'd been a captain on hoss back in dat war. It come into my 'membrance de song of Moses; 'de Lord had triumphed glorily and de hoss and his rider have been throwed into de sea'."

"You been good to listen. Dis is the fust time I can git to speak my mind like dis mornin'. All de' people seem runnin' here and yonder, after dis and after dat. Dere is a nudder old slave, I'se gwine to bring him down here Saturday and talk to you again."

Project 1885-1
FOLKLORE
Spartanburg, S. C.
Sept. 15, 1937
Edited by:
Elmer Turnage

# C. B. BURTON

## Stories From Ex-Slaves

"I works on de shares and makes a fair living on a rented farm; don't own no land. I was born in Newberry County, near de old Longshore store, about 12 miles northwest of Newberry Courthouse on de Henry Burton place. My parents belonged to Henry Burton in slavery time. He was our marster. I married Betty Burton, a nigger girl whose parents belonged to Marse Henry Burton, too.

"We had a good marster and mistress. Dey give us a good place to sleep and lots to eat. He had a big four-acre garden where he raised lots of vegetables fer his slaves. He had plenty meat, molasses and bread. We ground our corn and wheat and made our own feed.

"Marster wouldn't let anybody bother his slaves. He wouldn't 'low his overseers or de padrollers to whip 'em. He never whipped one.

"We had no school and no church; but was made to go to de white folks church and set in de gallery. When Freedom come, de niggers begin to git dere own church, and built small brush huts called 'brush harbors'.

"We didn't do work on Saturday afternoons, but went hunting and fishing den, while de women folks cleaned up around de place fer Sunday. De marster liked to hunt, and he hunted foxes which was plenty around dere den. Now dey is all gone.

"We danced and had gigs. Some played de fiddle and some made whistles from canes, having different lengths for different notes, and blowed 'em like mouth organs."

Source: C. B. Burton (79), Newberry, S. C.
Interviewer: G. L. Summer, Newberry, S. C. (9/10/37)

Project #-1655
Phoebe Faucette
Hampton County
Folklore

# GEORGE ANN BUTLER
## Ex-Slave 75 Years

West of the paved highway at Garnett one may reach, after several miles, the old Augusta Road that follows along the Savannah River from Augusta to a landing point a little south of Garnett. Miles from the busy highway, it passes, in quiet majesty, between fields and woods, made rich by the river's overflow and heavy dews. Nature has done her best in producing beautiful evergreen trees of immense size and much luxuriant shrubbery of many kinds. Live oaks, magnolias, yellow slash pines, hollies, and many evergreen shrubs keep the woods even in winter, a fascinating wilderness to hunters and nature lovers. On this road George Ann Butler lives, and has lived for the seventy-five years of her life.

"I was born an' raised on de Greenwood place. It belonged to ole man Joe Bostick. He owned all dese places 'long dese here road. He own de Bostick place back yonder; den he own de Pipe Creek place next dat; den Oaklawn; den joinin' dat was Greenwood. De Colcock's

Elmwood was next. My Husband was birth right here on de Pipe Creek, an' been here ever since. He kin tell you more'n I kin. I was George Anne Curry before I marry.

"I can't remember so much 'bout slavery time. I was crawlin' over de floor when slavery time—dey tell me. But atter de war, I 'members. Couldn't find no corn seed! Couldn't find no cotton seed! Couldn't find no salt! You knows it was hard times when dere wasn't no salt to season de vegetables. Had to go down to de salt water an' get de water an' boil it for salt. Dat been a long way from here. Must be fifty or sixty mile! An' dey couldn't go so fast in dem days. Sufferin' been in de neighborhood atter de war pass!

"Cotton was de thing 'way back yonder. An' right 'long dis road dey'd haul it. Haul it to Cohen's Bluff! Haul it to Matthews Bluff! Haul it to Parichucla! Don't haul it dis way no more! Send de cotton to de railroad! But in dem days it was de ships dat carried it to Savannah. Cotton seem to be play out now—dey plant so much.

"I hear 'em tell 'bout de war, an' havin' to drill an' step when dey say step, an' throw up dey hands, when dey say throw up de hand. Everything had to be done jes' so! De war was sure a terrible thing."

Source: George Anne Butler, R. F. D. Garnett, S. C.

Project #-1655
Phoebe Faucette
Hampton County

# ISAIAH BUTLER

## Ex-Slave 79 Years

"Yes, dis is Isaiah Butler, piece of him. Ain't much left of him now. Yes, I knows all 'bout dis heah country from way back. I was born and raised right on dis same place here; lived here all my life 'sides from travellin' round a little space. Dere was a rice field not far from dis house here, where I plowed up more posts that had been used as landmarks! Dis place was de Bostick place, and it jined to de Thomson place, and de Thomson place to Edmund Martin's place dat was turned over to Joe Lawton, his son-in-law. Bill Daniel had charge of de rice field I was telling you 'bout. He was overseer, on de Daniel Blake place. Den dere was de Maner place, de Trowell, de Kelly, and de Wallace places. Back in dem times dey cultivated rice. Had mules to cultivate it! But cotton and corn was what dey planted most of all; 4,000 acres I think dey tell me was on dis place. I know it supposed to be more than ten miles square. Nobody know de landmarks 'cept me. When de Bostick boys came back from out west last year, dey had to come to me to find out where dere place was. Dey didn't know nuttin' 'bout it.

Dey used to use twenty plow, and de hoe hands was over a hundred, I know.

"I 'member when de Yankees come through. I was no more'n a lad, nine or ten years old. Bostick had a big gin-house, barn, stables, and such like. And when de soldiers come a goat was up on de platform in front of de door to de loft of de barn. Dere were some steps leadin' up dere and dat goat would walk up dem steps same as any body. De fuss thing de Yankees do, dey shoot dat goat. Den day start and tear up eberyt'ing. All de white folks had refugeed up North, and dey didn't do nuttin' to us niggers.

"Fore dat time I was jes' a little boy too young to do nuttin'. Jes' played aroun' in de street. Ole Mr. Ben Bostick used to bring clothes an' shoes to us and see dat we was well cared for. Dere was nineteen houses in de street for us colored folks. Dey wuz all left by de soldiers. But in de year 1882 dere come a cyclone (some folks call it a tornado), and knocked down every house; only left four standing. Pieces of clothes and t'ings were carried for four or five miles from here. It left our house; but it took everyt'ing we had. It took de walls of de house, jes' left de floorin', an' it wus turn 'round. Took everyt'ing! I'd jes' been married 'bout a year, and you know how dat is. We jes' had to scuffle and scuffle 'roun' till de Lord bless us.

"Dere wuz plenty of deer, squirrel, possum, an' rabbits in dem times; no more dan dere is now, but dere wuz no hinderance den as now. De deer come right up to my door now; dey come all 'roun' dis house, and we cain't do nuttin'. De other day one wuz over dere by dat peachtree, an' not long ago four of 'em come walkin' right through dis yard. I don't go fishin' no more. Folks say de streams is all dried up. But I used to be a good fisherman, me an' me ole woman. She's spryer'n me now. I used to allus protect her when we wuz young, an' now its her dat's acarin' for me. We had our gardens in de ole days, too. Oh, yes'm. Little patches of collards, greens an' t'ings, but now I ain't able to do nuttin', jes' hang 'roun' de place here.

"My father used to belong to General Butler, Dennis Butler was his name. My mother was a Maner, but originally she wuz draw out of de Robert estate. Ole Ben Bostick fuss wife wuz a Robert. Dey wuz sure wealthy folks. One of 'em went off to sail. Bill F. Robert wuz his name. He had so much money dat he say dat he goin' to de end of de world. He come back an' he say he went so close hell de heat draw de pitch from de vessel. But he lost his eyesight by it. Wa'n't (it was not) long after he got back dat he went stone blind.

"My ole boss, preacher Joe Bostick wuz one of de best of men. He wuz hard of hearin' like I is, an' a good ole man. But de ole lady, ole "Miss Jenny", she wuz very rough. She hired all de overseers, and she do all. If'n anybody try to go to de old man wid anyt'ing, she'd talk to 'em herself an' not let 'em see de old man.

"In slavery time de slaves wuz waked up every morning by de colored over-driver blowin' a horn. Ole man Jake Chisolm wuz his name. Jes' at daybreak, he'd put his horn through a crack in de upper part of de wall to his house an' blow it through dat crack. Den de under-driver would go out an' round 'em up. When dey done all dey day-work, dey come home an' cook dey supper, an' wash up. Den dey blow de horn for 'em to go to bed. Sometime dey have to out de fire an' finish dey supper in de dark. De under-driver, he'd go out den and see who ain't go to bed. He wouldn't say anyt'ing den; but next mornin' he'd report it to de overseer, an' dem as hadn't gone to bed would be whipped.

"My mother used to tell me dat if any didn't do dey day's work, dey'd be put in de stocks or de bill-bo. You know each wuz given a certain task dat had to be finish dat day. Dat what dey call de day-work. When dey put 'em in de stocks dey tie 'em hand and foot to a stick. Dey could lie down wid dat. I hear of colored folks doin' dat now to dare chillun when dey don't do. Now de bill-bo wuz a stabe (stave) drove in de ground, an' dey tied dere hands and den dere feet to dat, standin' up. Dey'd work on Saturday but dey wuz give Sundays. Rations wuz give out on Mondays. Edmund Lawton went over to Louisiana to work on de Catherine Goride place, but he come back, 'cause he say dey blow dey horn for work on Sunday same as any other day, and he say he wa'n't goin' to work on no Sunday. Dey didn't have a jail in dem times. Dey'd whip 'em, and dey'd sell 'em. Every slave know what, 'I'll put you in my pocket, sir!' mean.

"De slaves would walk when dey'd go anywhere. If'n dey buy a bunch of slaves in New Orleans, dey'd walk by night and day. I 'member when one young girl come back from refugin' wid de white folks, her feet were jes' ready to buss open, and dat wuz all. You couldn't travel unless de boss give you a pass. De Ku Klan had "patrol" all about in de bushes by de side of de road at night. And when dey caught you dey'd whip you almost to death! Dey'd horsewhip you. Dey didn't run away nowhere 'cause dey knowed dey couldn't.

"If'n you wanted to send any news to anybody on

another plantation, de overseer'd write de message for you and send it by a boy to de overseer of de other plantation, and he'd read it to de one you wrote to.

"When de war wuz over, ole man Jones cone over frum Georgia and sell t'ings to de colored folks. He'd sell 'em everyt'ing. He took all de colored folks' money!

"I learned to read when I wuz goin' to school when I wuz about fifteen years old, but I learned most I know after I wuz married, at night school, over on de Morrison place. De colored folks had de school, but 'course Mr. Morrison was delighted to know dey wuz havin' it. As for church, in de olden times, people used to, more or less, attend under de bush-arbor. In 1875 when I jined de church, ole man John Butler wuz de preacher.

"Ghosts? I'se met plenty of um! When I wuz courtin' I met many a one—One got me in de water, once. And another time when I wuz crossing a stream, I wuz on de butt end of de log, an' dey wuz on de blossom end, an' we meet jes' as close as I is to you now. I say to him, same as to anybody, 'I sure ain't goin' to turn back, and fall off dis log. Now de best t'ing for you to do is to turn 'round and let me come atter (after) you. You jes' got to talk to 'em same as to anybody. It don't pay to be 'fraid of 'em. So he wheel 'round. (Spirits can wheel, you know.) And when he get to de end of de log, I say, 'Now you off and I off. You kin go on 'cross now.' Dey sure is a t'ing, all right! Dey look jes' like anybody else, 'cept'n it's jes' cloudy and misty like it goin' to pour down rain. But it don't do to be 'fraid of 'em. I ain't 'fraid of nuttin', myself. I never see 'em no more. Guess I jes' sorta out-growed 'em. But dere sure is sech a t'ing, all right! De white folks'd see 'em, too. I 'member hearin' ole Joe Bostick, de preacher, say to a man, by de name of Tinlin, 'Did you hear dat hog barkin' last night? Well, de spirit come right in de house. Come right up over de mantlepiece.' I wuz in de field workin' same as I allus done, and I hear'd ole Joe horse a snortin'. Ole Joe didn't want nuttin'. He jes' want to see what I wuz doin'.

"Abraham Lincoln done all he could for de colored folks. But dey cain't none of 'em do nuttin' without de Lord."

Source: Isaiah Butler, Garnett, S. C.

Project #-1655
Phoebe Faucette
Hampton County
Approx. 800 Words

# SOLBERT BUTLER
## Ex-Slave Of 82 Years

Miles from the highway old Solbert Butler lives alone under the shadow of the handsome winter home of an aged northerner upon the same soil that he has seen pass from Southerner to Negro, to Southerner, to Northerner. Though shrunken and bent with age he still enjoys talking.

"I lives in de Deer Country. A couple of months ago, I saw eight in a drove at one time, like a drove of sheep, or sech like. You can't raise nuthin' 'round here. Dey'll eat up your garden. And de wild turkey! And de partridge! But you can't shoot 'em without de Cassels give you a license to do it. Now he comin' next month and dere'll be more shootin'! But he aint able to hunt none hisself. He kin ride 'bout in de woods in de car. Dey are blessed people, though!

"Dis used to be de Bostick place. Old Massa Ben Bostick lived fourteen miles from here. Dere was Ben Bostick, Iva Bostick, Joe Bostick, Mr. Luther, Eddie Bostick, an' Jennie

Jo Bostick. De place was divided up between 'em. O-oh! I couldn't number de plantations old Mr. Bostick owned. I think he owned fifteen plantations! He was de millinery (millionaire)! Oh, de Bosticks, O-oh!! De house dey live in, dey call um—what was it dey call um—de Paradise house. No one go to dat house but only de rich.

"At Christmas dey'd go up dere. And oh, I couldn't number it! Oh, it was paradise. He was good to 'em. An' he whip 'em good, too! Tie 'em to de fence post and whip 'em. But I didn't' have anythin' of dat. I was a little boy. Jes' 'bout six year old when de war broke out. But I got plenty of whippin's all right.

"Massa take me as a little boy as a pet. Took me right in de carriage! Had a little bed right by his own an' take care of me. Every morning dey bring in dey tray, an' go back. My uncle was a carriage man. Dey kept two fine horses jes' for de carriage. Massa'd come up to de Street every Monday morning with big trays of rations. He'd feed his colored folk, den go on back."

(Another old ex-slave from the same plantation had said that on Mondays the week's rations were given out.)

"Dey planted cotton, corn, peas, potatoes, rice—an' dey'd lick you! All de time, dey'd lick you. After dey'd lick 'em until de blood come out, den dey'd rub de red pepper and salt on 'em. Oh, my God! Kin you say dem as done sech as dat aint gone to deir reward? My uncle was so whip he went into de woods, an' live dere for months. Had to learn de independent life. Mr. Aldridge was de overseer. Old Mr. Aldridge gone now. But dere can't be no rest for him. Oh my God no! He do 'em so mean dat finally ole Massa hear 'bout it. And when he do hear 'bout it, he discharged him. He had everything discharged—to de colored driver. Den he got Mr. Chisolm. After Mr. Chisolm come in, everythin' jes' as sweet an' smooth as could be! Dere's a nice set of people for you—de Chisolms. Two of 'em livin' now. One at Garnett, an' one at Luray, I believe.

"I refugeed wid Massa. Dey come together in Virginia. Dey surrendered in Virginia. Set de house afire. And set all dey houses. Dey burned Massa's cotton. Over 200 bales! But if'n de colored folks begged for some, dey let 'em have some. I stayed right wid Massa. He carried me everywhere he went. Carried me all de way to Mill Haven, Georgia.

"After de war de colored folks jes' took an' plant de crop an' make de livin' wid de hoe. Didn't have no mule, no ox, or thin' like dat. When ole Massa come back, he took de cotton, an' give de colored folks de corn. De Yankees kill all de hog. Kill all de cow. Kill all de fowl. Left you nothin' to eat. If de colored folk had any chicken, dey jes' had to take dat an' try to raise 'em somethin' to eat.

"I'se a Methodist. I was converted under Elder Drayton—come from Georgia at St. Luke Methodist Church on de Blake Plantation. De Blake Plantation right dere. It jines dis one. De ole Methodist white folk's church where I was baptized been take down. It was called de Union Church. But de cemetery still dere. It right up dere not a mile down de road. Dere was a good ole preacher name of Rev. Winborn Asa Lawton. An' de camp meetin'! Oh, Lord, Lord! Dey had over a thousand dere. Come from Orangeburg. Come from Aiken! An' come way from Cheraw! Come from Charleston, Beaufort, and Savannah! De colored folks got a church now up here on what used to be de Pipe Creek place of ole Ben Bostick where de white folks used to have a Baptist church. De colored folks church call it Kenyon Church. Dat's de church dey white folks moved to Lawtonville, den to Estill. But when de colored folks built, dey built de church to face de East. Built on de same foundation; but face it east, facing a little road dat had sprung up and wind 'round dat way right in close to de church. But de white folks church was face west, facing de Augusta road. Dat big space twixt de road and de church was a grove.

"Ghosts? I used to 'em. I see 'em all de time. Good company! I live over dere by myself, an' dey comes in my house all de time. Sometime I walk along at night an' I see 'em. An' when you see 'em you see a sight. Dey play. Dey dance 'round an' 'round. Dey happy all right. But dey'll devil you, too. When dey find out dat you scary, dey'll devil you. Dey don't do nothin' to me. Only talk to me. I'll be in my house an' dey'll come talk to me. Or I'll be walkin' down de road, an' meet 'em. Dey'll pass de time of day wid me, Like:

'Hey, Solbert! How far you goin', Solbert?'

'I'se jes' goin' down de road a little piece,' I'll say.

'Uh-huh'.

"Or sometime dey'll say, 'Mornin', Solbert. How you feeling?'

'I'se jes' so so'.

'Uh-huh'.

"Dey all favors. Dey all looks alike. You remembers

when dat car come down de road jes' now? Well, I see a bunch of 'em right den! Dey get out de road for dat car to pass. Oh, you can't see 'em. No matter how much I shows 'em to you—you can't see 'em. But me! Dey swell wid me. I see 'em all de time. De big house up dere. It full of 'em. De white folks see 'em, too. Dat is some of de white folks. I see de other day a white man dat has to work up here start toward de house when de ghosts was comin' out thick. When I tell him you ought to see him turn an' run. One of 'em push me over in de ditch one time. I say,

'Now what you done dat for?'

'Well, dat aint nothin''

'Aint nothin'. But don't you do dat no more.'

"I talks to 'em jes' de same as if dey was somebody. Some folks outgrows 'em. But not me. You have to be born to see 'em. If'n you be born wrapped in de caul, you kin see 'em. But if you aint, you can't see 'em."

Source: Solbert Butler, 82 years, R. F. D. Scotia, S. C.

Project 1885-1
District #4
Spartanburg, S. C.
May 31, 1937

# GRANNY CAIN
## Folklore: Ex-Slaves

"I was born on the other side of Maybinton, in Newberry County, South Carolina. Old Squire Kenner was my master and his wife, Lucy, my mistress. My pa was Joseph Gilliam, who was a slave of John Gilliam, and my mamma was Lou Kenner, who was a slave of Squire Kenner. I stayed with my mamma at Squire Kenner's and waited on my mistress, Mrs. Lucy Kenner, who was the best white woman I know of—just like a mother to me, wish I was with her now. I stayed there 'till my mistress died, was right by her bed.

"It sure was a good place to live. Dey didn't give us money for work but we had enough to eat and place to sleep and a few clothes. Squire had a big farm he got from the Hancocks, some of his kin. He didn't have overseers; he looked after his own farms. Master had a big garden and give us lots from it to eat. We hunted 'possums, rabbits, squirrels, wild turkeys, on the river. We lived right near Broad River.

"I remember de padderrolers; dey come to my pa's house and want to come in, but pa had an old musket gun and tole them if dey come in dey wouldn't go out alive—and dey went away.

"After the day's work was done, the slaves would set down and talk, and on Saturday afternoons, they would stay home, go fishing or wash up, and sometimes the chaps would go to de river and watch the boats full of cotton go by. On Sundays we go to church. They made us go to Baskets church, de white folks church, and set in the gallery. On Christmas Day we would get time off and master would give us good things to eat. We never had any corn-shuckings and cotton pickings there. All of the family and the slaves do that work on moon-shiney nights. We had some games we played, like Molly Bright, Hiding Switches, Marbles. We played on Sunday, too, unless the mistress calls us in and stops us.

"When a slave got sick we sent for the doctor. We never put much store in herb root tea and such like.

"The Yankees went through Maybinton but didn't get over as far as us. Some say they stole cattle and burned ginhouses.

"Squire Kenner was killed in the war, and when the war was over we stayed on with de mistress; she was like a mamma. She had a son who was killed in the war, too. Another son lived there and we worked for him after Mistress died, but he soon moved far away and sold out his plantation. His name was Howsen Kenner.

"I married Walter Cain at Mr. Walter Spearman's house, a good white man, and the white folks give us a good supper after the wedding. I had one child, 2 grand-children, and one great-grand-child. I joined the church before I married 'cause I wanted to do better, do right and live right, and get religion. I think everybody ought to join the church and live right. That is the reason the Lord blesses me in lots of ways today. We had good time in slavery—sometimes I wish I was back there—would have somebody to take of you and help you. If my mistress was living I would rather be back in slavery."

Source: Granny Cain (90), RFD, Newberry; by G. L. Summer, Newberry, S. C.

Project 1885-1
FOLKLORE
Spartanburg Dist. 4
Sept. 22, 1937
Edited by:
Elmer Turnage

# GRANNY CAIN

## Stories From Ex-Slaves

"I was born near the village of Maybinton, and lived on old Squire Kenner's plantation. Squire Kenner and his wife, mistress Lucy, was good to me. My mistress was so good I wish I was living with her now, I sho wouldn't have such a hard time getting something to eat. I am old and have rheumatism and can't get about good now.

"I live with some of my grand children, but they can't make so much for us. We manage to eat, though. We rent a two-room house about two miles from Newberry Courthouse.

"I don't know nothing about 40 acres of land for the slaves after the war. We just stayed on with the master 'til he died, for wages; then we hired out to other people for wages. I don't know nothing 'bout slaves voting after the war. There was no slave up-risings then in our section.

"Ever since the war was over, the slaves have worked for wages on plantations or moved to town and got little jobs here and there where they could. Some of the slaves would rent small farms from land owners or work the farms on shares. None of the slaves in our section come from Virginia."

Source: "Granny" Cain (90), Newberry County, S. C.
Interviewer: G. L. Summer, Newberry, S. C. 8/10/37.

Project 1885-1
FOLKLORE
Spartanburg Dist. 4
May 24, 1937
Edited by: Elmer Turnage

## LAURA CALDWEL

### Stories From Ex-Slaves

"I was born in Union County, S. C., not far from the ferry on Tyger River. My mother was a slave of George R. Tucker who lived on the Enoree River. I can't remember slavery times nor the war; but I remember about the end of the war when everybody was coming home.

"My mother was a weaver, going to the white folks' houses and weaving clothes for them for small pay. Carding and spinning was done by all the white families at home.

"The farms had large gardens and raised most everything to eat. Large patches of turnips, cabbage and green vegetables was the custom at that time."

Source: Laura Caldwell (77), Newberry, S. C.
Interviewer: G. L. Summer, Newberry, S. C. May 20, 1937

Project 1885-1
Folklore
Spartanburg, Dist. 4
Dec. 15, 1937
Edited by: Elmer Turnage

[HW: (Caldwell)]

# SOLOMON CALDWELL
## Stories From Ex-Slaves

"I own a little farm, about 22 acres, and I live on it wid my wife. I ain't been married but once, but we had 15 chilluns. Dey is all done married and left us. I is gitting so I can't do much work any more, 'specially plowing. I lives below Prosperity. I was born above dar, near Beaver Dam Creek on de old Davenport place.

"My daddy was Alfred Caldwell and my mammy was Suella Caldwell. She was a Nelson. Dem and me belonged to Marse Gillam Davenport. Marse Gillam sho was rapid. I saw him whip my mammy till you couldn't put a hand on her shoulder and back widout touching a whelp. Marse Gillam killed a man and dey put him in jail in Newberry, but he died befo' de trial come off. Atter dat, I was put in de hands of his son, Sam Davenport. Dis was atter freedom come. He was a purty good man, but my mammy was always careful. At night she say, 'Come in chilluns, I got to fasten de do' tight.' We lived in a little log house den. When we moved from dar we went to Dr. Welch's place, jes' dis side of it.

"De niggers never had any churches till atter de war; den dey used brush arbors or some old broke-down log house. We never had schools den, not till later. I never had a chance to go a-tall.

"I 'member de Ku Klux and how dey rid around in white sheets, killing all de niggers. De Red Shirts never killed but dey sometimes whipped niggers. My daddy voted de Republican ticket den, but I know'd two niggers dat was Democrats and rode wid de Red Shirts. Dey was old Zeb and old Jeff Bozard.

"We had a big camp meeting sometimes at a log house dat was called 'Hannah's Church'. It was named for a nigger man of slavery time. He bought de land for de church when freedom come and give it to dem. Dis church is on de other side of Bush River, near Mr. Boulware's place.

"In old times we had plenty to eat dat we raised on de farm. We had gardens, too. We raised hogs and made our own flour. We never worked on Saturday afternoons and Sundays. On Christmas we got together and tried to have extra things to eat, and maybe a few drinks.

"In old times we had lots of corn-shuckings and log-rollings. De niggers all around would come and help, den we would git a feast of lamb or pig that was cooked while we was working.

"Some old folks use to make medicines out of herbs.

I 'member my ma would take fever grass and boil it to tea and have us drink it to keep de fever away. She used branch elder twigs and dogwood berries for chills. Another way to stop chills from coming was to dip a string in turpentine, keep it tied around de waist and tie a knot in it every time you had a chill.

"Abraham Lincoln was a good man. Seems like all de niggers loved him lots. I don't know much about Jefferson Davis. Booker Washington was a good man. I 'member he was once in Newberry and I heard him preach in de old courthouse. (?)

"I joined de church when I was 12 years old. In dem days de old folks made chillun go to church when dey was 12 years old, and join den. Dat was de reason I joined. I was a Methodist but I joined de Baptist later, because, well, I saw dat was de right way."

Source: Solomon Caldwell (73), Newberry, S. C. RFD
Interviewer: G. L. Summer, Newberry, S. C. 12/7/37.

Project #1655
W. W. Dixon,
Winnsboro, S. C.

# NELSON CAMERON
## Ex-Slave 81 Years.

Nelson Cameron and his wife, Mary, together with a widowed daughter, Rose, and her six children, live in a four-room frame house, two miles south of Woodward, S. C., about sixty yards east of US highway #21. He cultivates about eighty acres of land, on shares of the crop, for Mr. Brice, the land owner. He is a good, respectable, cheerful old darkey, and devoted to his wife and grandchildren.

"Marse Wood, Ned Walker, a old Gaillard nigger says as how he was down here t'other day sellin' chickens, where he got them chickens I's not here for to say, and say you wanna see me. I's here befo' you and pleads guilty to de charge dat I'm old, can't work much any longer, and is poor and needy.

"You sees dere's a window pane out of my britches seat and drainage holes in both my shoes, to let de sweat out when I walks to Bethel Church on Sunday. Whut can you and Mr. Roosevelt do for dis old Izrallite a passin' thru de wilderness on de way to de Promise Land? Lak to have a little manna and quail, befo' I gits to de river Jordan.

"My old marster name Sam Brice. His wife, my mistress, tho' fair as de lily of de valley and cheeks as pink as de rose of Sharon, is called 'Darkie.' Dat always seem a misfit to me. Lily or Rose or Daisy would have suited her much more better, wid her laces, frills, flounces, and ribbons. Her mighty good to de slaves. Take deir part 'ginst de marster sometime, when him want to whup them. Sometime I sit on de door-steps and speculate in de moonlight whut de angels am like and everytime, my mistress is de picture dat come into dis old gray head of mine. You say you don't want po'try, you wants facts?

"Well, here de facts: My mammy name Clara. Don't forget dat. I come back to her directly. My young mistress was Miss Maggie. Her marry Marse Robert Clowney; they call him 'Red-head Bob.' Him have jet red hair. Him was 'lected and went to de Legislature once. No go back; he say dere too much ding dong do-nuttin' foolishness down dere for him to leave home and stay 'way from de wife and chillun half de winter months.

"Marse Sam never have so pow'ful many slaves. Seem lak dere was more women and chillun than men. In them days, pa tell me, a white man raise niggers just lak a man raise horses or cows. Have a whole lot of mares and 'pendin' on other man to have de stallion. Fust thing you know dere would be a whole lot of colts kickin' up deir heels on de place. Lakwise a white man start out wid a few women folk slaves, soon him have a plantation full of little niggers runnin' 'round in deir shirt-tails and a kickin' up deir heels, whilst deir mammies was in de field a hoeing and geeing at de plow handles, workin' lak a man. You ketch de point? Well I's one of them little niggers. My pa name Vander. Him b'long to one of de big bugs, old Marse Gregg Cameron. Marse Gregg, him 'low, always have more money and niggers than you could shake a stick at, more land than you could walk over in a day, and more cuss words than you could find in de dictionary. His bark was worser than his bite, tho'. Pa was de tan-yard man; he make leather and make de shoes for de plantation. After freedom date, de way he make a livin' for mammy and us chillun was by makin' boots and shoes and half solin' them for white folks at Blackstock, S. C. Marse Sam Brice mighty glad for mammy to contact sich a man to be de pappy of her chillun.

"Us live in a log house wid a little porch in front and de mornin' glory vines use to climb 'bout it. When they bloom, de bees would come a hummin' 'round and suck de honey out de blue bells on de vines. I 'members dat well 'nough, dat was a pleasant memory. Is I told you my mammy name Clara? My brothers and sisters, who they? George dead, Calvin dead, Hattie (name for pa's young mistress) dead, Samson, who got his ear scald off in a pot of hot water, is dead, too. I's existing still. I did mighty little work in slavery times. 'Members not much 'bout de Yankees.

"Freedom come, pa come straight as a martin to his gourd, to mammy and us pickaninnies. They send us to school at Blackstock and us walk fourteen miles, and back, every day to school. At school I meets Mary Stroud, a gal comin' from de Gaillard quarter. Her eyes was lak twin stars. Her hair lak a swarm of bees. All my studyin' books was changed to studyin' how to git dat swarm of bees in a hive by myself. One day I walk home from school with her and git old Uncle Tom Walker to marry us, for de forty cents I saved up. Us happy ever since. Nex' year I work for Ben Calvin, a colored man on de Cockerell place, jinin' de Gaillard place. Us did dat to be near her pappy, Uncle Morris Stroud.

"All thru them 'Carpet Bag' days my pappy stuck to de white folks, and went 'long wid de Ku Kluxes. His young mistress, Miss Harriet Cameron, marry de Grand Titan of all de Holy invisible Roman Empire. Him name was Col. Leroy McAfee. Pappy tell me all 'bout it. Marse Col. McAfee come down from North Ca'lina, and see Marse Feaster Cameron at old Marse Gregg Cameron's home and want Marse Feaster to take charge down in dis State. While on dat visit him fall in love wid Marse Feas's sister, Harriet, and marry her. You say Marse Tom Dixon dedicate a book to her, de Clansman? Well, well, well! To think of dat. Wish my pappy could a knowed dat, de Sundays he'd take dat long walk to Concord Church to put flowers on her grave. They all lie dere in dat graveyard, Old Marse Gregg, Marse Leroy, Miss Harriet, and Marse Feas. De day they bury Marse Feas de whole county was dere and both men and women sob when de red earth rumbled on his coffin top. Pappy had me by de hand and cried lak a baby, wid de rest of them, dat sad day.

"Does you 'member de time in 1884, when my pappy made you a pair of boots for $10.00 and when you pay him, him knock off one dollar and you pay him nine dollars? You does? Well dat is fine, for I sure need dat dollar dis very day.

"Does I 'member de day old Marse Gregg die? 'Course I does. It happen right here in Winnsboro. Him come down to 'tend John Robinson's Circus. Him lak Scotch liquor; de tar smell, de taste, and de 'fect, take him back to Scotland where him generate from. Them was bar-room days in Winnsboro. De two hotels had bar-rooms, besides de other nine in town. Marse Gregg had just finished his drink of Scotch. De parade of de circus was passing de hotel where he was, and de steam piano come by a tootin'. Marse Gregg jump up to go to de street to see it. When it pass, him say: 'It's a damn humbug' and drop dead."

Project #1855
W. W. Dixon
Winnsboro, S. C.

## THOMAS CAMPBELL
### Ex-Slave 82 Years Old.

"Good mornin' Marster Wood! Marster Donan McCants and Marster Wardlaw McCants both been tellin' me dat how you wants to see me but I's been so poorly and down at de heels, in my way of feelin', dat I just ain't of a mind or disposition to walk up dere to de town clock, where they say you want me to come. Take dis bench seat under de honey suckle vine. It shade you from de sun. It sho' is hot! I's surprise dat you take de walk down here to see a onery old man lak me.

"Yes sir, I was born, 'cordin' to de writin' in de Book, de 15th day of March, 1855, in de Horeb section of Fairfield District, a slave of old Marster John Kennedy. How it was, I don't know. Things is a little mixed in my mind. Fust thing I 'members, and dreams 'bout sometimes yet, is bein' in Charleston, standin' on de battery, seein' a big ocean of water, wid ships and their white sails all 'bout, de waves leapin' and gleamin' 'bout de flanks of de ships in de bright sunshine, thousands of white birds flyin' 'round and sometimes lighting on de water. My mammy, her name Chanie, was a holdin' my hand and her other hand was on de handle of a baby carriage and in dat carriage was one of de Logan chillun. Whether us b'long to de Logans or whether us was just hired out to them I's unable to 'member dat. De slaves called him Marster Tom. Us come back to Fairfield in my fust childhood, to de Kennedy's.

"Marster John Kennedy raise more niggers than he have use for; sometime he sell them, sometime he hire them out. Him sell mammy and me to Marster James B. McCants and I been in de McCants family ever since, bless God!

"Marse James was a great lawyer in his day. I was his house boy and office boy. When I get older I take on, besides de blackin' of his boots and shoes and sweepin' out de office, de position of carriage driver and sweepin' out de church. Marster James was very 'ligious. Who my pa was? Dat has never been revealed to me. Thank God! I never had one, if they was lak I see nigger chillun have today. My white folks was all de parents I had and me wid a skin as black as ink. My belly was always full of what they had and I never suffer for clothes on my back or shoes on my feets.

"Does I 'members de Yankees? Yes sir, I 'member when they come. It was cold weather, February, now dat I think of it. Oh, de sights of them days. They camp all 'round up at Mt. Zion College and stable their hosses in one of de rooms. They gallop here and yonder and burn de 'Piscopal Church on Sunday mornin'. A holy war they called it, but they and Wheeler's men was a holy terror to dis part of de world, as naked and hungry as they left it. I marry Savannah Parnell and of all our chillun, dere is just one left, a daughter, Izetta. Her in Tampa, Florida.

"Does I 'members anything 'bout de Ku Klux? No sir, nothin'. I was always wid de white folks side of politics. They wasn't concerned 'bout me. Marster James have no patience for dat kind of business anyhow. Him was a lawyer and believed in lettin' de law rule in de daylight and would have nothin' to do wid work dat have to have de cover of night and darkness.

"Does I 'member 'bout de red shirts? Sure I does. De marster never wore one. Him get me a red shirt and I wore it in Hampton days. What I recollect 'bout them times? If you got time to listen, I 'spect I can make anybody laugh 'bout what happen right in dis town in red shirt days. You say you glad to listen? Well, here goes. One time in '76, de democrats have a big meetin' in de court house in April. Much talk last all day. What they say or do up dere nobody know. Paper come out next week callin' de radicals to meet in de court house fust Monday in May. Marster Glenn McCants, a lawyer, was one of old marster's sons. He tell me all 'bout it.

"De day of de radical republican meetin' in de court house, Marster Ed Ailen had a drug store, so him and Marster Ozmond Buchanan fix up four quart bottles of de finest kind of liquor, wid croton-oil in every bottle. Just befo' de meetin' was called to order, Marster Ed pass out dat liquor to de ring leader, tellin' him to take it in de court house and when they want to 'suade a nigger their way, take him in de side jury rooms and 'suade him wid a drink of fine liquor. When de meetin' got under way, de chairman 'pointed a doorkeeper to let nobody in and nobody out 'til de meetin' was over, widout de chairman say so.

"They say things went along smooth for a while but

directly dat croton-oil make a demand for 'tention. Dere was a wild rush for de door. De doorkeeper say 'Stand back, you have to 'dress de chairman to git permission to git out'. Chairman rap his gavel and say, 'What's de matter over dere? Take your seats! Parliment law 'quire you to 'dress de chair to git permission to leave de hall'. One old nigger, Andy Stewart, a ring leader shouted: 'To hell wid Parliment law, I's got to git out of here.' Still de doorkeeper stood firm and faithful, as de boy on de burnin' deck, as Marster Glenn lak to tell it. One bright mulatto nigger, Jim Mobley, got out de tangle by movin' to take a recess for ten minutes, but befo' de motion could be carried out de croton-oil had done its work. Half de convention have to put on clean clothes and de court house steps have to be cleaned befo' they could walk up them again. You ask any old citizen 'bout it. Him will 'member it. Ask old Doctor Buchanan. His brother, de judge, was de one dat help Marster Ed Aiken to fix de croton-oil and whiskey.

"Well, dat seem to make you laugh and well it might, 'cause dat day been now long ago. Sixty-one years you say? How time gits along. Well, sixty-one years ago everybody laugh all day in Winnsboro, but Marster Ed never crack a smile, when them niggers run to his drug store and ask him for somethin' to ease their belly ache."

Code No.
Project, 1885-(1)
Prepared by Annie Ruth Davis
Place, Marion, S. C.
Date, October 5, 1937
No. Words
Reduced from –– words
Rewritten by ––

## SYLVIA CANNON

### Ex-Slave, Age 85

"Yes, mam, I been a little small girl in slavery time. I just can remember when I was sold. Me en Becky en George. Just can remember dat, but I know who bought me. First belong to de old Bill Greggs en dat whe' Miss Earlie Hatchel bought me from. Never did know whe' Becky en George went. Yes, mam, de Bill Greggs had a heap of slaves cause dey had my grandmammy en my granddaddy en dey had a heap of chillun. My mammy, she belong to de Greggs too. She been Mr. Gregg's cook en I de one name after her. I remembers she didn' talk much to we chillun. Mostly, she did sing bout all de time. Most of de old people sing bout;

'O Heaven, sweet Heaven,
When shall I see?
If you get dere fore me,

You tell my Lord I on de way.
O shall I get dere?
If you get dere fore I do,
You tell My Lord I on de way.
O Heaven, sweet Heaven,
When shall I see?
O when shall I get dere?"

"Oh, dat be a old song what my grandmammy used to sing way back dere."

"I don' know exactly how old I is cause de peoples used to wouldn' tell dey chillun how old dey was fore dey was grown. I just ain' able to say bout my right age, but I know my sister was older den me en she de one keep count us chillun age. She told me I be bout 84 or 85 years old, so my sister tell me. She done gone en left me en I try to keep count, but I don' know. Dere been bout 14 head of we chillun en dey all gone but me. I de last one. I can tell you dis much, I was just a little small girl when Miss Earlie Hatchel bought me en she wouldn' let me hold de baby cause she was 'fraid I would drop it. I just set dere on de floor en set de baby 'tween my legs, but my Lord, Miss Hatchel been so good to me dat I stay on dere wid her 8 years after freedom come. Miss Hatchel tell me I better stay on dere whe' I can get flour bread to eat. Yes, mam, never got a whippin in all my life. Miss Hatchel, she shake me by de shoulders once or twice, but never didn' whip me in all my life dat I knows of. Dat de reason, when my parents come after me, I hide under de bed. My mammy, she went in de name of Hatchel en all her chillun went in de name of Hatchel right down dere in de Effingham section."

"No, honey, don' nobody be here wid me. Stays right

here by myself. Digs in de garden in de day en comes in de house at night. Yes, mam, I thought dis house been belong to me, but dey tell me dis here place be city property. Rich man up dere in Florence learn bout I was worth over $1500.00 en he tell me dat I ought to buy a house dat I was gettin old. Say he had a nice place he want to sell me. I been learned dat what white folks tell me, I must settle down on it en I give him de money en tell him give me de place he say he had to sell me. I been trust white folks en he take my money en settle me down here on city property. He say, 'Mom Sylvia, you stay here long as you live cause you ain' gwine be here much longer.' I promise my God right den not to save no more money, child. People back dere didn' spend money like dey do dese days en dat how-come I had dat money. Dey would just spend money once a year in dat day en time. Yes, mam, I pay dat man over $900.00. Been payin on it long time en got it all paid but $187.00 en city find out what dat man had done. City tell me just stay on right here, but don' pay no more money out. Dey give me dat garden en tell me what I make I can have. Courthouse man tell me dat I ought to drop my thanks to de Heavenly Father dat I is free. If de town picks up any sick person, dey bring dem here en tell me do de best I can for dem. Tell me to keep good order so de people won' be shame to come en see bout me. Got two houses dere join together. Dere be four rooms in dis front one en three in de other house. Woman go up north en leave her things here en tell me if she ain' come back, I could have dem en she ain' come back yet. Been gone two years."

"Yes, mam, I been married twice. First husband die en den another sick man come along en ax de city for me. I work on him en make teas for him, but he die in bout two years. I beg de town to let me go out to de poor farm en stay, but dey say I done pay too much to move. Tell me stay on here en keep de house up de best way I can.

"No'um, I ain' able to do no kind of work much. No more den choppin my garden. Can' hardly see nothin on a sunny day. I raise my own seed all right cause sometimes I can' see en find myself is cut up things en dat make me has to plant over another time. City tell me do like I was raise en so I been choppin here bout 20 years."

"Oh, now go way from here. My son born in de year of de earthquake en if he had lived, I would been bless wid plenty grandchillun dese days. Yes, mam, I remember all bout de shake. Dey tell me one man, Mr. Turner, give way his dog two or three days fore de earthquake come en dat dog get loose en come back de night of de shake. Come back wid chain tied round his neck en Mr. Turner been scared most to death, so dey tell me. He say, 'Oh, Mr. Devil, don' put de chain on me, I'll go wid you.' Dat was his dog come back en he thought it was de devil come dere to put de chain on him. Yes, mam, dere was such a cuttin up every which a way cause de people thought it was de Jedgment comin. I went a runnin dere to de white folks house en such a prayin en a hollerin, I ain' never see de like fore den en ain' see it since den neither. Dere was stirrin everywhe' dat night en de water in de well was just a slashin. I tried to pray like de rest of de people. Some say dey was ready to get on de old ship of Zion. I cut loose from de white folks en went in de woods to pray en see a big snake en I ain' been back since. I know dat ain' been nothin but a omen en I quit off cuttin up. I know it ain' been no need in me gwine on like dat cause I ain' never do no harms dat I knows of."

"Yes, mam, white folks had to whip some of dey niggers in slavery time, dey be so mean. Hear tell bout some of dem would run away en go in de woods en perish to death dere fore dey would come out en take a whippin. Some was mean cause dey tell stories on one another en been swear to it. My mammy tell me don' never tell nothin but de truth en I won' get no whippin. I been raise up wid de white folks en I tell de truth, I can' hardly stand no colored people."

"Oh, honey, dere won' no such thing as cotton mill, train, sawmill or nothin like dat in my day. People had to set dere at night en pick de seed out de cotton wid dey own hands. Didn' hear tell bout no telephone nowhe' in dem days en people never live no closer den three en four miles apart neither. Got old Massa horn right in dat room dere now dat he could talk on to people dat be 16 miles from whe' he was. Come in here, child, en I'll let you see it. See, dis old horn been made out of silver money. You talks in dat little end en what you say runs out dat big end. Man ax me didn' I want to sell it en I tell him I ain' got no mind to get rid of it cause it been belong to old Massa. Den if I get sick, I call on it en somebody come. Wouldn' take nothin for it, honey."

"Times was sho better long time ago den dey be now. I know it. Yes, mam, I here frettin myself to death after dem dat gone. Colored people never had no debt to pay in slavery time. Never hear tell bout no colored people been put in jail fore freedom. Had more to eat en more to wear den en had good clothes all de time cause white folks furnish everything, everything. Dat is, had plenty to eat such as we had. Had plenty peas en rice en hog meat en rabbit en' fish en such as dat. Colored people sho fare better in slavery time be dat de white folks had to look out for dem. Had dey extra crop what dey had time off to work every Saturday. White folks tell dem what dey made, dey could have. Peoples would have found we colored people rich wid de money we made on de extra crop, if de slaves hadn' never been set free. Us had big rolls of money en den when de Yankees come en change de money, dat what made us poor. It let de white people down en let us down too. Left us all to bout starve to death. Been force to go to de fish pond en de huckleberry patch. Land went down to $1.00 a acre. White people let us clear up new land en make us own money dat way. We bury it in de ground en dat how-come I had money. I dig mine up one day en had over $1500.00 dat I been save. Heap of peoples money down dere yet en dey don' know whe' to find it."

    Source: Sylvia Cannon, age 85, ex-slave, Marion St., Florence,
S. C.
    Personal interview by Annie Ruth Davis, October, 1937.

Code No.
Project, 1885-(1)
Prepared by Annie Ruth Davis
Place, Marion, S. C.
Date, August 4, 1937
No. Words —
Reduced from — words
Rewritten by —

## SYLVIA CANNON

Ex-Slave, Age 85.
Florence, S. C.

"I lives here by myself cause my husband been dead three years. Moved here fore my chillun went to de war. I go to work en buy dis here home en get whe' I can' pay tax en people tell me not to move. Say, rent me bed en catch me a dollar, if it ain' a sin to rent your bed for a dollar. One of de big officers of de town tell me dat last week en he die next day. Government take my house en when dey carry sick peoples from de jail, dey bring em here fore dey die. It ain' but one night journey. Ain' gwine let dem be live enough to run away. Ain' got no kin to leave de house to en dey tell me stay on here. Dey say I work so hard to get dis house dat dey ain' gwine make me leave here."

(Aunt Sylvia has a sign in her front yard. It seems she

took the frame of a large picture and inserted a piece of pasteboard into it. She explained that this sign is a warning to evil doers not to molest her. She says that they must not come past this sign. The words on the sign are somewhat illegibly written. The interviewers were able to make out these words: "This is a house of the Lord. Don't go pass. This is a house of the Lord...." Sign is dated March 1, 1937).

"I don' know how old I is, but I remembers I was 8 years old when freedom come. I born down dere in de Effingham section on Mr. Gregg plantation. My half-sister say I must always remember de Christmas day cause dat de day I was born. Father en mother belong to de old Bill Greggs en dat whe' Miss Earlie Hatchel buy me from. After dat, I didn' never live wid my parents any more, but I went back to see dem every two weeks. Got a note en go on a Sunday evenin en come back to Miss Hatchel on Monday. Miss Hatchel want a nurse en dat how-come she buy me. I remembers Miss Hatchel puttin de baby in my lap en tell me don' drop him. Didn' have to do no work much in dem days, but dey didn' allow me to play none neither. When de baby sleep, I sweep de yard en work de garden en pick seed out de cotton to spin. Nursed little while for Miss Hatchel en den get free."

"I see em sell plenty colored peoples away in dem days cause dat de way white folks made heap of dey money. Coase dey ain' never tell us how much dey sell em for. Just stand em up on a block bout three feet high en a speculator bid em off just like dey was horses. Dem what was bid off didn' never say nothin neither. Don' know who bought my brothers, George en Earl. (She cried after this statement). I see em sell some slaves twice fore I was sold en I see de slaves when dey be travelin like hogs to Darlington. Some of dem be women folks lookin like dey gwine to get down dey so heavy."

"We fare good in dat day en time. Everybody round dere fare good. My Massa always was good to his slaves cause all de colored people say he was good man to us. Dey never whip me in all my life. Tell me if I don' know how to do anything to tell dem en dey show me how. I remembers Miss Hatchel caught en shook me one time en when I tell her husband, he tell her to keep his hands off his little Nigger. Dey all was good to me. When I start home to see my mamma, dey cry after me till I come back. Many a time my Missus go work in de field en let me mind de chillun."

"We live in de quarter bout ½ mile from de white folks house in a one room pole house what was daubed wid dirt. Dere was bout 20 other colored people house dere in de quarter dat was close together en far apart too. De ground been us floor en us fireplace been down on de ground. Take sticks en make chimney cause dere won' no bricks en won' no saw mills to make lumber when I come along. Oh, my white folks live in a pole house daubed wid dirt too. Us just had some kind of home-made bedstead wid pine straw bed what to sleep on in dem days. Sew croaker sack together en stuff em wid pine straw. Dat how dey make dey mattress. Didn' get much clothes to wear in dat day en time neither. Man never wear no breeches in de summer. Go in his shirt tail dat come down to de knees en a 'oman been glad enough to get one piece homespun frock what was made wid dey hand. Make petticoat out of old dress en patch en patch till couldn' tell which place weave. Always put wash out on a Saturday night en dry it en put it back on Sunday. Den get oak leaves en make a hat what to wear to church. We didn' never have but one pair of shoes a year en dey was dese here brogans wid thick soles en brass toes. Had shop dere on de plantation whe' white man made all de shoes en plows. Dey would save all de cowhide en soak it in salt two or three weeks to get de hair off it en dey have big trough hewed out whe' dey clean it after dey get de hair off it. After dat, it was turn to de man at de shop."

"I remembers when night come on en we go back to de quarter, we cook bread in de ashes en pick seed from de cotton en my mamma set dere en sew heap of de time. Den I see em when dey have dem hay pullings. Dey tote torch to gather de hay by en after dey pull two or three stacks of hay, dey have a big supper en dance in de road en beat sticks en blow cane. Had to strike fire on cotton wid two rocks cause dey didn' have no match in dem days."

"I tellin you my Missus sho was good to me in dat day en time. She been so good to me dat I stay dere wid her 20 year after I got free. Stay dere till I marry de old man Isenia Cannon. You see my old Massa got killed in de war. She tell me I better stay whe' I can get flour bread to eat cause she make her own flour en bake plenty biscuit in de oven. Den she kill hogs en a cow every Christmas en give us all de egg-nog en liquor we want dat day. Dig hole in de ground en roast cow over log fire. When I get hard up for meat en couldn' get nothin else, I catch rabbits en birds. Make a death trap wid a lid en bait it wid cabbage en corn en catch em dat way. Den another time, I dig deep hole in de ground en dob it wid clay en fill it up wid water. Rabbits hunt water in de night en fall in dere en drown. I used to set traps heap of times to keep de rabbits from eatin up de people gardens. Folks eat all kind of things durin de war. Eat honeysuckle off de low sweet bush after de flower falls off en pine mass dat dey get out de burr en sour weeds. Wouldn' nobody eat dem things dese days. Coase dey let de slaves have three acres of land to a family to plant for dey garden. Work dem in moonlight nights en on a Saturday evenin."

"Oh, yes, dey have white overseers den. I hear some people say dey was good people. At night de overseer would walk out to see could he catch any of us walkin widout a note en to dis day, I don' want to go nowhe' widout a paper. It just like dis, de overseer didn' have to be right behind you to see dat you work in dem days. Dey have all de fields name en de overseer just had to call on de horn en tell you what field to go work in dat day. Den he come along on a Saturday evenin to see what you done. If you ain' do what he say do, he put de Nigger dog on you en he run you all night till he find you. No matter whe' you hide, he find you en hold you till de overseer get dere. Bite you up if dey get reach of you. When de overseer come, he carry you to de stables en whip you. Dey dat ain' never got no whipping, you can' do nothin wid dem dese days."

"I got Miss Hatchel horn bout here now dat been through nearly 100 head of people. If you talk on it, dere de 100 head of automobiles to see what it is. I sold old Massa's sword last week for ten cents, but I ain' gwine do away wid his old horn. (4 ft. long, 15 in. cross big end 1 in. from top end. Mouth piece is gone. Catch about 15 in. from top). Can talk to anybody 15 to 16 miles away en dat how-come I don' want to sell it cause if anything happen, I can call people to come. Dis horn ain' no tin, it silver. It de old time phone. Got old Massa maul too en dis here Grandpa oxen bit dat was made at home."

"De white folks didn' never help none of we black people to read en write no time. Dey learn de yellow chillun, but if dey catch we black chillun wid a book, dey nearly bout kill us. Dey was sho better to dem yellow chillun den de black chillun dat be on de plantation. Northern women come dere after de war, but dey didn' let em teach nobody nothin."

"I go to church wid my white folks, but dey never have no church like dey have dese days. De bush was dey shelter en when it rain, dey meet round from one house to another. Ride to church in de ox cart cause I had to carry de baby everywhe' I go. White folks didn' have no horse den. De peoples sho been blessed wid more religion in dem days den dese days. Didn' never have to lock up nothin den en if you tell a story, you get a whippin. Now de peoples tell me to tell a story. I been cleanin up a lady porch en she tell me to tell anybody what come dere dat she ain' home. A lady come en ax fer her en I tell her she say anybody come here, tell em I ain' home. If you don' believe she here, look in de bedroom. Miss Willcox come out dere en beat me in de back. I tell her don' read de Bible en tell me to tell a story. I ain' gwine tell no story cause my white folks learnt me not to do dat. I knows people was better in dem times den dey is now. Dey teach you how you ought to treat your neighbor en never hear no bad stories nowhe'. Massa en Missus taught me to say a prayer dat go like dis:

"De angels in Heaven love us,
Bless mamma en bless papa,

Bless our Missus,
Bless de man dat feedin us,
For Christ sake."

"De peoples use herb medicines for dey cures in dem days dat dey get out de woods. I make a herb medicine dat good for anything out de roots of three herbs mix together. Couldn' tell you how I make it cause dat would ruin me. Town people try to buy de remedy from me, but Dr. McLeod tell me not to sell it. Dey offer me $1500.00 for it, but I never take it."

"You want my mind, my heart, de truth en I gwine tell you it just like I see it. Since de colored peoples got de law, dey get in all kind of devilment. Dat how-come if I had to go back, I would go back to slavery en stay wid my white folks."

Source: Sylvia Cannon, ex-slave, age 85, Florence. S. C.

Personal interview by H. Grady Davis and Mrs. Lucile Young, and written up in question and answer form. Rewritten in story form by Annie Ruth Davis.

## FUNERAL SONG

Star in de east en star in de west,
I wish de star was in my breast.
Mother is home, sweet home,
Mother is home, sweet home,
Want to join de angel here.
What a blessed home, sweet home,

What a blessed home, sweet home,
Want to join de angel here.

(You can sing bout father, brother, sister en all.)

Sylvia Cannon,

Ex-Slave, age 85,
May 21, 1937,
Florence, S. C.

## FUNERAL SONG

Come ye dat love de Lord,
En let your joys be known.
Hark from de tomb,
En hear my tender voice.
By de grace of God I'll meet you
On Canaan Happy Shore.
Oh, mother, where will I meet you on Canaan Happy Shore?
En by de grace of God I'll meet you on Canaan Happy Shore.

(Shaking hands, marching around grave. White en Colored marched from church to graveyard. Old people in de ox cart en young people walking. Didn' have coffins like dey do now. Build de coffin en black it wid smut. Blacksmith make de nails. Could see in de box.)

Sylvia Cannon,
Ex-Slave, age 85,
May 21, 1937,

# Florence, S. C.

United States

Project No. 1885-(1)
Prepared by Mrs. Genevieve Chandler
Place, Murrells Inlet, S. C.
Date, March 25, 1937
Typed by M. C., N. Y. A.
No Words ––
Reduced from Words ––
Rewritten by ––

# UNCLE ALBERT CAROLINA

[Hw: Georgetown Co.]
[Hw: Heaven's Gate Church]
(Verbatim Conversation):

When asked about the founding of Heaven's Gate colored Methodist church Rev. Albert Carolina answered:

"In the beginning of Freedom they separate us from whites.
'Sixty one the war begun;
Sixty four the war was o'er."

"Rev. Zacharias Duncan wuz the man. He the one built Heaven Gate church. Brother Henry Smith and Brother David Kidd and old man Jackson Heywood wuz the old ones built it. Some more been there. Can't think of them. Old man Jim Beaty wuz one. Can't remember no more. He wuz Allston man. (That means he was a slave owned by the Allstons) Uncle Dave Kidd, he owned a tract of land in the Savannah.

"Brought us up in Sabbus (Sabbath) school. Sunrise prayer-meeting. Ten o'clock Sunday school. Leven o'clock the service. Three o'clock service again. Eight at night—service again. Raise us taughen (taught) in the church. Steal off Slavery time in they own house and have class meeting. Driver come find'em, whip'em. Th' patrolls come riding down th' road. Four plait whip. Two big black dog. White pat-roller. Ketch without pass, they whip me. Crawling. (I was crawling). But I walk then and walk every since! Bo-cart. Dat's what they call it—'Bo-cart'. (Crude home made baby walker.) Bout seventy seven years since I start. Remember nother thing going on in them time. Mausser gin (give) the women a task. Didn't done it. Next day didn't done it. Saturday come, task time out! Driver! I tell yuh th' truth, you could hear those people, 'Murder! Murder!'

"Judge Kershaw was a fine man. His boy William—I and William born the same day.

"We never has met th' bed yet, without family prayer—and never get up without it. Didn't low them with a book in they hand. The Driver learn you at night if he like you. Try to out-wage (educate) you at night. Didn't have any school.

"Mother's father Indian. Brighter than, who? Who round here bright as my Grand-father? Hannah! Hair was long. Wouldn't stay home. Lives in th' swamp. Wouldn't stay out. Grandmother wuz African. She had a little bowl make out of clay."

Uncle Albert Carolina, age 87 (colored)
Murrells Inlet, S. C.
March 8th, 1937.

(A description followed of how his grand-parents built a kiln of clay pots and baked them.)

Project #-1655
Phoebe Faucette
Hampton County

# SILVIA CHISOLM
## Ex-Slave 88 Years Old

"Aunt Silvie", sitting out in the sunshine in the yard of a small negro cabin, on a warm day in January, seemed very old and feeble. Her answers to questions were rather short and she appeared to be preoccupied.

"I been fifteen year old when de Yankee come—fifteen de sixth of June. I saw 'em burn down me Massa's home, an' everythin'. I 'members dat. Ole man Joe Bostick was me Massa. An' I knows de Missus an' de Massa used to work us. Had de overseer to drive us! Work us till de Yankees come! When Yankee come dey had to run! Dat how de buildin' burn! Atter dey didn't find no one in it, dey burn! De Marshall house had a poor white woman in it! Dat why it didn't burn! My Massa's Pineland place at Garnett was burn, too. Dey never did build dis un (one) back. Atter dey come back, dey build deir house at de Pineland place.

"I wus mindin' de overseer's chillun. Mr. Beestinger was his name! An' his wife, Miss Carrie! I been eight year old when dey took me. Took me from me mother an' father here on de Pipe Creek place down to Black Swamp. Went down forty-two mile to de overseer! I never see my mother or my father anymore. Not 'til atter freedom! An' when I come back den I been married. But when I move back here, I stay right on dis Pipe Creek place from den on. I been right here all de time.

"Atter I work for Mr. Beestinger, I wait on Mr. Blunt. You know Mr. Blunt, ain't you? His place out dere now.

"Mr. Bostick was a good ole man. He been deaf. His chillun tend to his business—his sons. He was a preacher. His father was ole man Ben Bostick. De Pipe Creek Church was ole Missus Bostick's Mammy's church. When de big church burn down by de Yankees, dey give de place to de colored folks. Stephen Drayton was de first pastor de colored folks had. Dey named de church, Canaan Baptist Church. Start from a bush arbor. De white folks church was paint white, inside an' out. It was ceiled inside. Dis church didn't have no gallery for de colored folks. Didn't make no graveyard at Pipe Creek! Bury at Black Swamp! An' at Lawtonville! De people leave dat church an' go to Lawtonville to worship. Dey been worshipping at Lawtonville ever since before I could wake up to know. De Pipe Creek Church jes' stood dere, wid no service in it, 'til de Yankee burn it. De church at Lawtonville been a fine church. Didn't burn it! Use it for a hospital durin' de war!

"I'se 88 year old now an' can't remember so much. An' I'se blind! Blind in both eye!"

Source: Silvia Chisolm, R. F. D. Estill, S. C.

Project #1655
Stiles M. Scruggs
Columbia, S. C.

# TOM CHISOLM
## An Ex-Slave Who Climbed Up With White Folks.

Tom Chisolm, a sixty-two year old bricklayer, 11 Railroad Street, Columbia, S. C., is a son of Caesar Chisolm, who represented Colleton County in the South Carolina House of Representatives for ten years. Caesar was one of the few leading Negroes, who voted and spoke for the Democratic Party and was friendly to the leaders of white supremacy until he died in 1897. Tom relates the following story:

"My daddy was born in slavery and he was always treated good by his master, de late Jimeson Chisolm, of Colleton County. He could read and figure up 'most anything, when he was set free, and he had notions of his own, too. For instance, he marry my mammy. She die soon after I was born, and daddy say to me: 'Son, your mammy is gone, but you need not fear dat any other woman will ever boss you. I's through with wives.' And he never marry again.

"I come to Columbia with him, when he serve in de Legislature. When he tell de niggers and white folks, back in Colleton, dat he was not aimin' to run for de Legislature no more, they was sad. One time I go with him to Smoak's, where Congressman George D. Tillman was to speak on one of his campaigns. I felt pretty big, when Congressman Tillman smile and grasp de hand of my daddy and say: 'You's goin' to say a few words for me befo' I starts, eh, Chisolm?' 'I sho' will, if you laks,' say my daddy. Soon he mount de platform, and befo' he say a word, both de white and de niggers clap deir hands and stamp deir feets and smile. My daddy bow, smile, and say: 'Ladies and gentlemen: We, us, and company sent George Tillman to Congress long ago and knows what he has done. Now we's gwine to send him back, and I is a little in doubt as to whether he is gwine to take us to Washington, or bring Washington down here!' He say, he jus' git started. But de crowd was laughin', dancin', and huggin' de Congressman, and daddy laugh and set down.

"He introduce Master Duncan Clinch Heyward at Walterboro in 1902, when Master Heyward was making his first race for governor. He raise such laughter and pay so many witty compliments to Master Heyward, dat Governor Heyward, when he was 'lected, appoint my daddy to an office in Columbia, and we come to Columbia to live in 1903. My daddy retire at de same time dat Governor Heyward quit office, in 1907. He later wrote insurance on de lives of niggers, and he prosper.

"'Bout 1885, my daddy happen to be walkin' near de corner of Gervais and Pulaski streets, and two niggers meet dere at de time and begin to quarrel. My daddy stop and watch them awhile. One of them niggers kill de other, and some time afterward a nigger lawyer come to see my daddy and ask him: 'Wasn't you dere?' 'I sho' was,' say my daddy. De nigger lawyer laugh and slap daddy on de back and say: 'Come on.' Daddy come back in a few hours pretty tipsy. 'Dat lawyer spend a lot on me,' say daddy, 'but de fool never let me tell him jus' what I knows.'

"A day or two afterward he was in de witness box. De nigger lawyer say: 'Now, Mister Chisolm, tell your tale in your own way.' Daddy say: 'I saw de defendant and de man, now dead, as they meet. They glare at each other and begin to talk harsh and cuss each other. Then, one strike at de other and they back 'way and begin to reach in deir hind pockets.' Daddy stop, and de nigger lawyer fairly scream: 'Yes, yes, go on!' 'That all I saw,' say my daddy, 'cause I run to cover. I made it to de next corner in nothin' flat and pick up speed afterward. So I was two blocks 'way, when I hear de shootin'!' De nigger lawyer nearly faint. He say: 'Who bought you off?' Daddy say he would have told him at de start, if he'd had de chance.

"At another time, we was down on de 700 block of Wayne Street, at a nigger gatherin'. We often spend days down dere collectin' weekly insurance dues, and we knowed most of de people. Dere happen to be a young nigger dere, back from de West for a visit, and he was a great bragger. He was tellin' 'bout corn in Texas. 'Dere,' he said, 'corn grow twenty feet high, with stalks as big as the arm of John L. Sullivan, when he whupped Kilrain, and half a dozen big ears on each stalk.' De crowd was thunderstruck.

"My daddy cleared his throat and say: 'Dat am nothin' in de way of corn. One day I was walkin' past a forty-acre patch of corn, on de Governor Heyward plantation by de Combahee River and de corn was so high and thick, I decide to ramble through it. 'Bout halfway over, I hears a commotion. I walks on and peeps. Dere stands a four-ox wagon backed up to de edge of de field, and two niggers was sawin' down a stalk. Finally they drag it on de wagon and drive off. I seen one of them, in a day or two, and asks 'bout it. He say: 'We shelled 366 bushels of corn from dat one ear, and then we saw 800 feet of lumber from de cob.'

"Dat young man soon slip out from de crowd and has never been seen here since. I thinks daddy was outdone with me, 'cause I was not quickwitted and smart, lak him. He tell me once: 'You must learn two good trades, and I think carpenterin' and brick-layin' safest.' I done that, and I has never been sorry, 'cause I's made a good livin'. Governor Heyward was always a good friend of daddy, and he was proud to see us makin' good in de insurance business."

Project 1885-1
FOLKLORE
Spartanburg Dist. 4
May 24, 1937
Edited by:
Elmer Turnage

# MARIA CLELAND
## Stories From Ex-Slaves

"I was born near old Bush River Baptist Church, in Newberry County, S. C. I was the slave of John Satterwhite. My mother lived with them. I was a small girl when the war was on. My brother went to war with Marse Satterwhite. When de Ku Klux and paddrollers traveled around in that section, they made Mr. Satterwhite hold the niggers when they was whipped, but he most all the time let them loose, exclaiming, 'they got loose'—he did not want many of them whipped.

"My mother had a kitchen way off from the house, wid a wide fireplace where she cooked victuals. There was holes in back of de chimney with iron rods sticking out of them to hold de pans, pots, kettles or boilers.

"People there did not believe much in ghosts. They were not much superstitious, but one time some of the negroes thought they heard the benches in Bush River Baptist Church turn over when nobody was in the church.

"Negroes most always shouted at their religious meetings. Before de negroes had their own church meetings, the slaves went to the white folks' Bush River Baptist church and set up in the gallery. I moved to Newberry when I was young, after I got married."

Source: Maria Cleland, Newberry, S. C. (80 years old).
Interviewer: G. L. Summer, Newberry, S. C. (5/17/37)

Project #1655
W. W. Dixon
Winnsboro, S. C.

# PETER CLIFTON
## Ex-Slave, 89 Years Old.

"You want me to start wid my fust memory and touch de high spots 'til dis very day? Dat'll take a long time but I glad to find someone to tell dat to; I is! I 'members when I was a boy, drivin' de calves to de pasture, a highland moccasin snake rise up in de path. I see dat forked tongue and them bright eyes right now. I so scared I couldn't move out my tracks. De mercy of de Lord cover me wid His wings. Dat snake uncoil, drop his head, and silently crawl away. Dat was on de Biggers Mobley place 'tween Kershaw and Camden, where I was born, in 1848.

"My pappy name Ned; my mammy name Jane. My brudders and sisters was Tom, Lizzie, Mary, and Gill. Us live in a log house wid a plank floor and a wooden chimney, dat was always ketchin' afire and de wind comin' through and fillin' de room wid smoke and cinders. It was just one of many others, just lak it, dat made up de quarters. Us had peg beds for de old folks and just pallets on de floor for de chillun. Mattresses was made of wheat straw but de pillows on de bed was cotton. I does 'member dat mammy had a chicken feather pillow she made from de feathers she saved at de kitchen.

"My grandpappy name Warren and grandmammy name Maria. De rule on de place was: 'Wake up de slaves at daylight, begin work when they can see, and quit work when they can't see'. But they was careful of de rule dat say: 'You mustn't work a child, under twelve years old, in de field'.

"My master's fust wife, I heard him say, was Mistress Gilmore. Dere was two chillun by her. Master Ed, dat live in a palace dat last time I visit Rock Hill and go to 'member myself to him; then dere was Miss Mary dat marry her cousin, Dr. Jim Mobley. They had one child, Captain Fred, dat took de Catawba rifles to Cuba and whip Spain for blowin' up de Maine. You say you rather I talk 'bout old master and de high spots? Well, Master Biggers had a big plantation and a big mansion four miles southeast of Chester. He buy my mammy and her chillun in front of de court house door in Chester, at de sale of de Clifton Estate. Then he turn 'round and buy my pappy dere, 'cause my mammy and sister Lizzie was cryin' 'bout him have to leave them. Mind you I wasn't born then. Marster Biggers was a widower then and went down and courted de widow Gibson, who had a plantation and fifty slaves 'tween Kershaw and Camden. Dere is where I was born.

"Marster had one child, a boy, by my mistress, Miss Sallie. They call him Black George. Him live long enough to marry a angel, Miss Kate McCrorey. They had four chillun. Dere got to be ninety slaves on de place befo' war come on. One time I go wid pappy to de Chester place. Seem lak more slaves dere than on de Gibson place. Us was fed up to de neck all de time, though us never had a change of clothes. Us smell pretty rancid maybe, in de winter time, but in de summer us no wear very much. Girls had a slip on and de boys happy in their shirt tails.

"Kept fox hounds on both places. Old Butler was de squirrel and 'possum dog. What I like best to eat? Marster, dere is nothin' better than 'possum and yallow sweet 'taters. Right now, I wouldn't turn dat down for pound cake and Delaware grape wine, lak my mistress use to eat and sip while she watch my mammy and old Aunt Tilda run de spinnin' wheels.

"De overseer on de place was name Mr. Mike Melton. No sir, he poor man but him come from good folks, not poor white trash. But they was cussed by marster, when after de war they took up wid de 'publican party. Sad day for old marster when him didn't hold his mouth, but I'll get to dat later.

"Marster Biggers believe in whippin' and workin' his slaves long and hard; then a man was scared all de time of being sold away from his wife and chillun. His bark was worse then his bite tho', for I never knowed him to do a wicked thing lak dat.

"How long was they whipped? Well, they put de foots in a stock and clamp them together, then they have a cross-piece go right across de breast high as de shoulder. Dat cross-piece long enough to bind de hands of a slave to it at each end. They always strip them naked and some time they lay on de lashes wid a whip, a switch or a strap. Does I believe dat was a great sin? No sir. Our race was just lak school chillun is now. De marster had to put de fear of God in them sometime, somehow, and de Bible don't object to it.

"I see marster buy a many a slave. I never saw him sell but one and he sold dat one to a drover for $450.00, cash down on de table, and he did dat at de request of de overseer and de mistress. They was uneasy 'bout him.

"They give us Christmas Day. Every woman got a handkerchief to tie up her hair. Every girl got a ribbon, every boy a barlow knife, and every man a shin plaster. De neighbors call de place, de shin plaster, Barlow, Bandanna place. Us always have a dance in de Christmas.

"After freedom when us was told us had to have names, pappy say he love his old Marster Ben Clifton de best and him took dat titlement, and I's been a Clifton ever since.

"Go way, white folks! What everthing mate for? De birds, de corn tassle and de silk, man and woman, white folks and colored folks mates. You ask me what for I seek out Christina for to marry. Dere was sumpin' 'bout dat gal, dat day I meets her, though her hair had 'bout a pound of cotton thread in it, dat just 'tracted me to her lak a fly will sail 'round and light on a 'lasses pitcher. I kept de Ashford Ferry road hot 'til I got her. I had to ask her old folks for her befo' she consent. Dis took 'bout six months. Everything had to be regular. At last I got de preacher, Rev. Ray Shelby to go down dere and marry us. Her have been a blessin' to me every day since.

"Us have seven chillun. They's scattered east, west, north, and south. De only one left is just David, our baby, and him is a baby six foot high and fifty-one years old.

"Yes sir, us had a bold, drivin', pushin', marster but not a hard-hearted one. I sorry when military come and arrest him. It was dis a way, him try to carry on wid free labor, 'bout lak him did in slavery. Chester was in military district no. 2. De whole state was under dat military government. Old marster went to de field and cuss a nigger woman for de way she was workin', choppin' cotton. She turnt on him wid de hoe and gashed him 'bout de head wid it. Him pull out his pistol and shot her. Dr. Babcock say de wound in de woman not serious. They swore out a warrant for Marster Biggers, arrest him wid a squad, and take him to Charleston, where him had nigger jailors, and was kicked and cuffed 'bout lak a dog. They say de only thing he had to eat was corn-meal-mush brought 'round to him and other nice white folks in a tub and it was ladeled out to them thru de iron railin' into de palms of dere hands. Mistress stuck by him, went and stayed down dere. The filthy prison and hard treatments broke him down, and when he did get out and come home, him passed over de river of Jordan, where I hopes and prays his soul finds rest. Mistress say one time they threatened her down dere, dat if she didn't get up $10,000 they would send him where she would never see him again.

"Well, I must be goin'. Some day when de crops is laid by and us get de boll weevil whipped off de field, I'll get David to bring me and dat gal, Christina, you so curious 'bout, to Winnsboro to see you. Oh, how her gonna laugh and shake her sides when I get home and tell her all 'bout what's down on dat paper! You say it's to be sent to Washington? Why, de President and his wife will be tickled at some of them things. I's sure they will. Dat'll make Christina have a great excitement when I tell her we is to be talked 'bout way up dere. I 'spect it will keep her wake and she'll be hunchin' me and asking me all thru de night, what I give in.

"Oh, well, I's thankful for dis hour in which I's been brought very near to de days of de long long ago. Maybe I'll get a pension and maybe I won't. Just so de Lord and de President take notice of us, is enough for me."

Project 1885-1
From Field Notes.
Spartanburg, Dist. 4
April 29, 1937
Edited by:
Elmer Turnage

# HENRY COLEMAN
## Folk Lore: Folk Tales (Negro)

"I wuz born in Fairfield, dat is over yonder across Broad River, you knos what dat is, don't you? Yes sir, it wuz on Marse Johnson D. Coleman's plantation. And he had a plantation! Dese niggers here in Carlisle—and niggers is all dey is too—dey don't know what no plantation is. When I got big enough fer to step around, from de very fus, my maw took me in de big house. It still dat, cep it done bout fell down now, to what it wuz then. But some of Marse's folks, dey libs down dar still. Den you see, dey is like dese white folks up 'round here now. Dey ain't got no big money like dey had when I wuz a runnin' up. Time I got big enough fer to run aroun' in my shirt tail, my maw, she lowed one night to my paw, when he wuz settin by de fire, dat black little nigger over dar, he got to git hissef some pants kaise I'se gwine to put him up over de white fokes table. In dem times de doos and winders, dey nebber had no screen wire up to dem like dey is now. Fokes didn't know nothin bout no such as dat den. My Marster and all de other big white fokes, dey raised pea fowls. Is yu ebber seed any? Well, ev'y spring us little niggers, we coch dem wild things at night. Dey could fly like a buzzard. Dey roosted up in de pine trees, right up in de tip top. So de Missus, she hab us young uns clam up dar and git 'em when dey first took roost. Us would clam down and my maw, she would pull de long feathers out'n de tails. Fer weeks de cocks, dey wouldn't let nobody see 'em if dey could help it. Dem birds is sho proud. When dey is got de feathers, dey jus struts on de fences, and de fences wuz rail in dem days. If'n dey could see dereself in a puddle o' water after a rain, dey would stay dar all day a struttin' and carring on like nobody's business. Yes sir, dem wuz purty birds. After us got de feathers, de Missus, she'ud low dat all de nigger gals gwine to come down in de wash house and make fly brushes. Sometime de Missus 'ud gib some of de gals some short feathers to put in dere Sunday hats. When dem gals got dem hats on, I used to git so disgusted wid 'em I'd leave 'em at church and walk home by my sef. Anyway, by dat time all de new fly brushes wuz made and de Missus, she hab fans make from de short feathers for de white fokes to fan de air wid on hot days. Lawdy, I'se strayed fur from what I had started out fer to tell you. But I knowed dat you young fokes didn't know nothin' bout all dat. In dem days de dining room wuz big and had de windows open all de summer long, and all de doos stayed streched too. Quick as de mess of victuals began to come on de table, a little nigger boy was put up in de swing, I calls it, over de table to fan de flies and gnats off'en de Missus' victuals. Dis swing wuz just off'n de end of de long table. Some of de white fokes had steps a leadin' up to it. Some of 'em jus had de little boys maws to fech de young'uns up dar till dey got fru; den dey wuz fetched down again.

"Well, when I got my pants, my maw fetched me in and I clumb up de steps dat Marse Johnson had, to git up in his swing wid. At fus, dey had to show me jus how to hole de brush, kaise dem peacock feathers wuz so long, iffen you didn't mind your bizness, de ends of dem feathers would splash in de gravy er sumpin nother, and den de Missus table be all spattered up. Some o' de Marsters would whorp de nigger chilluns fer dat carelessness, but Marse Johnson, he always good to his niggers. Mos de white fokes good to de niggers round bout whar I comes from.

"It twad'nt long for I got used to it and I nebber did splash de feathers in no rations. But iffen I got used to it, I took to agoin to sleep up thar. Marse Johnson, he would jus git up and wake me up. All de white fokes at de table joke me so bout bein' so lazy, I soon stop dat foolishness. My maw, she roll her eyes at me when I come down atter de marster had to wake me up. Dat change like ever thing else. When I got bigger, I got to be house boy. Dey took down de swing and got a little gal to stand jus 'hind de Missus' chair and fan dem flies. De Missus low to Marse Johnson dat de style done change when he want to know how come she took de swing down. So dat is de way it is now wid de wimmen, dey changes de whole house wid de style; but I tells my chilluns, ain't no days like de ole days when I wuz a shaver.

"Atter de war, I come up to Shelton and got to de 'P' Hamilton place. I wuz grown den. I seed a young girl dar what dey called 'Evvie'. Her paw, he had b'longed to de Chicks, so dats who she wuz, Evvie Chick. Dar she sets in dat room by de fire. Now us got 'leven chilluns. Dey is scattered all about. Dey is good to us in our ole age. Us riz 'em to obey de Lawd and mine us. Dats all dey knows, and iffen fokes would do dat now, dey wouldn't have no sassy chilluns like I sees here in Carlisle.

"Evvie, what year wuz it we got married? Yes, dat's right. It wuz de year of de 'shake'. Is you heerd bout de 'shake'? Come out here Evvie and les tell him dat, kaise dese young fokes doan know nothin'. It wuz dark, and we wuz eatin' supper, when sumpin started to makin' de dishes fall out'n de cupboard. At fus we thought it wuz somebody a jumpin' up and down on de flo. Den we knowed dat it wuz sumpin else er makin' dem dishes fall out o' de cupboard. At fus we thought it wuz Judgment day, kaise ev'ry thing started fallin' worser and worser. De dishes fell so fast you couldn't pick'em up. Some of us went down to de spring. De white fokes, dey come along wid us and dey make us fetch things from de big house, like fine china dat de Missus didn't want to git broke up. She tole us dat it wuz er earthquake and it wasn't no day o' Judgment. Anyway, we lowed de white fokes might be wrong, so us niggers started to a prayin', and den all de niggers on de plantation dat heerd us, well de come along and jined wid us in de prayin' and singin'. Us wuz all a shakin' mos as bad as de earth wuz, kaise dat wuz a awful time dat we libbed through fer bout twenty minutes—de white fokes lowed it lasted only ten, but I ain't sho about dat. When we got back to de big house, de cupboard in de kitchen had done fell plum' down. In de nigger houses, de chimneys mos all fell in, and de chicken houses ev'rywhar wuz shuck down. While we wuz a lookin' aroun, and de wimmen fokes, dey wuz a takin' on mightily another shake come up. Us all took fer de spring agin; dis one lasted bout long as de first one. Us prayed and sung and shouted dis time. It sho stopped de earth a shakin' and a quiverin' some, kaise dat thing went on fer a whole week; ceptin de furs two wuz de heaviest. All de other ones wuz lighter. Iffen it hadn't been fur us all a beggin' de Lawd fer to sho us his mercy, it ain't no tellin' how bad dem shakes would er been. Miss Becky Levister, you know her, she live up yander in your uncle John's house now, she wuz wid us. She wuz jus a little girl den. Her paw wuz Mr. Kelly. He died for ever you wuz born. Not long ago I seed her. She lowed to me, 'uncle Henry, do you recollect in de time o' de shake? Lacken she think I'd fergit such as dat. It wuz in de time o' de worsest things dis ole nigger is ebber seed hisself, and I is gwine on 82 now. Miss Becky, she wuz a settin' in her car wid some one drivin' her, but she ain't fergot dis ole nigger. If I is up town and Miss Becky, she ride by, she look out and lows' 'Howdy uncle Henry', and I allus looks up and raises my hat. I likes mannerable white fokes, mysef, and den, I likes mannerable niggers fer as dat goes. Some of dese fokes, now both white—I hates to say it—and niggers, dey trys to act like dey ain't got no sense er sumpin'. But you know one thing I knos real fokes when I sees dem and dey can't fool me."

Aunt Evvie tells the following story about her father, Rufus Chick. The story is known by all of the reliable white folks of the surrounding neighborhood also: "My paw, Rufus Chick, lived on the Union side of Broad River, the latter days of his life. Maj. James B. Steadman had goats over on Henderson Island that my paw used to care for. He went over to the Island in a batteau. One afternoon, he and four other darkies were going over there when the batteau turned over. The four other men caught to a willow bush and were rescued. My paw could not swim, and he got drowned. For three weeks they searched for his body, but they never did find it. Some years after, a body of a darky was found at the mouth of the canal, down near Columbia. The body was perfectly petrified. This was my paw's body. The canal authorities sent the body to a museum in Detroit. It was January 11, 1877 when my father got drowned.

"When I wuz a young fellow I used to race wid de horses. I wuz de swifes runner on de plantation. A nigger, Peter Feaster, had a white horse of his own, and de white fokes used to bet amongst de selves as much as $20.00 dat I could outrun dat horse. De way us did, wuz to run a hundred yards one way, turn around and den run back de hundred yards. Somebody would hold de horse, and another man would pop de whip fer us to start. Quick as de whip popped, I wuz off. I would git sometimes ten feet ahead of de horse 'fore dey could git him started. Den when I had got de hundred yards, I could turn around quicker dan de horse would, and I would git a little mo' ahead. Corse wid dat, you had to be a swift man on yer feets to stay head of a fas horse. Peter used to git so mad when I would beat his ole horse, and den all de niggers would laf at him kaise de white fokes give me some of de bettin money. Sometimes dey would bet only $10.00, sometimes, $15 or $20. Den I would race wid de white fokes horses too. Dey nebber got mad when I come out ahead. After I got through, my legs used to jus shake like a leaf. So now, I is gib plum out in dem and I tributes it to dat. Evvie, she lowed when I used to do dat after we wuz married, dat I wuz gwine to give out in my legs, and sho nuf I is."

"Uncle" Henry says that his legs have given out in the bone.

Source: Henry Coleman and his wife, Evvie, of Carlisle, S. C.
Interviewer: Caldwell Sims, Union, S. C.

United States

Project 1885-1
District #4
Spartanburg, S. C.
May 31, 1937

## TUFF COLEMAN
### Folklore: Ex-Slaves

"I was born about 1857 and my wife about 1859. I lived on Squire Keller's farm, near the Parr place, and after the squire died I belonged to Mrs. Elizabeth (Wright) Keller. My mother died when I was a boy and my father was bought and carried to Alabama. My father was Gilliam Coleman and my mother, Emoline Wright. My master and mistress was good to me. The old Squire was as fine a man as ever lived on earth. He took me in his home and took care of me. After the war the mistress stayed on the place and worked the slaves right on, giving them wages or shares.

"The slaves were not whipped much; I 'member one man was whipped pretty bad on Maj. Kinard's place. He had a colored man to do whipping for him—his name was Eph. There was no whiskey on the place, never made any. Us did cooking in the kitchen wid wide fireplaces.

"When the Yankees came through at the end of the war, they took all the stock we had. The mistress had a fine horse, its tail touching the ground, and we all cried when it was taken; but we got it back, as some men went after it.

"I married in 1874 to Ellen T. Williams. She belonged to Bill Reagan. After I married I worked in the railroad shops at "Helena", and sometimes I fired the engine on the road, for about eight years. Then I went into the ministry. I was called by the Spirit of the Lord, gradually, and I preached 51 years. I have been superannuated two years.

"I have one child, a son, who is in the pullman service at Washington, D. C.

"I owned my little house and several acres and am still living on it."

> Source: Rev. Tuff Coleman and wife (80 and 78), Newberry, S. C.
> Interviewer: G. Leland Summer, Newberry, S. C.

Code No.
Project, 1885-(1)
Prepared by Annie Ruth Davis
Place, Marion, S. C.
Date, May 27, 1937
No. Words --
Reduced from -- words
Rewritten by --

## MOM LOUISA COLLIER

### Ex-Slave, 78 years.

"I born en raise up dere in Colonel Durant yard en I in my 78th year now. Dat seem lak I ole, don' it? Coase Colonel Durant hab plenty udder colored peoples 'sides us, but dey ne'er lib dere in de yard lak we. Dey lib up in de quarters on de plantation. My pappy name Ben Thompson en he hadder stay dere close to de big house cause he wus de Colonel driver. De Colonel hab uh big ole carriage wha' to ride in den. It hab uh little seat in de front fa my pappy to set in en den it hab two seat 'hind de driver whey de Colonel en he family is ride. I kin see dat carriage jes uz good right now dat my white folks hab to carry em whey dey is wanna go."

"Den my mammy come from de udder side uv Pee Dee en she name, Lidia Bass. She was de servant 'round de yard dere en dat count fa we to ne'er stay in de quarters wid de udder colored peoples 'fore freedom declare. I ne'er hadder do no work long uz I lib dere in de yard cause I ain' been but five year ole when freedom declare. My grandmammy lib right dere close us en Colonel Durant hab she jes to look a'ter aw de plantation chillun when dey parents wuz workin'. Aw uv de plantation peoples 'ud take dey chillun dere fa my grandmammy to nu'se."

"I 'member one day dere come uh crowd uv peoples dere dat dey tell us chillun wuz de Yankees. Dey come right dere t'rough de Colonel yard en when I see em, I wuz 'fraid uv em. I run en hide under my grandmammy bed. Don' know wha' dey say cause I ain' ge' close 'nough to hear nuthin wha' dey talk 'bout. De white folks hadder herry (hurry) en put t'ings in pots en bury em or hide em somewhey when dey hear dat de Yankees wus comin' cause dey scare dem Yankees might take dey t'ings lak dey is carry 'way udder folks t'ings. I hear em say dey ne'er take nuthin from de Colonel but some uv he wood."

"My white folks was well-off peoples en dey ain' ne'er use no harsh treatment on dey plantation peoples. De Colonel own aw dis land 'bout here den en he see dat he overseer on de plantation provide plenty uv eve't'ing us need aw de time. I hear tell 'bout some uv de white folks 'ud beat dey colored peoples mos' to death, but I ain' ne'er see none uv dat no whey. I is 'member when dey'ud sell some uv de colored peoples way offen to annuder plantation somewhey. Jes been bid em offen jes lak dey wuz cattle. Some uv de time dey'ud sell uh man wife 'way en den he hadder ge' annuder wife."

"A'ter freedom declare, we ne'er lib dere at de big house no more. Move in de colored settlement en den we ain' eat at de big house no more neither. Dey le' us hab uh garden uv we own den en raise us own chicken en aw dat. I 'member de Colonel gi'e us so mucha t'ing eve'y week en it hadder las' us from one Saturday to de next. My mammy 'ud go to de Colonel barn eve'y week en ge' she portion uv meal en meat. Dat de way dey pay de hand fa dey work den. Ne'er gi'e em no money den."

"Peoples wha' lib on Colonel Durant plantation ain' know nuthin but to lib on de fat uv de land. Dey hab plenty cows den en dey gi'e us plenty uv milk eve'y day. I 'member we chillun use'er take we tin cup en go up to de big house en ge' us milk to drink en den some uv de cows 'ud be so gentle lak dat we chillun is follow em right down side de path. Den when dere ne'er wuz nobody lak de Colonel overseer 'bout to see us, we is ketch de cow en ge' some more milk. I al'ays 'ud lub to drink me milk dat way. We is eat plenty green peas en 'tatoes en fish in dem days too en dey is use 'tatoe pie right smart den."

"Aw de colored peoples on Colonel Durant plantation hab good bed wha' to sleep on en good clothes to put on dey back. Coase we ne'er hab no bought fu'niture in dem days, but we hab bedstead wha' dey make right dere en benches en some uv de time dey is make wha' dey call 'way back chair. Den we is make us own bed outer hay cause de white folks ne'er spare de colored peoples no cotton den. Hadder cut de hay in de fall uv de year en dry it jes lak dey dries it fa to feed de cattle on. Den dey hadder take sack en sew em up togedder en put de hay in dese. Dey sleep right smart in dem days. Don' mucha people sleep on straw bed dese day en time en dey don' dress lak dey use'er neither. I 'member de long dress dey is wear den. Hadder hold em up when dey walk so dey won' tetch de floor 'bout em. Den some uv dem is wear wha' dey call leggens. Dey'ud gather em 'round de knee en le' em show 'bout de ankle. Dey wuz pretty, dat dey wuz. De white folks'ud make de plantation clothes outer calico en jeanes cloth en dat time. De jeanes cloth be wha' dey make de boy clothes outer. Dey is weave aw dey cloth right dere on de plantation en den dey use'er dye de thread en weave aw sorta check outer de different color thread. Wha' dey make de dye outer? Dey ge' bark outer de woods en boil de color outer it en den dey boil de thread in dat. Dat how dey is make dey dye. Ne'er see de peoples hab no hat lak dey hab now neither. Aw de colored peoples wear wha' dey call shuck hat den cause dey been make outer shuck. Dat aw de kinder hat we is hab."

"Peoples use'er ge' aw kinder useful t'ing outer de woods in dem days 'way back dere. Ne'er hadder buy no me'icine tall den. Ain' ne'er been no better cough cure no whey den de one my ole mammy use'er make fa we chillun. She larnt 'bout how it made when she stay 'round de Missus en dat how come I know wha' in it. Jes hadder go in de woods en ge' some cherry, call dat wild cherry, en cut some uv de wild cherry bark fust (first) t'ing. A'ter dat yuh hadder find some uv dese long-leaf pine en ge' de bud outer dat. Den yuh hadder go to whey dere some sweet gum grow en ge' de top outer dem en ge' some mullen to put wid it. Ain' ne'er no cough stand aw dat mix up togedder in no day en time. Dey gi'e dat to de peoples fa dat t'ing wha' dey use'er call de grip cough. Den dey use'er make uh t'ing dat dey call "bone set" tea. I forge' how dey make it but dey gi'e it to de peoples when dey hab de fevers. It been so bitter dat it'ud lift yuh up 'fore yuh is ge' it aw down de t'roat. Ain' see no fever me'icine lak dat nowadays."

"Yas'um, I 'members when dey hab plenty uv dem cornshucking to one annuder barn. De peoples'ud come from aw de plantation 'bout dere. Dem corn-shuckings wuz big times, dat dey wuz. Gi'e eve'body aw de "hopping-john" dey kin eat. Jes cook it aw in uh big pot dere in de yard to de big house. Ain' nuthin ne'er eat no better den dat "hopping-john" is eat."

"Den de peoples use'er come from aw de plantation 'bout en hab big dancing dere. Dat when I lub to be 'bout. Dey hab uh big fire build up outer in de yard en dat wha' dey dance 'round 'bout. Call dat uh torch fire. Dey'ud hab fiddle en dey dance wha' dey call de reel dance den. I 'member I use'er lub to watch dey feet when dat fiddle 'ud ge' to playing. I jes crawl right down on me knees dere whey I'ud see dey feet jes uh going."

"I ne'er hab mucha schooling 'fore freedom declare cause I been raise up on de plantation. Dis child (her daughter) pappy wuz de house boy to de big house en he ge' more schooling den I is. De Missus larnt he how to read en write she self. A'ter freedom declare, I go to school to uh white man up dere to de ole Academy en den I is go to annuder school down dere to uh blacksmith shop. I go to uh white man dere too. Ne'er hab no colored teacher den cause dey ain' hab 'nough schooling den. Dese chillun don' know nuthin 'bout dem times. I tell dese chillun I don' know wha' dey wanna run 'bout so mucha cause dere plenty t'ing to see dat pass right dere by us house eve'y day. I t'ink dis uh better day en time to lib en cause dis uh brighter day now dat we hab."

Source: Mom Louisa Collier, age 78, colored, Marion, S. C

Personal interview, May 1937.

Project #1655
W. W. Dixon
Winnsboro, S. C.

## JOHN COLLINS
### Ex-Slave, 85 Years Old.

John Collins lives in a two-room frame cottage by the side of US 21, just one mile north of the town of Winnsboro, S. C. on the right side of the highway and a few hundred yards from the intersection of US 21 and US 22. The house is owned by Mr. John Ameen. His son, John, who lives with him, is a farm hand in the employ of Mr. John Ameen, and is his father's only support.

"They tells me dat I was born in Chester County, just above de line dat separates Chester and Fairfield Counties. You know where de 'dark corner' is, don't you? Well, part is in Fairfield County and part is in Chester County. In dat corner I first see de light of day; 'twas on de 29th of February, 1852. Though I is eighty-five years old, I's had only twenty-one birthdays. I ketches a heap of folks wid dat riddle. They ask me: 'How old is you Uncle John?' I say: 'I is had twenty-one birthdays and won't have another till 1940. Now figure it out yourself, sir, if you is so curious to know my age!' One time a smart aleck, jack-leg, Methodist preacher, of my race, come to my house and figured all day on dat riddle and never did git de correct answer. He scribbled on all de paper in de house and on de back of de calendar leaves. I sure laughed at dat preacher. I fears he lacked some of dat good old time 'ligion, de way he sweated and scribbled and fussed.

"My daddy was name Steve Chandler. My mammy was called Nancy. I don't know whether they was married or not. My daddy was sent to Virginia, while de war was gwine on, to build forts and breastworks around Petersburg, so they say, and him never come back. I 'members him well. He was a tall black man, over six feet high, wid broad shoulders. My son, John, look just lak him. Daddy used to play wid mammy just lak she was a child. He'd ketch her under de armpits and jump her up mighty nigh to de rafters in de little house us lived in.

"My mammy and me was slaves of old Marse Nick Collins. His wife, my mistress, was name Miss Nannie. Miss Nannie was just an angel; all de slaves loved her. But marster was hard to please, and he used de lash often. De slaves whisper his name in fear and terror to de chillun, when they want to hush them up. They just say to a crying child: 'Shet up or old Nick will ketch you!' Dat child sniffle but shet up pretty quick.

"Marster didn't have many slaves. Best I 'member, dere was about twenty men, women, and chillun to work in de field and five house slaves. Dere was no good feelin's 'twixt field hands and house servants. De house servants put on more airs than de white folks. They got better things to eat, too, than de field hands and wore better and cleaner clothes.

"My marster had one son, Wyatt, and two daughters, Nannie and Elizabeth. They was all right, so far as I 'member, but being a field hand's child, off from de big house, I never got to play wid them any.

"My white folks never cared much about de slaves having 'ligion. They went to de Universalist Church down at Feasterville. They said everybody was going to be saved, dat dere was no hell. So they thought it was just a waste of time telling niggers about de hereafter.

"In them days, way up dere in de 'dark corner', de white folks didn't had no schools and couldn't read or write. How could they teach deir slaves if they had wanted to?

"De Yankees never come into de 'dark corner'. It was in 1867, dat us found out us was free; then we all left. I come down to Feasterville and stayed wid Mr. Jonathan Coleman. From dere, I went to Chester. While I was living dere, I married Maggie Nesbit. Us had five chillun; they all dead, 'cept John. My wife died two months ago.

"I is tired now, and I is sad. I's thinking about Maggie and de days dat are gone. Them memories flood over me, and I just want to lay down. Maybe I'll see you sometime again. I feel sure I'll see Maggie befo' many months and us'll see de sunrise, down here, from de far hebben above. Good day. Glad you come to see me, sir!"

Project 1885-1
Folklore
Spartanburg, Dist. 4
Nov. 29, 1937
Edited by:
Elmer Turnage

# BOUREGARD CORRY
## Stories From Ex-Slaves

"Time is but time, and how is I to know when I was born when everybody knows dat dey never had no calendars when I come here. Few it was dat ever seed even a Lady's Birthday Almanac. I is 75 years old. I was dat last January on de 13th day [HW: 1862]. I was born in old Union County about 4 miles south of Gaffney.

"Marse Mike Montgomery had a place dat reached from town way yonder to Broad River whar de Ninety-nine Islands lays. Now, de way de road lays, dey counts it twelve miles from Gaffney. When I was a boy it was lots further dan dat.

"Never know'd why, but de Red Shirts whipped my pa, Tom Corry. Dey jes' come and got him out'n his house. He come back in de house. Chilluns was not give no privileges in dem days, so I never axed no questions, kaise I was fear'd. Chilluns jes' trots into your business dese days.

"My pa say he was a slave on dem Ninety-nine Islands. All I know is what he told me. Mr. Mike Montgomery built lots of boats. Dey carried from 50 to 60 bales of cotton down at one time. De cotton was carried in de fall. De Smith place jined de Montgomery place and dat run into de Nancy Corry place. I have forded de river dar lots of times. Broad River is shallow, deepest place in it back den was at de mouth of King Creek, jes' below Cherokee Falls. It ain't so broad dar.

"Pa was de boatman for Mr. Mike. De boat was big and long, and dey always started off early in de morning wid a load of cotton. Old man Dick Corry had to stand in de boat jes' behind pa. Dey had two steermen. So many rocks in de shallow water dat it kept de steermen busy dodging rooks. Dey pushed de boat off de rocks wid long poles. Dey had to work away from de rocks. Sometimes dey had to get out in de water and roll some rocks from dere path if de water wasn't cold.

"Wharever night caught dem, dar dey stopped and pitched a camp. Dey fished and killed wild ducks or birds dat was plentiful den, and cooked dem along wid bread and other things fetched from home. On de way from Columbia dey had lots of store-bought things to eat. Store-bought things was a treat den. Now ducks and things is a treat. Times sho changes fast.

"Spring was took up wid farming. Every man, white and black, had a family back in dem days. Dat dey did, rich or poor, white or black, all raised families. Men farmed and hauled manure and cleaned up de plantation lots and fields and grubbed in de spring. Women cooked and washed and ironed and spun and kept house and made everybody in de house clothes, and made all de bed clothes. Dey stayed home all of de time. Men got through work and set down at home wid deir wives and never run around. Now all goes. Dat's all dey does dese days is go.

"We had plenty of bread and milk and we raised hogs and killed all kinds of wild things like turkey, ducks and birds, and caught fish. Men had guns dat dey used every day, and dey hit things, too. Folks kept in practice, wid guns and had shooting matches.

"After dey stopped boating, wagons come in. Den things begin to change. Dey still is changing. Wagons went to Spartanburg to take cotten. Folks never went to Columbia no more. Spartanburg begin to grow and it sho still is at it."

Source: Bouregard Corry (N, 75), Rt. 2, Gaffney, S. C.
Interviewer: Caldwell Sims, Union, S. C. (11/22/37).

United States

Project #1655
W. W. Dixon
Winnsboro, S. C.

# CALEB CRAIG
## Ex Slave 86 Years Old.

Caleb Craig lives in a four-room house, with a hall, eight feet wide, through the center and a fireplace in each room. He lives with his grandson, who looks after him.

"Who I is? I goes by de name of C. C. All de colored people speaks of me in dat way. C. C. dis and C. C. dat. I don't 'ject but my real name is Caleb Craig. Named after one of de three spies dat de Bible tell 'bout. Him give de favorite report and, 'cause him did, God feed him and clothe him all de balance of him life and take him into de land of Canaan, where him and Joshua have a long happy life. I seen a picture in a book, one time, of Joshua and Caleb, one end of a pole on Joshua's shoulder and one end on Caleb's shoulder, wid big bunches of grapes a hangin' from dat pole. Canaan must to been a powerful fertile land to make grapes lak dat.

"Would you believe dat I can't write? Some of them adultery (adult) teachers come to my house but it seem a pack of foolishness; too much trouble. I just rather put my money in de bank, go dere when I want it, set dat C. C. to de check, and git what I want.

"When I born? Christmas Eve, 1851. Where 'bouts? Blackstock, S. C. Don't none of us know de day or de place us was born. Us have to take dat on faith. You know where de old Bell house, 'bove Blackstock, is? Dere's where I come to light. De old stagecoach, 'tween Charlotte and Columbia, changed hosses and stop dere but de railroad busted all dat up.

"My mammy name Martha. Marse John soon give us chillun to his daughter, Miss Marion. In dat way us separated from our mammy. Her was a mighty pretty colored woman and I has visions and dreams of her, in my sleep, sometime yet. My sisters would call me Cale but her never did. Her say Caleb every time and all de time. Marse John give her to another daughter of his, Miss Nancy, de widow Thompson then, but afterwards her marry a hoss drover from Kentucky, Marse Jim Jones. I can tell you funny things 'bout him if I has time befo' I go.

"Us chillun was carried down to de June place where Miss Marion and her husband, Marse Ed P. Mobley live. It was a fine house, built by old Dr. June. Marse Ed bought de plantation, for de sake of de fine house, where he want to take Miss Marion as a bride.

"Dere was a whole passle of niggers in de quarter, three hundred or maybe more. I didn't count them, 'cause I couldn't count up to a hundred but I can now. Ten, ten, double ten, forty-five, and fifteen. Don't dat make a hundred? Sho' it do.

"Clothes? Too many dere, for to clothe them much. I b'long to de shirt-tail brigade 'til I got to be a man. Why I use to plow in my shirt-tail! Well, it wasn't so bad in de summer time and us had big fires in de winter time, inside and outside de house, whenever us was working'. 'Til I was twelve years old I done nothin' but play.

"Money? Hell no! Excuse me, but de question so surprise me, I's caught off my guard. Food? Us got farm produce, sich as corn-meal, bacon, 'lasses, bread, milk, collards, turnips, 'tators, peanuts, and punkins.

"De overseer was Mr. Brown. My marster was much talked 'bout for workin' us on Sunday. He was a lordly old fellow, as I 'member, but dere was never anything lak plowin' on Sunday, though I do 'member de hands workin' 'bout de hay and de fodder.

"Marse Ed, a great fox hunter, kep' a pack of hounds. Sometime they run deer. Old Uncle Phil was in charge of de pack. Him had a special dog for to tree 'possums in de nighttime and squirrels in de daytime. Believe me, I lak 'possum de best. You lak 'possum? Well, I'll git my grandson to hunt you one dis comin' October.

"Marse Ed didn't 'low patarollers (patrollers) on de June place. He tell them to stay off and they knowed to stay off.

"Slave drovers often come to de June place, just lak mule drovers and hog drovers. They buy, sell, and swap niggers, just lak they buy, sell, and swap hosses, mules, and hogs.

"Us had preachin' in de quarters on Sunday. Uncle

Dick, a old man, was de preacher. De funerals was simple and held at night. De grave was dug dat day.

"A man dat had a wife off de place, see little peace or happiness. He could see de wife once a week, on a pass, and jealousy kep' him 'stracted de balance of de week, if he love her very much.

"I marry Martha Pickett. Why I marry her? Well, I see so many knock-knee, box-ankle, spindly-shank, flat nose chillun, when I was growin' up, dat when I come to choose de filly to fold my colts, I picks one dat them mistakes wasn't so lakly to appear in. Us have five chillun. Lucy marry a Sims and live in Winnsboro, S. C. Maggie marry a Wallace and live in Charlotte, N. C. Mary marry a Brice and live in Chester, S. C. Jane not married; she live wid her sister, Mag, in Charlotte. John lives 'bove White Oak and farms on a large place I own, not a scratch of pen against it by de government or a bank.

"I live on 27 acres, just out de town of Winnsboro. I expects no pension. My grandchillun come and go, back'ards and fo'ards, and tell me 'bout cities, and high falutin' things goin' on here and dere. I looks them over sometime for to see if I didn't do sumpin' for deir figures, in s'lectin' and marryin' Martha, dat's more important to them than de land I'll leave them when I die. When Martha die, I marry a widow name Eliza but us never generate any chillun. Her dead. Not 'nough spark in me to undertake de third trip, though I still is a subject of 'tentions.

"What 'bout Marse Ed and Marse Jim Jones? Well, you see, Marse Jim was close wid his money. Marse Ed was a spender. I 'tend Marse Ed to a chicken main once. Marse

Jim rode up just as Marse Ed was puttin' up $300.00 on a pile brass wing rooster, 'ginst a black breasted red war hoss rooster, dat de McCarleys was backin'. Marse Ed lost de bet. But him never told Marse Jim, dat befo' he rode up, him had won $500.00 from them same men. After de main was over, Marse Jim, bein' brudder-in-law to Marse Ed, rode home to dinner wid him. After dinner they was smokin' deir cigars befo' de parlor fire dat I was 'viving up. Marse Jim lecture Marse Ed for throwin' 'way money. Marse Ed stretch out his long legs and say: 'Mr. Jones does you 'member dat day us 'tended de circus in Chester and as us got to de top of de hill a blind begger held out his cup to us and you put in a quarter?' Mr. Jones say he does 'member dat. Marse Ed went on: 'Well, Mr. Jones, I had a dream last night. I dream us comin' through de Cumberland Mountains wid a drove of mules from Kentucky. You was ridin' a piebald hoss, de same one you rode into South Carolina de fust time you come here. You had on a faded, frazzled grey shawl, 'bout lak de one you had on today. Us was in front, de outriders behind, when us got to de gap in de mountains. De drove stampede just as us git in de gap. Us was both kilt. You got to heaven befo' I did. When I did git dere, you was befo' de High Court. They examine you and turn over de leaves of a big book and find very little dere to your credit. At last they say, I think it was de 'Postle Peter dat ask de question. Him say: 'Everything is recorded in dis book. Us can find nothin'. Do you happen to 'member anything you did to your credit down dere on earth?' Then you stand up wid dat old shawl 'round your shoulders and say: 'Aha! I do 'member one thing. One day I was in Chester and put a quarter of a dollar in a blind man's tin cup.' De 'postle then tell de recording angel to see if him could find dat deed. Him turn over de leaves 'til him found it on de page. Then de twelve 'postles retire and 'liberate on your case. They come back and de judge pass sentence which was: 'The sentence of de High Court is, that in view of your great love of money, James Jones, it is de sentence of de court dat you be given back de quarter you give de blind beggar in Chester and dat you, James Jones, be sent immediate on your way to hell.' Then they both laugh over dat and Marse Jim got real happy when he find out Marse Ed quit de main wid $200.00 to de good."

    Address:
    Caleb Craig,
    Winnsboro, S. C.

    That part of the suburb of Winnsboro called "Mexico".
    Just east of the
    Southern Railway Company and north of Winnsboro
    Cotton Mills.

Project #1655
W. W. Dixon
Winnsboro, S. C.

# DINAH CUNNINGHAM
## Ex-Slave 84 Years Old.

Dinah Cunningham lives about seven miles west of Ridgeway, S. C., on the Hood place about a hundred yards off the old Devil's Race Track road. She lives with her daughter and son-in-law and their three children. They live in a two-room frame house with a shed room annex. In the annex, Dinah and the smaller children sleep. They are kind to Dinah, who is feeble and can do no farm labor. Dinah is as helpless about the home as a child.

"I's come up here 'bout seventeen miles for to let you see me. 'Spect you don't see much in dis old worn out critter. Now does you?

"Well, here I is, and I wants you white folks to help me, 'cause I's served you from generation to generation. Wid de help of de Lord and trustin' in Jesus de Lamb, I knows I's goin' to git help. When is they gwine to start payin' off? I's heard them say how you got to be on de roll and signed up befo' de fourth day of July. So here I is!

"I was born de fust day of March, 1853, out from Ridgeway, sunrise side. My marster was David Robertson and my mistress name Sally. Her was mighty pretty. Her was a Rembert befo' she marry Marse Dave. They had one child dat I was de nurse for and her name was Luray. Her marry Marse Charlie Ray.

"De onliest whippin' I got was 'bout dat child. I had de baby on de floor on a pallet and rolled over on it. Her make a squeal like she was much hurt and mistress come in a hurry. After de baby git quiet and go to sleep, she said: 'Dinah, I hates to whip you but de Good Book say, spare de rod and spoil de child.' Wid dat, she goes out and git a little switch off de crepe myrtle bush and come back and took my left hand in her left hand, dat had all de rings on de fingers, and us had it 'round dat room. I make a big holler as she 'plied dat switch on dese very legs dat you sees here today. They is big and fat now and can scarcely wobble me 'long but then, they was lean and hard and could carry me 'long like a deer in de woods.

"My white folks was no poor white trash, I tells you! Good marse and good mistress had heap of slaves and overseers. One overseer name Mr. Welch. De buckra folks dat come visitin', use to laugh at de way he put grease on his hair, and de way he scraped one foot back'ards on de ground or de floor when they shake hands wid him. He never say much, but just set in his chair, pull de sides of his mustache and say 'Yas sah' and 'No sah', to them dat speak to him. He speak a whole lot though, when he git down in de quarters where de slaves live. He wasn't like de same man then. He woke everybody at daylight, and sometime he help de patrollers to search de houses for to ketch any slaves widout a pass.

"Us had all us need to eat, sich as was good for us. Marse like to see his slaves fat and shiny, just like he want to see de carriage hosses slick and spanky, when he ride out to preachin' at Ainswell and sometime de Episcopal church at Ridgeway. My young mistress jine de Baptist church after she marry, and I 'member her havin' a time wid sewin' buckshots in de hem of de dress her was baptized in. They done dat, you knows, to keep de skirt from floatin' on top of de water. You never have thought 'bout dat? Well, just ask any Baptist preacher and he'll tell you dat it has been done.

"When de Yankees come, they went through de big house, tore up everything, ripped open de feather beds and cotton mattresses, searchin' for money and jewels. Then they had us slaves ketch de chickens, flung open de smoke-house, take de meat, meal, flour, and put them in a four-hoss wagon and went on down to Longtown. Them was scandlous days, boss! I hope never to see de likes of them times wid dese old eyes again.

"I 'member 'bout de Ku Klux just one time, though I heard 'bout them a heap. They come on de Robertson place all dressed up wid sheets and false faces, ridin' on hossback, huntin' for a republican and a radical nigger, (I forgits his name, been so long) but they didn't find him. They sho' was a sight and liked to scared us all to death.

"Was I ever married? Sure I was, I marry Mack Cunningham. Us was jined in de holy wedlock by Marse Alex Matherson, a white trial justice. Ask him and he'll tell you when it was. I's got some chillun by dat husband. There is William at Charlotte, and Rosy at Ridgeway. Rosy, her marry a man name Peay. Then there is Millie Gover at Rembert and Lila Brown at Smallwood, de station where

Marse Charlie Ray and my Mistress Luray was killed by a railroad train runnin' into de automobile they was in. Then there is my daughter, Delia Belton, at Ridgeway, and John L., a son livin' and farmin' at Cedar Creek.

"I b'longs to de Mt. Olivet Church dat you knows 'bout. White folks comes there sometime for to hear de singin'. They say us can carry de song better than white folks. Well, maybe us does love de Lord just a little bit better, and what's in our mouth is in our hearts.

"What you gwine to charge for all dat writin' you got down there? If you writes much more maybe I ain't got enough money to pay for it. I got a dollar here but if it's more than dat you'll have to wait on me for de balance. You say it don't cost nothin'? Well, glory hallelujah for dat! I'll just go 'round to de colored restaurant and enjoy myself wid beef stew, rice, new potatoes, macaroni and a cup of coffee. I wonder what they'll have for dessert. 'Spect it'll be some kind of puddin'. But I'd be more pleased if you would take half of this dollar and go get you a good dinner, too. I would like to please you dat much!

"May de good Lord be a watch 'tween me and you 'til us meets again."

Project #-1655
Phoebe Faucette
Hampton County
FOLKLORE

# LUCY DANIELS

"Aunt Lucy is a tall well-built old woman who looks younger than her years. She delights in talking, and was glad to tell what she knew about the olden times.

"I don't know how old I been when de war end. If I been in de world I wasn't old enough to pick up nuthin'. Miss Lulie Bowers say I'll be 78 first of March coming. Miss Lulie was my 'young Missus'. I love Miss Lulie, and I thinks she thinks a heap of me—my young Missus, and her father, my young Massa. He good to his darkies. He was a rich man—even after de war. Miss Lulie say she was de only young lady that could go off to college after de war. Miss Lulie help me powerful. She give me shoes, and beddin. She and me grow up together. She is in de bed sick now. I jes' come from dere. Had de doctor to see her.

"I hear 'em tell 'bout how de soldiers burn 'em out. My mother would tell me. My father had gone off to fight. Say dey'd tie de hams an' de things on de saddle—and burn de expensive houses. White folks jes' had to hide everything. She talk 'bout all de men was gone and de women had to pile up, four or five in one house to protect deyselves. My father say when dey been 'rough-few-gieing' (refugeeing) de Beaufort Bridge been burn down. He say he been so hungry one time he stop to a old lady's house and ask her for something to eat. She say she didn't have nothing but some dry bread. He take de bread, but he say it been so hard, he threw some of it away. But he say he so hungry he wish he hadn't throw it away. It was a hard time. Used to have to weave cloth and dye thread. Had a loom to weave on and a spinning wheel. My grandmother say de Yankees come to her house and take everything, but she say one little pullet run out in de weeds and hide and de soldiers couldn't find her. She say dat pullet lay and hatch and dat how dey got start off again. Dey scramble and dey raise us some how or another.

"I had nine chillun for my first husband and one for my second husband. I raise 'em all 'till dey grown; but all dead now 'cept three. My husband died last year, I had to work for my chillun. But my second husband, he help me wid 'em.

"Dat's all I kin tell you, Miss. I don't remember so much. Chillun in those days weren't so bright as dey is now, you know."

Source: Lucy Daniels, 78 ex-slave, Luray, S. C.

Project 1885-1
Folklore
Spartanburg, Dist. 4
Nov. 30, 1937
Edited by:
Elmer Turnage

# JOHN N. DAVENPORT
## Stories From Ex-Slaves

"My family belonged in slavery time to old Marse Pierce Lake who was de Clerk of Court in town, or de Probate Judge. He lived at de old Campbell Havird House and I lived dar wid him. My mother belonged to dis Lake family and she was named Martha Lake. I don't know who my father was, but I was told he was a white man.

"We slaves had good enough quarters to live in, and dey give us plenty to eat. De house I live in now is fair, but it has a bad roof. It is my wife's chillun's place. My wife had it and left it to dem. She was Ellen Gallman, a widow when I married her. Only my blind daughter now live wid me. I was married five times and had eighteen chilluns by three wives. Each of my wives died befo' I married agin. I didn't separate from any. My mother's father lived wid Marse Lake. He and his wife come from Virginia.

"I was a boy in slavery and worked and piddled round de house. Sometimes I had to work de corn or in de garden. We had plenty to eat. As de old saying is, 'We lived at home and boarded at de same place.' We raised everything we had to eat, vegetables, hogs, cows and de like. Marster had a big garden, but he didn't let his slaves have any garden of deir own. We made all our clothes, homespun. My mother used to spin at night and work out all day; lots of niggers had to do dat.

"Marse Lake was good to his niggers, but he had to whip dem sometimes, when dey was mean. He had six or eight slaves, some on de upper place and some on de home place. We got up at daylight and worked all day, except for dinner lunch, till it was sundown.

"We never worked at night in de fields. Sometimes Marse would have corn-shuckings and de neighbors would come in and help catch up wid shucking de corn; den dey would have something to eat. De young folks would come, too, and help, and dey would dance and frolic.

"I didn't learn to read and write. Marse never said anything about it. My sister learned when some of de white women school teachers boarded at Marse Lake's house. De teachers learn't my sister when she was de maid of de house, and she could read and write good. Didn't have a school or church on de plantation. Atter de war, some of de niggers started a brush arbor. Befo' de war, some of us niggers had to come to town wid de white folks and go to deir church and set in de gallery.

"De patrollers was sometimes mean. If dey catch'd a nigger away from home widout a pass dey sho whipped him, but dey never got any of us. Dey come to our house once, but didn't git anybody.

"We had to work all day Saturdays, but not Sundays. Sometimes de fellows would slip off and hunt or fish a little on Sunday. Women would do washing on Saturday nights, or other nights. We had three days holiday when Christmas come, and we had plenty good things to eat, but we had to cook it ourselves. De marster would give de chillun little pieces of candy.

"Chillun had games like marbles and anti-over. Dey played anti-over by a crowd gitting on each side of de house and throwing a ball from one side to de other. Whoever got de ball would run around on de other side and hit somebody wid it; den he was out of de game. We never believed much in ghosts or spooks. I never saw any.

"Some of de folks had remedies for curing, like making hot tea from a weed called 'bone-set'. Dat weed grows wild in de woods. It was good for chills and fever. De tea is awful bitter. Little bags of asafetida was used to hang around de little chillun's necks to ward off fever or diptheria.

"We used to call de cows on de plantation like dis: 'co-winch, co-winch'. We called de mules like dis: 'co, co', and de hogs and pigs, 'pig-oo, pig-oo'. We had dogs on de place, too, to hunt wid.

"When freedom come, de marster told us we could go away or stay on. Most of us stayed on wid him. Soon atter dis, he got mad at me one day and told me to git off de place. I come to town and stayed about two weeks, piddling around to git along. I found out whar my mother was—she had been sold and sent away. She was in Saluda (Old Town). I went to her and stayed two weeks; den she come to Newberry and rented a little cabin on Beaver Dam Creek, near Silver Street.

"I remember hearing about de Yankees. When dey come through here dey camped in town to keep order and peace. I remember de Ku Klux, too, how some of 'em killed niggers. I voted in town on de Republican ticket. I am still a Republican. None of my friends held office, but I remember some of dem. Old Lee Nance was one, and he was killed by a white man.

"Since de war, de niggers have worked mostly on farms, renting and wage-hands. Some of dem have bought little places. Some moved to town and do carpenter work, and others jes' piddle around.

"Some of de dances de niggers had was, 'Jump Jim Crow'; one nigger would jump up and down while tripping and dancing in de same spot. Some times he say, 'Every time I jump, I jump Jim Crow.' We had what was called a 'Juber' game. He would dance a jig and sing, 'Juber this, Juber that, Juber killed a yellow cat'.

"I never thought much about Abraham Lincoln nor Jefferson Davis. Only seed de pictures of dem. Reckon dey was all right. Don't know nothing about Booker Washington, neither.

"I was 25 years old when I joined de church. I joined because I thought I ought to, people preaching Christ and him crucified; and I thought I ought to do right. Think everybody ought to join de church and be religious.

"What I think of de present generation is hard to say.

Dey is not like de old people was. De old generation of chilluns could be depended on, but de present niggers can't be.

"No, de slaves never expected anything when de war was over, dem in de neighborhood didn't. Some say something about gitting 40 acres of land and a mule, but we never expected it. None ever got anything, not even money from de old marsters or anybody."

Source: John N. Davenport (N, 89), Newberry, S. C. RFD
Interviewer: G. L. Summer, Newberry, S. C. (11/3/37)

United States

Project 1886-1
FOLKLORE
Spartanburg Dist. 4
June 8, 1937
Edited by:
Elmer Turnage

# MOSES DAVENPORT
## Stories From Ex-Slaves

"I was born, March 10, 1848, on Little River in Newberry county, S. C. My master in slavery time was Gilliam Davenport. He was good to his slaves, not strict; good to his cattle, and expected his negroes to be good to them. But he was quick to resent anything from outsiders who crossed his path.

"All that part of the country was good for hunting. The deer, fox, and wild turkey have gone; though a few years ago, some men brought some foxes there and turned them loose, thinking they would breed, but they gradually disappeared. The kildees were many. That was a sign of good weather. When they flew high and around in a circle, it was a sign of high winds.

"Fishing in the rivers was much done. They fished with hooks on old-time canes. They had fish baskets, made of wooden splits, with an opening at the end like the wire baskets now used. If they were set anytime, day or night, a few hours afterwards would be enough time to catch some fish.

"An old sign was: when the youngest child sweeps up the floor, somebody was coming to see you. If a dish-rag was dropped on the floor, somebody was coming who would be hungry."

Source: Moses Davenport (89), Newberry, S. C.
Interviewer: G. L. Summer, Newberry, S. C. (5/10/37)

Code No.
Project, 1886-(1)
Prepared by Annie Ruth Davis
Place, Marion, S. C.
Date, July 28, 1937
No. Words --
Reduced from -- words
Rewritten by --

## CHARLIE DAVIS

### Ex-Slave, 88 Years

"I couldn' tell how old I is only as I ask my old Massa son en he tell me dat I was born ahead of him cause he had de day put down in he family book. I had one of dem slavery bible, but I have a burnin out so many times dat it done been burn up. I belong to Mr. George Crawford people. Mr. George de one what die up here one of dem other year not far back. Dey who been my white folks."

"I can tell you a good deal bout what de people do in slavery time en how dey live den, but I can' tell you nothin bout no jump about things. My Massa didn' 'low us to study bout none of dem kind of frolickings in dat day en time."

"I gwine tell you it just like I experience it in dem days. We chillun lived well en had plenty good ration to eat all de time cause my mammy cook for she Missus dere to de big house. All she chillun lived in a one room house right dere in de white folks yard en eat in de Missus big kitchen every day. Dey give my mammy en she chillun just such things as de white folks had to eat like biscuit en cake en ham en coffee en hominy en butter en all dat kind of eatin. Didn' have no need to worry bout nothin 'tall. My Massa had a heap of other colored peoples dere besides we, but dey never live dat way. Dere been bout 80 of dem dat live up in de quarter just like you see dese people live to de sawmill dese days. Dey live mighty near like us, but didn' have no flour bread to eat en didn' get no milk en ham neither cause dey eat to dey own house. Didn' get nothin from de dairy but old clabber en dey been mighty thankful to get dat. Oh, dey had a pretty good house to live in dat was furnish wid dey own things dat dey make right dere. Den dey had a garden of dey own. My Massa give every one of he plantation family so much of land to plant for dey garden en den he give em every Saturday for dey time to tend dat garden. You see dey had to work for de white folks all de other week day en dey know when dey hear dat cow horn blow, dey had to do what de overseer say do. Never couldn' go off de place widout dey get a mit (permit) from de overseer neither else dey tore up when dey come back. No 'mam, didn' dare to have nothin no time. Didn' 'low you to go to school cause if you was to pick up a book, you get bout 100 lashes for dat. No 'mam, didn' have no church for de colored peoples in dem days. Just had some of dese big oaks pile up one on de other somewhe' in de woods on dat whe' we go to church. One of de plantation mens what had more learnin den de others was de one what do de preachin dere."

"My Massa wasn' never noways scraggeble to he

colored peoples. Didn' cut em for every kind of thing, but I is see him beat my stepfather one time cause he run away en stay in de woods long time. Oh, he beat him wid a switch or a stick or anything like dat he could get hold of."

"Didn' never know nothin bout doing no hard work in us chillun days. When I was a boy, I mind de crows out de field. Oh, crows was terrible bout pickin up peoples corn in times back dere. You see if dey let de crows eat de corn up, dey had to go to de trouble of planting it all over again en dat how-come dey send we chillun in de field to mind de crows off it. We just holler after em en scare em dat way. Crows was mighty worser in dem days den dey is dis day en time."

"I sho remembers when freedom was declare cause I was bout 16 year old den. When dem Yankees talk bout comin round, my Massa take all we colored boys en all he fast horses en put em back in de woods to de canebrake to hide em from de Yankees. It been many a year since den, but I recollects dat we was settin dere lookin for de Yankees to get as any minute. Wasn' obliged to make no noise neither. Oh, we had big chunk of lightwood en cook meat en hoecake en collards right dere in de woods. Den my Massa take one of dem oldest plantation boys to de war wid him en ain' nobody never hear tell of him no more. He name Willie. O my Lord, when dey hear talk bout de Yankees comin, dey take all de pots en de kettles en hide em in holes in de fields en dey put dey silver bout some tree so dey know whe' dey bury it. Den dey hide de meat en de corn to de colored peoples house en when dey hear talk of de Yankees gwine away, dey go en get em again. Dem Yankees never destroy nothin bout dere, but dey is make my Massa give em a cart of corn en a middlin of meat. Yes'um, I look at dem Yankees wid me own eyes. Dey was all dressed up in a blue uniform en dey was just as white as you is. Oh, dey said a lot of things. Say dey was gwine free de niggers en if it hadn' been for dem, we would been slaves till yet. Coase I rather be free den a slave, but we never have so much worryations den as people have dese days. When we get out of clothes en get sick in dat day en time, we never had to do nothin but go to us Massa. Now, we have to look bout every which a way."

"My Massa ask my mother was she gwine live with him any longer after freedom was declare en she say she never have no mind to leave dere. We live on dere for one year en den we studied to get another place. I believes heap of dem white folks died just on account of us get freed. Dey never didn' want us to be free."

"I heard a 'oman say somebody had conjured her, but I don' believe in none of dat. I knows I got to die some of dese days en dat might come before me. I don' bother wid none of dat kind of thing, but I'll tell you bout what I has experience. I had two dogs dere en somebody poison em cause dey tell me somebody do dat. Oh, I know dey was poison. De police say de dog was poison. A 'oman do it dat had chillun what was afraid of my dog en dat how-come she poison it. I sho think she done it cause it just like dis, anything peoples tell me, I believes it."

"I have seen dem things peoples say is a ghost when I was stayin here to Lake View. I plant a garden side de road en one night I hear somethin en I look out en dere was a great big black thing in me garden dat was makin right for de house. I call me wife en tell her to look yonder. De thing was comin right to de house en my wife hurry en light up de lamp. I hear de peoples say if you didn' light up de lamp when you see a spirit, dat it would sho come in en run you out. I had done paid some money on de place but after I see dat thing, I didn' have no mind to want it. Had de best garden en chickens dere I ever had, but I never bother no worry bout dat. Just pick right up en leave dere to come here en I been here ever since. I knows dat been somethin come dere to scare me out dat house. Dat ain' been nothin else but a spirit. Ain' been nothin else."

Source: Charlie Davis, age 88, colored, Marion, S. C. Personal interview, July 1937.

Project #1655
Henry Grant
Columbia, S. C.

# CHARLIE DAVIS'S MUSINGS.

Charlie Davis, now seventy-nine years old, was a small boy when the slaves were freed. He lives alone in one room on Miller's Alley, Columbia, S. C., and is healthy and physically capable of self-support.

"I has been wonderin' what you wanted to talk to dis old nigger 'bout since I fust heard you wanted to see me. I takes it to be a honor for a white gentleman to desire to have a conversation wid me. Well, here I is, and I bet I's one of de blackest niggers you's seen for a season. Somehow, I ain't 'shame of my color a-tall. If I forgits I is dark complected, all I has to do is to look in a glass and in dere I sho' don't see no white man.

"Boss, I is kinda glad I is a black man, 'cause you knows dere ain't much expected of them nowhow and dat, by itself, takes a big and heavy burden off deir shoulders. De white folks worries too much over dis and over dat. They worries 'cause they ain't got no money and, when they gits it, they worries agin 'cause they is 'fraid somebody is gwine to steal it from them. Yes, sir, they frets and fumes 'cause they can't 'sociate wid big folks and, when they does go wid them, they is bothered 'cause they ain't got what de big folks has got.

"It ain't dat way wid most niggers. Nothin' disturbs them much, 'cept a empty stomach and a cold place to sleep in. Give them bread to eat and fire to warm by, then, hush your mouth; they is sho' safe then! De 'possum in his hollow, de squirrel in his nest, and de rabbit in his bed, is at home. So, de nigger, in a tight house wid a big hot fire, in winter, is at home, too.

"Some sort of ease and comfort is 'bout what all people, both white and black, is strivin' for in dis world. All of us laks dat somethin' called 'tentment, in one way or de other. Many white folks and some darkies thinks dat a pile of money, a fine house to live in, a 'spensive 'motorbile, fine clothes, and high 'ciety, is gwine to give them dat. But, when they has all dis, they is still huntin' de end of de rainbow a little ahead of them.

"Is de black man nervous or is he natchally scary? Well, sir, I is gwine to say yes and no to dat. A nigger gits nervous when he hears somethin' he don't understand and scared when he sees somethin' he can't make out. When he gits sho' 'nough scared, he moves right then, not tomorrow. Lak de wild animals of de woods, he ain't 'fraid of de dark, much, if he is movin' 'bout, but when he stops, no house is too tight for him, in summer or winter. If he sees a strange and curious sight at night, he don't have to ask nobody what to do, 'cause he knows dat he has foots. It is good-bye wid old clothes, bushes, and fences, when them foots gits to 'tendin' to deir business. When you hears a funny and strange noise and sees a curious and bad sight, I b'lieves you fust git nervous and then dat feelin' grows stronger fas', 'til you git scared. I knows de faster I moves, de slower I gits scared.

"From my age now, you can tell dat I was mighty little in slavery time. All I knows 'bout them terrible times is what I has heard. I come pretty close to them ticklish times, but I can't help from thinkin', even now, dat I missed a 'sperience in slavery time dat would be doin' me good to dis very day. Dere ain't no doubt dat many a slave learnt good lessons dat showed them how to work and stay out of de jail or poorhouse, dat's worth a little.

"I has heard my mammy say dat she b'long to de Wyricks dat has a big plantation in de northwestern part of Fairfield County and dat my daddy b'long to de Graddicks in de northern part of Richland County. Dese two plantations was just across de road from each other. Mammy said dat de patrollers was as thick as flies 'round dese plantations all de time, and my daddy sho' had to slip 'round to see mammy. Sometime they would ketch him and whip him good, pass or no pass.

"De patrollers was nothin' but poor white trash, mammy say, and if they didn't whip some slaves, every now and then, they would lose deir jobs. My mammy and daddy got married after freedom, 'cause they didn't git de time for a weddin' befo'. They called deirselves man and wife a long time befo' they was really married, and dat is de reason dat I's as old as I is now. I reckon they was right, in de fust place, 'cause they never did want nobody else 'cept each other, nohow. Here I is, I has been married one time and at no time has I ever seen another woman I wanted. My wife has been dead a long time and I is still livin' alone. All our chillun is scattered 'bout over de world somewhere, and dat somewhere is where I don't know. They ain't no help to me now, in my old age. But, I reckon they ain't to be blamed much, 'cause they is young, full of warm blood and thinks in a different way from de older ones. Then, too, I 'spects they thinks deir old daddy would kinda be in deir way, and de best thing for them to do is to stay away from me. I don't know, it just seems lak de way of de world.

"I come from de Guinea family of niggers, and dat is de reason I is so small and black. De Guinea nigger don't know nothin', 'cept hard work, and, for him to be so he can keep up wid bigger folks, he has to turn 'round fas'. You knows dat if you puts a little hog in a pen wid big hogs, de little one has got to move 'bout in a hurry amongst de big ones, to git 'nough to eat, and de same way wid a little person, they sho' has to hustle for what they gits. I has no head for learnin' what's in books, and if I had, dere wasn't no schools for to learn dat head, when I come 'long. I has made some money, 'long through de years, but never knowed how to save it. Now I is so old dat I can't make much, and so, I just live somehow, dat's all.

"President Roosevelt has done his best to help de old, poor, and forgotten ones of us all, every color and race, while dis 'pression has been gwine on in dis country. Is us gwine to git dis new pension what is gwine 'bout, or is dat other somebody gwine to think he needs it worser than us does? Dat's de question what 'sorbs my mind most, dese days. I don't need much, and maybe I don't deserve nothin', but I sho' would lak to git hold of dat little dat's 'tended for me by dat man up yonder in Washington. (Roosevelt)

"Does I b'lieve in spirits and hants? My answer to dat question is dis: 'Must my tremblin' spirit fly into a world unknown?' When a person goes 'way from dis world, dere they is, and dere they is gwine to stay, 'til judgment."

United States

Code No.
Project, 1885-(1)
Prepared by Annie Ruth Davis
Place, Marion, S. C.
Date, January 21, 1938
No. Words --
Reduced from -- words
Rewritten by --

# HEDDIE DAVIS

## Ex-Slave, 72 Years

Lizzie Davis sends word for Heddie Davis to come over to her little shack to join in the conversation about old times and Heddie enters the room with these words: "Sis, I gwine hug your neck. Sis, I did somethin last night dat I oughtn't done en I can' hardly walk dis mornin. Pulled off my long drawers last night en never had none to change wid. I can' bear to get down en pray or nothin like dat, my knee does ache me so bad. I gwine up town yonder en get some oil of wintergreen en put on it. Yes'um, dat sho a good thing to strike de pain cause I heard bout dat long years ago. Sis, ain' you got no coffee nowhe' dis mornin? God knows, de Lord sho gwine bless you, Sis."

"What honey? No'um, I won' here in slavery time. I was just tereckly after it. Well, I come here a Lewis, but I inherited de Davis name when I married. Old man Peter Lewis was my daddy, en my mother—she was a North Carolina woman. Oh, I heard dat man talk bout de old time war so much dat I been know what was gwine fly out his mouth time he been have a mind to spit it out. My daddy, he belonged to de old man Evans Lewis en he been de one his boss pick to carry to de war wid him. Yes'um, he stayed up dere to Fort Sumter four years a fightin en hoped shoot dem old Yankee robbers. My old man, he had one of dem old guns en I give it to his brother Jimmie. He lives way up yonder to de north en he carried dat gun wid him just cause I give it to him, he say. He marry my younger sister en she grayer den I is. Think dey say dey lives to Rockingham, North Carolina. Yes, honey, my daddy was sho in dat wash out dere to Fort Sumter. Lord, have mercy, I never hear tell of crabs en shrimps in all my life till my daddy come back en tell bout a old woman would be gwine down de street, dere to Charleston, cryin, 'Shrimps, more shrimps.' But, my Lord, I can' half remember nothin dese days. If I had de sense I used to have, I would give de Lord de praise. Honey, he said a lot of stuff bout de war. Told a whole chance of somethin. Tell us bout de parade en everything, but I is forgetful now en I just can' think. De Bible say dat in de course of your life, you will be forgetful in dat how I is. Just can' think like I used to. You see, I gwine in 70 now.

"Oh, I was born dere to Mullins in January on de old man Evans Lewis' plantation. Den we moved dere to de Mark Smith place after freedom settle here. Dat long high man, dat who been us boss. His wife was name Sallie en de place was chock full of hands. No, mam, my white folks didn' care bout no quarter on dey plantation. Colored people just throwed 'bout all over de place. Oh, I tell you, it was a time cause de niggers was dere, plenty of dem. Some of dey house was settin side de road, some over in dat corner, some next de big house en so on like dat all over de place. Oh, dey lived all right, I reckon. Never didn' hear dem say dey got back none. Hear dey live den better den de people lives now. Oh, yes'um, I hear my parents say de white folks was good to de colored people in slavery time. Didn' hear tell of nobody gettin nothin back on one another neither. No, child, didn' never hear tell of nothin like dat. Seems like de people don' work dese days like dey used to nohow. Well, dey done somethin of everything in dat day en time en work bout all de time. Ain' nobody workin much to speak bout dese days cause dey walks bout too much, I say. I tell you, when I been a child gwine to school, soon as I been get home in de evenin en hit dat door-step, I had to strip en put on my everyday clothes en get to work. Had to pick up wood en potatoes in de fall or pick cotton. Had to do somethin another all de time, but never didn' nobody be obliged to break dey neck en hurry en get done in dem days. Chillun just rushes en plays too much dese days, I say. No, Lord, I don' want to rush no time. I tellin you, when I starts to Heaven, I want to take my time gettin dere.

"Lord, child, I sho hope I gwine to Heaven some of dese days cause old Satan been ridin me so tough in dis here world, I ain' see no rest since I been know bout I had two feet. My husband, he treat me so mean, if he ain' in Heaven, he in de other place, I say. Den all dem chillun, Lord a mercy, dey will kill you. I raised all mine by myself en I tell you, dey took de grease out of me.

"My daddy, he was a prayin man. Lord knows, he was a prayin man. Seems like de old people could beat de young folks a prayin up a stump any day. I remember, my daddy come here to de white people church to Tabernacle one night en time dem people see him, dey say, 'Uncle Peter, de Lord sho send you cause ain' nobody but you can pray dese sinners out of hell here tonight.' God knows dat man could sing en pray. Lord, he could pray. Oh, darlin child, dat man prayed bout all de time. Prayed every mornin en every night en when us would come out de field at 12 o'clock, us had to hear him pray fore he ever did allow us to eat near a morsel. Sis, I remember one day, when dey first started we chillun a workin in de field, I come to de house 12 o'clock en I was so hungry, I was just a poppin. God knows, people don' serve de Lord like dey used to."

"Sis, you wants dat one patch, too. Lord Jesus, dere ain' no limit to dis one. Sis, I must be come here on Saturday cause everywhe' I goes, I has to work. Hear talk, if you born on a Saturday, you gwine have to work hard for what you get all your days. I been doin somethin ever since I been big enough to know I somebody. Remember de first thing I ever do for a white woman. Ma come home en say, 'Heddie, get up in de mornin en wash your face en hands en go up to Miss Rogers en do everything just like she say do.' I been know I had to do dat, too, cause if I never do it, I know I would been whip from cane to cane. When I got dere, I open de gate en look up en dere been de new house en dere been de old one settin over dere what dey been usin for de kitchen den. I won' thinkin bout nothin 'cept what Miss Rogers was gwine say en when I been walk in dat gate, dere a big bulldog flew up in my head. I stop en look at him en dat dog jump en knock me windin en grabbed my foot in his mouth. Yes'um, de sign dere yet whe' he gnawed me. White folks tell me I been do wrong. Say, don' never pay no attention to a dog en dey won' bother up wid you. But, honey, dat dog had a blue eye en a pink eye. Ain' never see a dog in such a fix since I been born. I tell you, if you is crooked, white folks will sho straighten you out. Dat dog taught me all I is ever wanted to know. Lord, Miss Mary, I been love dat woman. De first time I ever see her, she say, 'You ain' got no dress to wear to Sunday School, I gwine give you one.' Yes, mam, Miss Mary dress me up en de Lord knows, I ain' never quit givin her de praise yet.

"Yes'um, de Yankees, I hear my daddy talk bout when dey come through old Massa's plantation en everything what dey do. Say, dere was a old woman dat was de cook to de big house en when dem Yankees come dere dat mornin, white folks had her down side de cider press just a whippin her. Say, de Yankees took de old woman en dressed her up en hitched up a buggy en made her set up in dere. Wouldn' let de white folks touch her no more neither. Oh, de place was just took wid dem, he say. What dey never destroy, dey carried off wid dem. Oh, Lord a mercy, hear talk dere was a swarm of dem en while some of dem was in de house a tearin up, dere was a lot of dem in de stables takin de horses out. Yes'um, some was doin one thing en some another. En Pa tell bout dey had de most sense he ever did see. Hitched up a cart en kept de path right straight down in de woods en carted de corn up what de white folks been hide down dere in de canebrake. Den some went in de garden en dug up a whole lot of dresses en clothes. En dere was a lady in de house sick while all dis was gwine on. Oh, dey was de worst people dere ever was, Pa say. Took all de hams en shoulders out de smokehouse en like I tell you, what dey never carried off, dey made a scaffold en burned it up. Lord, have mercy, I hopes I ain' gwine never have to meet no Yankees."

Source: Heddie Davis, colored, age 72, Marion, S. C.
Personal interview by Annie Ruth Davis, Jan., 1938.

Project #1655
W. W. Dixon
Winnsboro, S. C.

## HENRY DAVIS
### Ex-Slave 80 Years Old.

Henry Davis is an old Negro, a bright mulatto, who lives in a two-room frame house on the farm of Mr. Amos E. Davis, about two miles southwest of Winnsboro, S. C.

In the house with him, are his wife, Rosa, and his grown children, Roosevelt, Utopia, and Rose. They are day laborers on the farm. At this period, Henry picks about seventy-five pounds of cotton a day. His children average one hundred and fifty pounds each. The four together are thus enabled to gather about five hundred and twenty-five pounds per day, at the rate of sixty-five cents per hundred. This brings to the family, a daily support of $3.41. This is seasonal employment, however; and, as they are not a provident household, hard times come to Henry and his folks in the winter and early summer.

"I was born on de old Richard Winn plantation dat my master, Dr. W. K. Turner, owned and lived on. I was born de year befo' him marry Miss Lizzie Lemmon, my mistress in slavery time.

"My mother was name Mary and took de name of Davis, 'cause befo' freedom come, her was bought by my master, from Dr. Davis, near Monticello.

"I had a good many marsters and mistresses. Miss Minnie marry Dr. Scruggs. Miss Anna marry Mr. Dove. Miss Emma marry Mr. Jason Pope. Marse Willie K. marry a Miss Carroll up in York, S. C., and Marse Johnnie marry Miss Essie Zealy. My brothers and sisters was Minton, Ike, Martha, and Isabella.

"Who I marry and all 'bout it? How come you want to know dat? I 'clare! You think dat gwine to loosen me up? Well, I marry de 'Rose of Sharon' or I calls her dat when I was sparkin' her, though she was a Lemmon. Her was name Rose Lemmon. Lots of times she throw dat in my face, 'Rose of Sharon' when things go wrong. Then her git uppish and sniff, 'Rose of Sharon, my eye! You treats me lak I was a dogwood rose on de hillside or worse than dat, lak I was a Jimson weed or a rag weed.'

"My mammy and us chillun live in de yard not far from de kitchen. My mammy do de washin' and ironin'. Us chillun did no work. I ride 'round most of de time wid de doctor in his buggy and hold de hoss while he visit de patients. Just set up in de buggy and wait 'til him git ready to go to another place or go home.

"I 'member de Yankees comin' and searchin' de house, takin' off de cows, mules, hosses, and burnin' de gin-house and cotton. They say dat was General

Sherman's orders. They was 'lowed to leave de dwellin' house standin', in case of a doctor or preacher.

"Miss Lizzie had a whole lot of chickens. Her always keep de finest pullets. She make pies and chicken salad out of de oldest hens. Dat February de Yankees got here, she done save up 'bout fifty pullets dat was ready to lay in March. A squad of Yankees make us chillun ketch every one and you know how they went 'way wid them pullets? They tie two on behind, in de rings of de saddle. Then they tie two pullets together and hang them on de saddle pommel, one on each side of de hosses neck. Dat throw them flankin' de hosses withers. I 'members now them gallopin' off, wid them chickens flutterin' and hollerin' whare, whare, whare, whare, whare!

"After slavery time, us live on de Turner place nigh onto thirty years and then was de time I go to see Rosa and court and marry her. Her folks b'long to de Lemmons and they had stayed on at de Lemmon's place. De white folks of both plantations 'courage us to have a big weddin'. Her white folks give her a trousseau and mine give me a bedstead, cotton mattress, and two feather pillows. Dat was a mighty happy day and a mighty happy night for de 'Rose of Sharon'. Her tells young niggers 'bout it to dis day, and I just sets and smokes my pipe and thinks of all de days dat am passed and gone and wonder if de nex' world gwine to bring us back to youth and strength to 'joy it, as us did when Rose and me was young.

"Does I 'members anything 'bout patrollers? 'Deed, I do! Marster didn't 'ject to his slaves gwine to see women off de place. I hear him say so, and I hear him tell more than once dat if he ever hear de patrollers a comin' wid blood hounds, to run to de lot and stick his foots in de mud and de dogs wouldn't follow him. Lots of run'ways tried it, I heard, and it proved a success and I don't blame them dogs neither."

Project #1655
W. W. Dixon
Winnsboro, S. C.

# JESSE DAVIS
## Ex-Slave 85 Years Old.

Jesse Davis, one of the fast disappearing landmarks of slavery times, lives with his wife and son, in one of the ordinary two-room frame houses that dot, with painful monotony, the country farms of white landowners. The three attempt to carry on a one-horse farm of forty acres, about thirty acres in cotton and the remainder in corn. The standard of living is low. Jesse is cheerful, his wife optimistic with the expression that the Lord will provide, and their son dutiful and hopeful of the harvest. Their home is about ten miles southwest of Winnsboro, in the Horeb section of Fairfield County.

"Dere is some difficulty 'bout my age. Nigh as I can place it, I was born befo' de Civil War. I 'members 'tendin' to and milkin' de cows, and keepin' de calf off, drawin' water out de well, and bringin' in wood to make fires. I 'spects I's eighty-five, mountin' up in years.

"I lives on Mr. Eber Mason's place wid one of my chillun, a son name Mingo. Us all work on de place; run a farm on shares. I can't do much work and can't support myself. It's mighty hard to be 'pendent on others for your daily rations, even if them others is your own bone and flesh. I'd 'preciate sumpin' to help my son and wife carry on. Dats why I wants a pension. Do you 'spect God in His mercy will hear de prayer of dis feeble old believer? I don't beg people but de Bible give me a right to beg God for my daily bread. De Good Book say: 'Take no consarnment 'bout your raiment'. You can see from what I's got on, dat me nor nobody else, is much consarned 'bout dis raiment.

"My mammy b'long to de Smiths. My master was Dr. Ira Smith. My mistress was him wife, Miss Sarah. Deir chillun was: Marse Gad, Marse Jim, and Marse Billie. Marse Jim was de baker of dis town all his life, after de way of old-time oven-cookin', 'til Boy bread and Claussen bread wagons run him out of business. Him is now on de 'lief roll and livin' in de old McCreight house, de oldest house in Winnsboro.

"Dere was my young misses, Miss Lizzie and Miss Lennie. My mammy name Sarah, just lak old mistress name Sarah. Her b'long to marster and mistress but my pappy no b'long to them. Him b'long to de big bugs, de Davis family. Him was name Mingo, and after slavery him and all us take de name, de secon' name, Davis, and I's here today, Jesse Davis. See how dat work out to de name? Good Book again say: 'Good name better than riches; sweeter to de ear than honey-comb to de tongue.'

"You is well 'quainted wid Marse Amos Davis, ain't you? Well, his people was pappy's people. I had a brudder name Gabriel, tho' they called him Gabe. Another one name Chap; he got kilt while clearin' up a new ground.

Sister Fannie marry a Ashford nigger. Marse Ira, de doctor, have a plantation near Jenkinsville, S. C.

"When de Yankees come thru, they come befo' de main army. They gallop right up, jump down and say: 'Hold dese hosses! Open dat smoke-house door!' They took what they could carry 'way. 'Bout dat time marster rode up from a sick call him been 'tendin' to. Course you know him was a doctor. They surround him, take his watch, money, and hoss, and ride 'way.

"De main army come nex' day, Saturday mornin' 'bout 8 o'clock. They spread deir tents and stay and camp 'til Monday mornin'. When they leave they carry off all de cows, hogs, mules, and hosses. Then they have us ketch de chickens, got them all, 'cept one old hen dat run under de house, and they didn't wait to git her. Marster have to go 'way up to Union County, where him have kin folks, to git sumpin' to eat.

"My marster was not big rich lak de Davises, de Means, and de Harpers, but him have all them people come to see him. Him know a heap of things dat they 'preciate. De way to dye cloth was one of dese secrets. Marster have a madder bed. Him take de roots of dat madder put them in de sun just lak you put out pieces of apples and peaches to make dried fruit. When them roots git right dry, him have them ground up fine as water-ground meal. He put de fine dust in a pot and boil it. When he want red cloth, he just drop de cloth in dat pot and it come out all red to suit you. Want it blue, him have a indigo patch for dat.

"I never hear anything 'bout alum dese days. Well, de slaves could take peach tree leaves and alum and make yellow cloth and old cedar tops and copperas and make tan cloth. Walnut stain and copperas and make any cloth brown. Sweet-gum bark and copperas and make any cloth a purple color. I 'member goin' wid one into de woods to git barks. One day old marster come 'cross a slippery elm tree. Him turn and command me to say right fast: 'Long, slim, slick saplin' and when I say long, slim, sick slaplin', him 'most kill hisself laughin'. You try dat now! You find it more harder to say than you think it is. Him give me a piece of dat bark to chew and I run at de mouth lak you see a hoss dat been on de range of wild clover all night and slobberin' at da bits.

"Yes sah, I b'longs to de church! My wife and son, Mingo, just us three in de house and de whole household jined de Morris Creek Baptist Church. What's my favorite song? None better than de one dat I'll h'ist right now. Go ahead? I thanks you. Listen:

> 'Am I born to die
> To lay dis body down
> A charge to keep I have
> A God to glorify.'

"You lak dat? Yes? You is praisin' me too highly I 'spect, but since you lak dat one just listen at dis one; maybe you change your mind, 'cause I's gwine to h'ist it a wee bit higher and put more of de spiritual in it. Ready? Yes? I stand up dis time.

> 'All de medicine you may buy
> All de doctors you may try
> Ain't gonna save you from de tomb
> Some day you got to lay down and die.
> De blood of de Son can only

Save you from de doom!
Some day you got to lay down and die.'

"You lak dat one? You just ought to hear my wife, Mingo, and Me, singin' dat 'round de fire befo' us go to bed.

"Well, I'll toddle 'long now. Good-bye."

Project, 1885-(1)
Prepared by Annie Ruth Davis
Place, Marion, S. C.
Date, February 4, 1938

# LIZZIE'S 'SPONSIBILITY

## I.

The first scene of "Lizzie's 'Sponsibility" is that of the small, one room dwelling place of Lizzie Davis, aged colored woman of Marion, S. C. A disorderly, ill-lighted, crudely furnished room, saturated with the odor of food. Behind the front door stands a gayly colored iron bed, over which is thrown a piece of oilcloth to keep the rain from leaking on it. In the center of the room are several little quaint home-made stools and two broken rockers, while in one corner sits a roughly finished kitchen table, the dumping place of all small articles. Still in another corner, almost hidden from sight in the darkness, is the dim outline of an old trunk gaping open with worn out clothing, possibly the gift of some white person. A big fireplace in one side of the wall not only furnishes heat for the little room, but also serves as a cooking place for Lizzie to prepare her meals. On its hearth sits a large iron kettle, spider, and griddle, relics of an earlier day. The room is dimly lighted by the fire and from two small doors, together with a few tiny streaks that peep through at various cracks in the walls and top of house.

It is about 9 o'clock on a cold, drizzly morning in January, 1938. The little two room house, in which Lizzie rents one room for herself, displays an appearance of extreme coldness and dilapidation, as a visitor approaches the doorway on this particular morning. It is with somewhat of an effort that the visitor finally reaches the barred door of Lizzie's room, after making a skip here and there to keep from falling through the broken places in the little porch and at the same time trying to dodge the continual dripping of the rain through numerous crevices in the porch roof. Within is the sound of little feet scuffling about on the floor, the chatter of tiny children mixed with mumblings from Lizzie, and the noise of chairs and stools being roughly shoved about on the floor.

A rap on the door brings Lizzie, crippled up since she was twelve years of age, hobbling to the door. Taking her walking stick, she lifts the latch gently and the door opens slightly. A gray head appears through the crack of the door and Lizzie, peeping out from above her tiny rim spectacles, immediately recognizes her visitor. She offers her usual cheerful greeting and begins hastily to push the large wooden tubs from the door to make room for her visitor to enter, though it is with unusual hesitancy that she invites her guest to come in on this occasion.

Lizzie—Come in, Miss Davis. I feelin right smart dis mornin. How you been keepin yourself? Miss Davis, I regrets you have to find things so nasty up in here dis mornin, but all dis rainy weather got me obliged to keep dese old tubs settin all bout de floor here to try en catch up de water what drips through dem holes up dere. See, you twist your head up dat way en you can tell daylight through all dem cracks. Dat how I know when it bright enough to start to stir myself on a mornin.

Yes'um, I tell Miss Heddie here de other day dat I had promise you I was gwine study up some of dem old time songs to give you de next time you come back. Miss Heddie, she lookin to a right sharp age, I say. Yes'um, she been here a time, honey. I tell her to be gettin her dogs together cause I was sho gwine point her out to you de next time I see you.

I tell you, Miss Davis, I got a 'sponsibility put on me here to look after all dese chillun. Yes'um, it sho a 'sponsibility cause I think dere five of dem dere, en it de truth in de Lord sight, dey has me settin up so straight to keep a eye on dem dat I can' never settle my mind on nothin. Dey won' let me keep nothin clean. Ain' no use to scrub none, I say. You see, cripple up like I is, I ain' able to get no work off nowhe' en I keeps dem while dey parents work out. Dey mammas have a job to cook out en dey brings dem here bout 6 o'clock in de mornin for me to see after till dey get home in de afternoon. Cose dey helps me along, but it takes what little dey give me to keep dem chillun warm cause I has to try en keep a fire gwine, dey be so little. Dere Bertha Lee en Joseph, dey start gwine to school dis year en I has to see dey gets fix decent en march dem off to school every mornin. Dem other three dere, dey name: Possum en June en Alfred. Ain' but just one girl en dat—

(Lizzie's attention turns to June, who comes in crying from the back yard, where all the children went to play during Lizzie's conversation with her visitor).

Lizzie—What de matter wid you, June?

June—Aun' Izzie, Possum knock me wid de ax.

Lizzie—Great King! What a peculiar thing to hit you wid. How-come he to do dat?

June—He was bustin up dem stick out dere side de wood pile.

Lizzie—Oh, well, you just go en butt up on de ax. Dat ain' no fault of he own den. Clean up dat face en gwine on way from here.

(June, crying to himself, remains seated on the little stool).

Lizzie—Let me see now, Miss Davis, I tryin to get some of dem old time songs together to turn for you what you been axin me bout de other time you come here. Yes'um, I tryin to blow my dogs—

(Possum enters the room).

Possum—Aun' Izzie, I was bustin up dem splinters dat my daddy brung for you to cook wid en June come en set right under de ax.

Lizzie—Um-huh, ain' I tell you so? Whe' de ax, Possum? Fetch it here en put it in de corner. Ain' none of you had no business wid dat ax nohow. Ain' I tell you to mind your way round dat ax?

(Possum runs back out in the yard).

Lizzie—Like I tellin you, Miss Davis, if de people had a song in de old days, dey would put it down on a long strip called a ballad, but honey, I been through de hackles en I can' think of nothin like I used to could. Is anybody sing dis one for you, Miss Davis? It a old one, too, cause I used to hear—

(Alfred comes in to tell his tale).

Alfred—Aun' Izzie, June set on Possum's pile of splinters dat he was makin en Possum let de ax fall right on June's head.

Lizzie—Dey is cases, Miss Davis. I tellin you, dese chillun just gets everything off my mind. Most makes me forget to eat sometimes. Dere Miss Julia Woodberry, poor creature, she been down mighty sick en I ain' been able to go en see bout her no time. Don' know what ailin her cause I don' gets bout nowhe' much. No, mam, dese chillun don' have no manners to go visitin en I can' left dem here widout nobody to mind bout dat dey don' run—

Joseph—Aun' Izzie, I ain' gwine wear no coat to school dis mornin.

Lizzie—Boy, is you crazy? What de matter wid you, ain' you know de ground been white wid Jack Frost dis mornin? En you clean up dat nose fore you get dere to school, too. You ain' say your ma send you here widout no pocket rag to wipe your nose wid? You ma, she know better den to 'spect me to hunt rags for you. Come here en let me fasten up dat coat round de neck. You look like a turkey buzzard wid it gapin open dat way. Whe' Bertha Lee? It time both you been in dat road gwine to school dere.

(Bertha Lee and Joseph go out the door to leave for school).

Lizzie—Lord a mercy, Miss Davis, my mind just a windin. How dat song turn what I had for you?

> One for Paul,
> En one for Sidas—

Lizzie—Joseph, how-come you ain' tell dese chillun good-bye?

Joseph—Good-bye Possum, good-bye June, good-bye Alfred.

Possum, June, Alfred—Good-bye Joseph.

Lizzie—Is you got dat one now, Miss Davis? What de next? Great Jeruselum! Dem chillun done carry dat tune way wid dem. I can' turn dat one to save my neck. Just can' come to de turn table as de old man would say. (12 o'clock mill whistle blows, time teller for many colored people of the community). Lord a mercy, what dat whistle say? It done come 12 o'clock en dat pot ain' thought bout to kick up none yet. I tell you, honey, it sho a 'sponsibility I got put on me here to cook for all dese chillun en see dey ration is cook mighty done, too, so as dey won' be gwine round gruntin wid dey belly hurtin all de evenin.

(Lizzie begins to stir up the fire to make the pot boil and her visitor decides to return later to hear the songs).

Date, February 7, 1938

## II

It is a damp, chilly mornin about three weeks later, when Lizzie's visitor returns to hear her sing old time songs. June, Bertha Lee, and Alfred are playing in the street before the little house.

Visitor—Is Aun' Lizzie at home?

June, Alfred, Bertha Lee—Yes'um, she in dere. She in de house.

Visitor—You children better mind how you run about in all this damp weather, it might make you sick.

June—Possum's got de chicken pox.

Alfred—Possum's got de chicken pox.

June—Me sick, too.

Bertha Lee—I got a cold.

Alfred—I sick, too.

Visitor—Poor little Possum. Is he sick much?

Alfred—Yes'um, he stay right in dat room dere. (Room next to Lizzie's room with a separate front door).

Bertha Lee—He mamma had de chicken pox first en den Possum, he took down wid it.

June—Dere he now! Dere Possum! (Possum appears from around the corner of the house with both hands full of cold fish).

(Alfred goes to Lizzie's door to tell her that she has a visitor)

Alfred—Aun' Izzie, somebody out dere wanna see you.

Lizzie—Holy Moses! Who dat out dere? Boy, you ain' tellin me no story, is you? Mind you now, you tell me a story en I'll whip de grease out you.

Bertha Lee—Aun' Izzie, ain' nobody but Miss Davis out dere.

(Lizzie hobbles to the door on her stick).

Lizzie—How you is, Miss Davis? I ain' much to speak bout dis mornin. I tell you de truth, Miss Davis, dese chillun keeps me so worried up dat I don' know whe' half my knowin gone, I say. Great Lord a mercy, dere Possum out dere in de air now en he been puny, too.

Visitor—The children tell me Possum has the chicken pox.

Lizzie—No'um, he ain' got no chicken pox, Miss Davis. Dey thought he had it cause he mamma been ailin dat way, but I don' see nothin de matter wid him 'cept what wrong wid he mouth. Possum, stand back dere way from Miss Davis, I say. Yes'um, he been sorta puny like dis here last week. He mamma must been feed him too much en broke he mouth out dat—

June—Miss Davis, I know how to spell my name.

Bertha Lee—I know how to spell my name, too. Me likes to go to school.

Visitor—Oh, I think it is nice to like to go to school. What do you do at school?

June—Pull off your hat.

Bertha Lee—Us writes.

Visitor—Lizzie, how about those old time songs you promised to study up for me? You ought to have a mind running over with them by this time.

Lizzie—Lord, Lord, honey, I had study up a heap of dem old tunes here de other day, but I tellin you de truth, Miss Davis, dese chillun got me so crazy till nothin won stick—

(Willie, age 10, comes over to play with the children and begins to whistle.).

Lizzie—Willie, ain' you know it ill manners to whistle in anybody house? Dere now, it impolite to walk by anybody house whistlin, too. You is too big a boy for dat. Ain' gwine stand for you learnin dese chillun no such manners for me to beat it out dem. No, boy, mind yourself way from here now, I got to hunt up dat tune for Miss Davis. Yes'um, I got one of dem old tune poppin now. Let me see—Great Happy! Dat pot done gwine out all my sparks. (Lizzie rushes in the house to look after a pot that she hears boilin over on the fire).

June—Bertha Lee, de lady don' know whe' us sleeps, do she?

Bertha Lee—Dere us house over dere.

(Bertha Lee gets up to point the house out and June

immediately slides into her seat on the bench next to the visitor).

Bertha Lee—Move way, June.

June—No, dis place whe' I been.

Bertha Lee—June, go further, I say.

June—No, Bertha Lee, dis whe' I been.

Bertha Lee—No, go further. (June holds his place) I go tell Aun' Izzie den.

Visitor—Tell Lizzie I'm waitin to hear that tune she promised to sing.

Bertha Lee—Aun' Izzie, June settin in my place.

Lizzie—Fetch yourself on back out dere now, Bertha Lee, en settle your own scrap. Ain' you shame of yourself en you bigger den June, too? Go way from here, I say. I ain' got no time to monkey up wid you. I got to get dese collards boilin hard, else dey ain' gwine get done time you chillun start puffin for your dinner. Go way, I tell you. Miss Davis, I comin toreckly.

(Bertha Lee returns to the porch quietly and takes her place on the opposite side of the visitor, while June clings to his place).

June—Miss Davis, does you know Mr. Rembert?

Visitor—Is he your father?

Bertha Lee and June—No, he ain' us daddy.

June—Mr. Rembert, he bought me everything I got. He shoe horses. Don' you know him now?

Bertha Lee—He bought June's sweater, but dem my overalls he got on.

June—Dem dere pretty buttons you got on you, Miss Davis.

Bertha Lee—Sho is, en dem little chain dere.

June—Me got a sweater just like her coat.

Bertha Lee—Ain' just like it.

June—It most like it.

Bertha Lee—No, it ain' cause dis here wool.

(Lizzie returns to the porch and sits on a little stool near her door).

Lizzie—Lord, Miss Davis, dat tune done left me. Now, de next time dat I get a tune in my mind. I gwine sho get somebody to place it for me. It de Lord truth, my mind gwine just so wid so much of chillun worryations till—

June—Me can sing.

Possum—Aun' Izzie, I ain' got nothin to eat.

(Lizzie returns to her room again to stir up the fire and get Possum some bread).

Bertha Lee—Sing den, June.

June—Un-uh, I can'. Aun' Izzie might hear me.

Bertha Lee—I gwine sing den.

June—

"I sees de lighthouse—amen,
I sees de lighthouse—amen,
I sees de lighthouse—amen."

(Lizzie and Possum return to porch. Possum has three muffins).

Lizzie—Clean up your nose dere, Alfred. Miss Davis, I ready. Sho got a mind to turn dat tune dis— —

Alfred—Possum wouldn' fetch me no bread, Aun' Izzie.

Lizzie—Dere dey go again, Miss Davis. No, you can' have none of Possum's bread. Gwine on in dere en catch you a piece out your own pan. You eat up Possum's bread en den he'll be de one howlin bout he ain' got none.

(Alfred goes in the room and comes back with a biscuit).

Lizzie—I pretty certain I ready now, Miss Davis. Let dem all get dey belly full en den dey head won' be turnin so sharp. Dat how-come I tries—

Possum—Aun' Izzie, Alfred eatin June's bread.

Lizzie—Alfred, look here, boy, you know dat ain' none of your bread. You sho gwine get a lickin for dat. (Lizzie slaps him). Your ma, she ain' never left nothin but corn hoecake in your pan since you been born en you know dat, too. Dem chillun carries me in de clock sometimes, Miss Davis. Dis one en dat one callin me en de Lord help me, I forgets what I doin—Clean up dat nose dere, boy.

June—My nose clean.

Lizzie—Possum know I talkin to him. Get on in dere

en tell Miss Mammie to give you a pocket rag, Possum. (Miss Mammie is Possum's aunt who came to spend the day with them).

Bertha Lee—

"Peter Rabbit, Ha! Ha! Ha!
Make Your Ears Go, Flop! Flop! Flop!"

Lizzie—I has to ax you to bear wid me, Miss Davis. I sorry you come here on a dead shot en ain' gettin no birds. Lord knows, I tryin to get my mind—

June—Oo, Aun' Izzie, Joseph been cuttin out Willie's book.

(Lizzie's attention is attracted to Willie, who looks worried about his torn book.)

Lizzie—Great mercy, boy, you ought to have a pain in de chest. Look, you settin dere wid your bosom wide open. Fasten up your neck dere, I say.—Possum, come here, is you do like I tell you? Is you ax Miss Mammie for somethin to clean up dat nose wid?

Possum—Yes'um.

Lizzie—Look out now, I'll whip you for tellin a story. Whe' de rag? No, you ain' ax her neither. Gwine on en clean up dat nose fore I wear you out.

(Possum goes around corner of house).

Lizzie—Help me Lord not to forget it dis time. I sho got dat tune——

June—Aun' Izzie, Aun' Izzie, Possum fall in de tub of water what settin under de pump.

(Possum appears from around the corner of the house just at that moment drenched and almost frozen).

Lizzie—Great Lord a mercy! Possum, you looks like a drowned possum sho enough. Why ain' you do like I tell you to do? You know I don' never allow you chillun ramblin round dat pump tub no time. Ain' nobody want to drink out no tub you wash your snotty nose in. Fetch yourself in dere to de fire en dry yourself fore you is catch a death of cold. Gwine on, boy. Don' stand dere en watch me like a frizzle chicken. Dere Mr. John Fortune comin now. I gwine tell him to catch Possum en cook him up.

Possum—I gwine run.

Lizzie—You say you gwine run?

Possum—No'um, I ain' say I gwine run.

Lizzie—Mind you now, Possum, you know what I tell you bout a story-teller.

Mammie—Miss Lizzie, I just don' believe he know right from wrong.

Lizzie—Well, I gwine learn him den. Ain' nothin I despises worser den a story-teller. (Lizzie slaps Possum on the shoulder several times and sends him in the house to dry, shivering from both cold and fear.).

Lizzie—Miss Davis, Mr. John Fortune helps me out wonderfully wid dese chillun. Say, when dey bad, he gwine cook dem up en eat dem. Yes, mam, I tellin de truth, honey, dese chillun keeps me settin here listenin wid all my ears en lookin wid all my eyes, but dey is right sorta entertainin like. Yes'um, dey got so much of sense till dey done took what little I is had.

(Alfred comes running in and leans up on Lizzie).

Lizzie—Clean up dat snotty nose, Alfred. You ought to been name Snotty wid your mouth all de time lookin like you ain' hear tell of no pocket rag. Move way from dere, June. Don' blow your nose settin side Miss Davis.

Date, February 10, 1938

## III

It is three days later. Lizzie is sitting on her little porch enjoying the warm sunshine of a bright February day. The children have gone just across the street to play on the sidewalk and while Lizzie keeps a watchful eye on them, she is trying once more to call back to her mind some of the old time songs that she used to sing in her early days. Her visitor sits on a bench nearby ready to make notes of these old songs as she sings them. Lizzie's attention is not only distracted by the children at intervals but also by different ones of her friends constantly passing along the street in front of the small home.

Lizzie—Lord, Miss Davis, look like everything a hustlin dis mornin. Yes'um, dis here Monday mornin en everybody is a bustlin gwine to see bout dey business. Seems like everything just gwine on, just gwine on. I tell you de truth, Miss Davis, I studied so hard bout dem songs de other night, I beg de Massa to show me de light en he hop me to recollect dis one for you. See, when you gets to de age I is, you is foolish—

(Joseph runs across the street to tell Lizzie something).

Joseph—Aun' Izzie, Possum teachin June to hit Jerry.

Lizzie—Uh-huh, I gwine sho beat him, too. (Lizzie turns to her visitor) Possum, he teachin June to knock dat little one wid de speckle coat on.

Visitor—Is he another child that you are taking care of?

Lizzie—No'um, he grandma raise him en de poor little creature, he don' have nobody to play wid. Look like nobody don' care when he come or whe' he go. I say, I tries to collect mine up en take care of dem cause it dis way, if you don' take time en learn chillun, dey old en dey ain' old; dey fool en dey ain' fool. Yes'um, I tryin to drill dem, Miss Davis, but it does take time en a little whip, too. Has to punish dem right smart sometimes. I tellin you, dem chillun sho a 'sponsibility. Dem what put all dem gray hair up dere on my topknot. I tell dis one en dat one to set to a certain place till I say to get up en den I'll get my studyin on somethin else en de child, he'll be out yonder—

(Heddie Davis, age 72, a neighbor of Lizzies, comes over to join in the conversation).

Lizzie—Here come de hoss (horse). Come in, Miss Heddie. Miss Davis wants us to sing one of dem old back tunes dis mornin.

Heddie—Well, I is studied up one tune what I been hear de old people sing when I wasn' nothin much more den a puppy—Lord a mercy, Miss Lizzie, dere dem people comin from de trial. Look, dere dey fetchin dat girl to Dr. Graham now. En my Lord, got de poor child's head all wrapped up dat way. Dat man, he ought to have he head plucked. He know better den to cut dat child so close de senses. Don' know what de matter wid de people nohow.

Lizzie—Ain' nothin but de devil, Miss—

(Boy, about 8 years old, comes across the street and hands Lizzie a bundle).

Pickle—Miss Lizzie, ma say dere your sewin.

Lizzie—Thank you, son, thank you a thousand times again. Tell your mamma de old hen a scratchin bout out dere in de yard now huntin de nest en ain' gwine be no long time fore I can be catchin her a chicken to put in de pot. Yes, Lord, I got to start savin dem egg dis very day for de settin. (Lizzie turns to her visitor on the porch and continues her conversation). Miss Rosa, she does do all my sewin for me en I generally gives her eggs for her kindness. I sorry dere so much of huntin egg de same day.

(Little boy, Pickle, looks disappointed and continues to hang around).

Bertha Lee—Aun' Izzie, sing somethin.

Lizzie—You want me to sing so bad, sugar, en I ain' know nothin neither. Heddie, turn me one.

Heddie—Gwine on en spill dat one yourself what you been tell me bout de other mornin en quit your pickin on me.

Lizzie—Well, I tryin to get myself together, but dere so much of travelin en so much of chillun, I can' collect—

Alfred—Aun' Izzie, can I go to whe' Jerry gone?

Lizzie—No, boy, you know I ain' got no mind to let you go runnin off dat way. (Lizzie calls to Mammie in the room). Mammie, look dere to de clock. I gettin in a fidget to get some of dese chillun way from here.

(Pickle still hangs around).

Lizzie—Joseph, come here.

Joseph—Un-uh.

Lizzie—Boy, don' you grunt at me dat way. Come here, I say. Go dere in de chicken house en hunt dat one egg en give it to Pickle to carry to he mamma.—Got to scatter dese chillun way from here—

Joseph—Here de egg, Aun' Izzie.

Lizzie—Fetch it dere to Pickle den. Boy, tell your mamma I sorry I ain' had no egg to send her 'cept just dat one nest egg. Tell her, when she buss dat egg, she better look right sharp en see is de hen ain' got it noways addle like cause—

Bertha Lee—Aun' Izzie, how my nose is?

Lizzie—Look bad. Gwine on in dere en clean your face up. I know you ain' gwine to school wid all dem crumbs stuck bout on your mouth. Joseph, gwine on in de house dere en put you on some more clothes. Gwine on in dere, I say. Don' stand dere on de street en strip.

Heddie—No, boy, don' pull off in no public.

Bertha Lee—Aun' Izzie, I gwine carry my bread to school wid me.

Lizzie—Hunt you a paper den. You can' go dere to school wid no handful of bread makin all dem chillun start mouthin round you. Joseph, get me a paper to put dis here child's bread in.

Joseph—Here, Bertha Lee. Here de paper.

Lizzie—Lord, Miss Davis, it a time. I tell you de truth, honey, dis here 'sponsibility got me tied both hand en foot. Ain' no rest nowhe'. I hates it you come here en ain' gettin nothin what you been aimin to catch. I gwine be ready toreckly though. Let me get dese chillun in de road en dem songs gwine start travelin out my head faster den lightnin—

Bertha Lee—Aun' Izzie, make Joseph come on.

Lizzie—Joseph, get in dat road dere side Bertha Lee. Now, you chillun make your tracks dere to school straight as you can go en if you stop dere to dat lady house en get a pecan, I gwine whip you hard as I can.

Joseph and Bertha Lee—Good-bye Possum, good-bye June, good-bye Alfred.

Possum, June, Alfred—Good-bye Joseph, good-bye Bertha Lee.

Lizzie—Here dat tune come buzzin now, Miss Davis. Is you got dis one?

**Sunday Mornin Band!**

"Oh, my sister,
How you walk on de cross?
Sunday mornin band!
Oh, your feet might slip
En your soul get lost.
Sunday mornin band!
Oh, what band,
Oh, what band,
Do you belong?
What band! What band!
Sunday mornin band!"

Heddie—Sis, you is done took de one I been how. I been expectin you was comin out wid one of dem old time reels you used to be a singin en a jiggin bout all de time.

Lizzie—Oh, I been know a heap of dem reels. Hoped sing dem behind de old folks back many a day cause us chillun wasn' never allowed to sing reels in dem days. See, old back people was more religious den dey is now. Yes, mam, dey been know what spell somethin in dat day en time. When dey would speak den, dey meant somethin, I tell you. People does just go through de motion dese days en don' have no mind to mean what dey talk. No, child, us didn' dar'sen to let us parents hear us sing no reels den. What dem old people didn' quarrel out us, dey whip out us. My father never wouldn' let we chillun go to no frolics, but us would listen from de house en catch what us could. I used to could turn a heap of dem reels, too, but he was so tight on us till everything bout left me. Lord, Heddie, give me a thought. You is de jiggin hoss. Hope me out, Heddie, hope me out.

(Heddie begins song and Lizzie joins in and finishes it).

> "The blackest nigger I ever did see,
> He come a runnin down from Tennessee,
> His eye was red en his gum was blue,
> En God a mighty struck him,
> En his shirt tail flew.
> Meet me at de crossroads,
> For I'm gwine join de band.
> Um-huh! Um-huh! Um-huh!"

Lizzie—Great Lord a mercy, Miss Davis, dem kind of tune, dem sinful en wicked songs, dey what I used to turn fore I been big enough to know what been in dem. No, honey, I thank de good Lord to point me way from all dat foolishness en wickedness en I ain' gwine back to it neither.

> "Lord, I know dat my time ain' long,
> Oh, de bells keep a ringin,
> Somebody is a dying,
> Lord, I know dat my time ain' long.
> (Repeat three times)
> Lord, I know dat my time ain' long,
> Oh, de hammer keep a knockin,
> Keep a knockin on somebody coffin,
> Lord, I know dat my time ain' long."
> (Repeat three times).

Lizzie—Lord, I sho know my time ain' long. De Lord say de way of de righteous prevaileth to eternal life en I know I right, people. Lord, I know I right. 'Sponsibility or no 'sponsibility, Lord, I seekin de Kingdom.

Source: Lizzie Davis, colored, 70-80 years, Marion, S.C. Personal interview by Annie Ruth Davis, Marion, S. C.

Code No.
Project, 1885-(1)
Prepared by Annie Ruth Davis
Place, Marion, S. C.
Date, December 13, 1937
No. Words --
Reduced from -- words
Rewritten by --

## LIZZIE DAVIS

### Ex-Slave, Age 70 to 80

"No, mam, I couldn' exactly tell you how old I is cause my father, he been dead over 20 years en when us had a burnin out dere to Georgetown, Pa's Bible was destroyed den. Cose I don' remember myself, say, slavery time, but I can tell dat what I is hear de olden people talk bout been gwine on in dat day en time. No, mam, I want to suggest to you de best I can cause I might have to go back up yonder en tell it to be justified some of dese days."

"Oh, I been know your father en your grandfather en all of dem. Bless mercy, child, I don' want to tell you nothin, but what to please you. Lord, I glad to see your face. It look so lovin en pleasin, just so as I is always know you. Look like dere not a wave of trouble is ever roll 'cross your peaceful bosom."

"Now, like I speak to you, I don' know rightly bout my age, but I can tell you when dat shake come here, I been a missie girl. Oh, my Lord, I been just as proud en crazy in dem days. Wasn' thinkin nothin bout dat dese dark days was headin here. Yes, mam, I is always been afflicted ever since I been twelve years old, so dey tell me. You see, dat muscle right back dere in my foot, it grow crooked just like a hook. De doctor, he say dat if dey had kept me movin bout, it wouldn' been grow dat way. But my poor old mammy, she die while us was livin down dere to old man Foster Brown's plantation en dere won' no other hand gwine trouble dey way no time to lift me up. Oh, my mammy, she been name Katie Brown cause my parents, dey belonged to de old man Foster Brown in dey slavery day. Dat how-come I been raise up a country child dere on Mr. Brown's plantation. Another thing, like as you might be a noticin, I ain' never been married neither. No, mam, I ain' never been married cause I is always been use a stick in walkin in my early days en never didn' nobody want me. Yes, mam, I know I every bit of 70 or gwine on 80 years old to my mind en I think it a blessin de Lord preserve me dis long to de world. Cose I often wonders why de good Massa keep me here en take dem what able to work for demselves."

"Yes, honey, wid God harness on me, I come here to dis town a grown woman to live en I been livin right here by myself in dis same house near bout 20 years. Cose dere a little 12-year-old country girl dat stays here wid me while de school be gwine on so as to get some learnin. Yes'um, I pays $2.00 every month for dis here room en it ain' worth nothin to speak bout. Pap Scott's daughter stay in dat other room over dere. No, mam, dere ain' but just dese two rooms to de house. You, see, my buildin does leak en I has a big time some of dese days. See here, child, I has dis piece of oilcloth cross my bed en when it rains on a night, I sleeps in dat chair over dere en lets it drop on de oilcloth. Den when it comes a storm, my Lord, dere such a racket! I be settin here lookin for dat top up dere to be tumblin down on me de next crack en seems like it does give me such a misery in my head. Yes, mam, dat misery does strike me every time I hear tell bout dere a darkness in de cloud."

"Well, drawed up as I is, I ain' able to get no work worth much to speak bout dese days. It dis way, child, don' nobody like to see no old ugly crooked up creature like me round bout whe' dey be no time. Cose I sets here en does a washin now en den whe' de people gets push up, but don' get no regular work. Now, dem people over dere, I does dey washin mostly, but dey don' never be noways particular en stylish like en I don' have nothin much to worry wid. See, de lady, she don' go bout nowhe' much."

"Oh, Lord, dere my stove right dere, I say. Yes, mam, I cooks right here in de fireplace all de time. I got dat pot on dere wid some turnips a boilin now en it gettin on bout time I be mixin up dat bread, too, fore dat child be comin home from school hungry as a louse. I say, I got dis here old black iron spider en dis here iron griddle, too, what I does my bakin on cause you see, I come from way back yonder. Dem what de olden people used to cook on fore stoves ever been come here. Yes, mam, de spider got three legs dat it sets on en de griddle, dat what I makes dese little thin kind of hoecake on. See, when I wants to bake in de spider, I heaps my coals up in a pile dat way so as to set de spider on dem en pours de batter in de spider en puts de lid on. Den I rakes me up another batch of coals en covers de lid over wid dem. Do dat to make it get done on de top. Yes, mam, dat de kind of a spider dat de people used to cook dey cake in. Now, when I has a mind to cook some turnips or some collards, I makes dis here boil bread. Honey, dat somethin to talk bout eatin wid dem turnips. Ain' no trouble to mind it neither. First, I just washes my hands right clean like en takes en mixes up my meal en water together wid my hand till I gets a right stiff dough. Den I pinches off a piece de dough bout big as a goose egg en flattens it out wid my hand en drops it in de pot wid de greens. Calls dat boil dumplings. I think bout I got a mind dat I gwine cook some of dem in dat turnip pot directly, too. No, mam, I don' never eat dinner till it come bout time for de little girl to be expectin to be from school. Oh, my blessed, dem olden people sho know how to cook in dem days. Never didn' hear speak bout de cookin upsettin de people in dat day en time like it sets de people in a misery dese days. Dat how-come, I say, I ain' noways ailin in de inside cause it be dat I lives de olden way. Yes, child, de slavery people sho had de hand to cook. Dere ain' never been nothin cook nowhe' dat could satisfy a cravin like dat ash cake dat de people used to cook way back dere, I say. Oh, dey would mix up a batter just like dey was gwine make a hoecake en wrap it all up in oak leaves or a piece of dis here heavy brown paper en lay it in de hot ashes. Den dey would rake some more hot ashes all over de top of it. Yes'um, de dampness out de hoecake would keep de wrappin wet en when it would get done, de paper would peel right off it. I tell you, honey, I mighty glad I been come along in dat day en time. Mighty thankful I been a child of de olden ways."

"Yes, child, de people what been raise de slavery way, dey been have a heap of curious notions en some of dem was good, I say. Yes, mam, dere one sign dat I remembers bout en I follows dat up right sharp dese days. I sho watches dat closely. Say, somebody have a mouthful of rations en sneeze, it a sign of death. I finds dat to be very true to speak bout. Yes'um, I notices dat a good one, Miss Davis."

"Den I got another one comin. Always say, when you see bout a dozen buzzards moesin (flying) round a house en den dey break off en make a straight shoot for a graveyard, dere somebody out dat house gwine be bury dere soon. Cose dat what I hear talk bout, but I ain' watched dat so much."

"No, mam, dat ain' half de signs what de olden people used to have cause dat all what dey know to tell dem what to do en what was gwine happen. Dem what was wise, dey followed dem signs closely, too. Yes, you come back another time, child, en I'll see can I scratch up a heap of dem other sign to tell you. When I gets to talkin to you bout old times, my mind, it just gets to wanderin over dem old fields whe' I run bout as a little small child en I can' half remember nothin to speak to you bout."

Source: Lizzie Davis, colored, Marion, S. C.—Age 70 to 80.
Personal interview by Annie Ruth Davis, Dec., 1937.

Code No.
Project, 1885-(1)
Prepared by Annie Ruth Davis
Place, Marion, S. C.
Date, December 21, 1937
No. Words --
Reduced from -- words
Rewritten by --

## LIZZIE DAVIS

### Ex-Slave, Age --

"My parents, dey was sho raise in de South. Been come up on de old man Foster Brown's plantation. Ain' you know whe' Mr. Foster Brown used to live? Yes, mam, down dere in dat grove of pecans dat you see settin side de road, when you be gwine down next to Centenary. I remember, I hear my father tell bout dat his mammy was sold right here to dis courthouse, on dat big public square up dere, en say dat de man set her up in de wagon en took her to Georgetown wid him. Sold her right dere on de block. Oh, I hear dem talkin bout de sellin block plenty times. Pa say, when he see dem carry his mammy off from dere, it make he heart swell in his breast.

"Yes'um, I hear my father talk bout how dey would shoot de great big bomb guns in slavery time. Seems like, he say dat de shootin fuss been come from Fort Sumter. Oh, my Lord, I hear talk dat de people could hear dem guns roarin all bout dis here country. I know dat word been true cause I hear my parents en de olden people speak bout dat right dere fore we chillun. Say, when dey would feel dat rumblin noise, de people would be so scared. Didn' know what was gwine happen. Cose I speak bout what I catch cause de olden people never didn' allow dey chillun to set en hear dem talk no time. No, mam, de olden people was mighty careful of de words dey let slip dey lips.

"Oh, we chillun would have de most fun dere ever was romancin (roaming) dem woods in dat day en time. I used to think it was de nicest thing dat I been know bout to go down in de woods side one of dem shady branch en get a cup of right cool water to drink out de stream. I tell you, I thought dat was de sweetest water I is ever swallowed. Den we chillun used to go out in de woods wid de crowd en get dese big oak leaves en hickory leaves en make hats. Would use dese here long pine needles en thorns for de pins dat we would pick up somewhe' dere in de woods. En we would dress de hats wid all kind of wild flowers en moss dat we been find scatter bout in de woods, too. Oh, yes'um, we thought dey was de prettiest kind of bonnets. Den we would get some of dese green saplin out de woods often times to make us a ridin horse wid en would cut down a good size pine another time en make a flyin mare to ride on. Yes, mam, dat what we would call it. Well, when we would have a mind to make one of dem flyin mare, we chillun would slip a ax to de woods wid us en chop down a nice little pine tree, so as dere would be a good big stump left in de ground. Den we would chisel de top of de stump down all round de edges till we had us a right sharp peg settin up in de middle of de stump. After dat was fixed, we would cut us another pole a little bit smaller den dat one en bore a hole in de middle of it to make it set down on dat peg. Oh, my Lord, one of us chillun would get on dis end en dere another one would get on de other end en us chillun would give dem a shove dat would send dem flyin round fast as I could say mighty-me-a-life. My blessed a mercy, child, it would most bout knock de sense out dem what been on dere. Yes, mam, everybody would be crazy to ride on de flyin mare. All de neighbor's chillun would gather up en go in de woods en jump en shout bout which one turn come to ride next. I tellin you, dem was big pleasures us had in dat day en time en dey never cost nobody nothin neither."

"Well, Mr. Brown, he was mighty good to his colored people, so I hear my parents say. Would allow all his niggers to go to de white people church to preachin every Sunday, Cose my father, he was de carriage driver en he would have task to drive de white folks to church on a Sunday. Yes'um, dem what been belong to Mr. Brown, dey had dey own benches to set on right up dere in de gallery to de white people church, but I hear talk dat some of dem other white people round bout dere never wouldn' let dey colored people see inside dey church no time. Lord, I talk bout how de people bless wid privilege to go to church like dey want to in dis day en time en don' have de mind to serve de Lord like dey ought to no time. Cose dere a man comes here every Sunday mornin in a car en takes me out to church. Ain' no kin to me neither. He late sometimes en de preacher be bout out wid de sermon, but I goes anyhow en gets all I can. Look like de Lord bless me somehow, cripple up as I is, I say."

"De shake! Oh, I remember it well cause I been a grown girl den. Everybody thought it was de Jedgment en all de people was runnin out en a hollerin. I thought it was de last myself en I livin here to tell de people, I was sho scared. I been out to de well bout 12 o'clock de next day en I could see de water in de well just a quiverin. Lord, Lord, dat water tremble bout four weeks after dat. Such a hollerin en a prayin as de people had bout dat shake. No'um I was livin down dere to Tabernacle den en dere wasn' none of de houses round us destroyed. No, child, won' no harm done nowhe' dat I knows of only as a heap of de people been so scared, dey never didn' grow no more."

"Yes'um, I think bout here de other night dat I had make you a promise to fetch you up some of dem signs de olden people used to put faith in. Dere one sign bout if you hear a dog howl or a cow low round your house on a night, it a pretty good sign you gwine lose somebody out dat house. I finds dat to be a mighty true sign cause I notices it very closely."

"Den dey used to say, too, if you get up in de mornin feelin in a good humor, de devil sho gwine get you fore night fall dat same day. Cose I don' pay so much attention to dat. If I get up feelin like singin, I has to sing cause it my time to sing, I say."

"Let me see, dere another one of dem omen dat I had shake up in my mind to tell you. Say, if you see a ground mole rootin round your house, it won' be long fore you gwine move from dat place. But I don' never see no ground moles hardly dese days. Don' think dey worries nobody much."

"I recollects, too, way back yonder de people used to say, if you see de smoke comin out de chimney en turn down en flatten out on de ground, it a sign of rain in a few days."

"Yes, mam, I think bout dis one more. If you dream bout you be travelin en come to a old rotten down buildin, it a sign of a old person death. Don' say whe' it a man or a woman, but it a sho sign dat a old person gwine die."

"Den people what lives in de country believes, if a fox comes round a house barkin en a scratchin, it a sign dey gwine lose somebody out dey family. Yes'um, de fox just comes right out de woods up to de yard en barks. You see, a dog won' never run a fox dat comes bout dem barkin. No, mam, when de dog hear dat, he just stands right under de house en growls at de fox. I know dat be a true sign cause us tried dat one."

"Now, I got another one of dem thought comin. Yes, my Lord, I hear talk dat if you get de broom en sweep your house out fore sunrise, you would sweep your friends out right wid de trash. Dat used to be a big sign wid de people, too. En it bad luck to take up ashes after de sun go down, dey say. Yes, I know bout plenty people won' do dat today."

"Well, honey, seems like when I calls back, de people in a worser fix den when I used to get 25 cents a day. Used to could take dat en go to a country store en get a decent dress to wear to church. Sell peck of us corn en get it in trade. Didn' never pay more den 50 cents for a load of wood in dem days en I remembers just as good eggs been sell for 10 cents a dozen en 15 cents bout Christmas time. Cose I ain' exactly decided what to speak bout de times cause it dis way to my mind. De people, dey have a better privilege dis day en time, but dey don' appreciate nothin like dey did back in my dark days. Yes, mam, de people was more thankful to man en God den dey is dese days. Dat my belief bout de way de world turnin, I say."

Source:
Lizzie Davis, colored, age between 70 and 80, Marion, S. C.
Personal interview by Annie Ruth Davis, Dec., 1937.

Project #1855
W. W. Dixon
Winnsboro, S. C.

## LOUISA DAVIS
### Ex-Slave 106 Years Old.

"Well, well, well! You knows my white folks on Jackson Creek, up in Fairfield! I's mighty glad of dat, and glad to see you. My white folks come to see me pretty often, though they lives way up dere. You wants to write me up? Well, I'll tell you all I recollect, and what I don't tell you, my daughter and de white folks can put in de other 'gredients. Take dis armchair and git dat smokin' ash tray; lay it on de window sill by you and make yourself comfortable and go ahead."

"I was born in de Catawba River section. My grand-pappy was a full blood Indian; my pappy a half Indian; my mother, coal black woman. Just whu I b'long to when a baby? I'll leave dat for de white folks to tell, but old Marster Jim Lemon buy us all; pappy, mammy, and three chillun: Jake, Sophie, and me. De white folks I fust b'long to refuse to sell 'less Marse Jim buy de whole family; dat was clever, wasn't it? Dis old Louisa must of come from good stock, all de way 'long from de beginnin', and I is sho' proud of dat."

"When he buy us, Marse Jim take us to his place on Little River nigh clean cross de county. In de course of time us fell to Marse Jim's son, John, and his wife, Miss Mary. I was a grown woman then and nursed their fust baby, Marse Robert. I see dat baby grow to be a man and 'lected to legislature, and stand up in dat Capitol over yonder cross de river and tell them de Law and how they should act, I did. They say I was a pretty gal, then, face shiny lak a ginger cake, and hair straight and black as a crow, and I ain't so bad to look at now, Marse Willie says."

"My pappy rise to be foreman on de place and was much trusted, but he plowed and worked just de same, mammy say maybe harder."

"Then one springtime de flowers git be blooming, de hens to cackling, and de guineas to patarocking. Sam come along when I was out in de yard wid de baby. He fust talk to de baby, and I asked him if de baby wasn't pretty. He say, 'Yes, but not as pretty as you is, Louisa.' I looks at Sam, and dat kind of foolishness wind up in a weddin'. De white folks allowed us to be married on de back piazza, and Reverend Boggs performed de ceremony."

"My husband was a slave of de Sloans and didn't get to see me often as he wanted to; and of course, as de housemaid then, dere was times I couldn't meet him, clandestine like he want me. Us had some grief over dat, but he got a pass twice a week from his marster, Marse Tommie Sloan, to come to see me. Bold as Sam git to be, in after years ridin' wid a red shirt long side of General Bratton in '76, dat nigger was timid as a rabbit wid me when us fust git married. Shucks, let's talk 'bout somthing else. Sam was a field hand and drive de wagon way to Charleston once a year wid cotton, and always bring back something pretty for me."

"When de war come on, Sam went wid young Marster Tom Sloan as bodyguard, and attended to him, and learned to steal chickens, geese, and turkeys for his young marster, just to tell 'bout it. He dead now; and what I blames de white folks for, they never would give him a pension, though he spend so much of his time and labor in their service. I ain't bearin' down on my kind of white folks, for I'd jump wid joy if I could just git back into slavery and have de same white folks to serve and be wid them, day in and day out."

"Once a week I see de farm hands git rations at de smoke house, but dat didn't concern me. I was a housemaid and my mammy run de kitchen, and us got de same meals as my marster's folks did."

"Yas sir; I got 'possum. Know how to cook him now. Put him in a pot and parboil him, then put him in a oven wid lots of lard or fat-back, and then bake him wid yaller yam potatoes, flanked round and round, and then wash him down wid locust and persimmon beer followed by a piece of pumpkin pie. Dat make de bestest meal I 'members in slavery days."

"Us got fish out of Little River nigh every Saturday, and they went good Sunday morning. Us had Saturday evenin's, dat is, de farm hands did, and then I got to go to see Sam some Sundays. His folks, de Sloans, give us a weddin' dinner on Sunday after us was married, and they sho' did tease Sam dat day."

"Like all rich buckra, de Lemons had hogs a plenty,

big flock of sheep, cotton gin, slaves to card, slaves to spin, and slaves to weave. Us was well clothed and fed and 'tended to when sick. They was concerned 'bout our soul's salvation. Us went to church, learn de catechism; they was Presbyterians, and read de Bible to us. But I went wid Sam after freedom. He took de name of Davis, and I jined de Methodist Church and was baptized Louisa Davis."

"Patroller, you ask me? 'Spect I do 'member them. Wasn't I a goodlookin' woman? Didn't Sam want to see me more than twice a week? Wouldn't he risk it widout de pass some time? Sure he did. De patrollers got after and run Sam many a time."

"After de war my pappy went to Florida. He look just like a Indian, hair and all, bushy head, straight and young lookin' wid no beard. We never heard from him since."

"De slaves wash de family clothes on Saturday and then rested after doin' dat. Us had a good time Christmas; every slave ketch white folks wid a holler, 'Christmas gift, Marster' and they holler it to each other. Us all hung our stockin's all 'bout de Big House, and then dere would be sumpin' in dere next mornin'. Lord, wasn't them good times!"

"Now how is it dese days? Young triflin' nigger boys and gals lyin' 'round puffin' cigarets, carryin' whiskey 'round wid them, and gittin' in jail on Christmas, grievin' de Lord and their pappies, and all sich things. OH! De risin' generation and de future! What is it comin' to? I just don't know, but dere is comin' a time to all them."

"I sho' like to dance when I was younger. De fiddlers

was Henry Copley and Buck Manigault; and if anybody 'round here could make a fiddle ring like Buck could, wouldn't surprise me none if my heart wouldn't cry out to my legs, 'Fust lady to de right and cheat or swing as you like, and on to de right'."

"Stop dat laughin'. De Indian blood in me have held me up over a hundred years, and de music might make me young again."

"Oh yes, us had ghost stories, make your hair stand on end, and us put iron in de fire when us hear screech owl, and put dream book under bed to keep off bad dreams."

"When de yankees come they took off all they couldn't eat or burn, but don't let's talk 'bout dat. Maybe if our folks had beat them and git up into dere country our folks would of done just like they did. Who knows?"

"You see dis new house, de flower pots, de dog out yonder, de cat in de sun lyin' in de chair on de porch, de seven tubs under de shed, de two big wash pots, you see de pictures hangin' round de wall, de nice beds, all dese things is de blessin's of de Lord through President Roosevelt. My grandson, Pinckney, is a World War man, and he got in de CCC Camp, still in it in North Carolina. When he got his bonus, he come down, and say, 'Grandma, you too old to walk, supposin' I git you a automobile?" I allow, 'Son, de Indian blood rather make me want a house.' Then us laugh. 'Well,' he say, 'Dis money I has and am continuin' to make, I wants you and mama to enjoy it.' Then he laugh fit to kill heself. Then I say, 'I been dreamin' of a tepee all our own, all my lifetime; buy us a lot over in Sugartown in New Brookland, and make a home of happiness for your ma, me and you'."

"And dis is de tepee you settin' in today. I feel like he's a young warrior, loyal and brave, off in de forests workin' for his chief, Mr. Roosevelt, and dat his dreams are 'bout me maybe some night wid de winds blowin' over dat three C camp where he is."

Project #1855
District #4
Spartanburg, S. C.
May 29, 1937

## WALLACE DAVIS
### Folklore: Ex-Slaves

"I was a slave of Bill Davis who lived at "Rich Hill", near Indian Creek, in Newberry County, S. C. I was born about 1856, I reckon. My daddy was Ivasum Davis and my mammy was Rhody Davis. Marse Bill was a good master, lived in a big house, give us a good place to live and plenty to eat. He hardly ever whipped us, and was never cruel to us. He didn't let his overseer whip us, and never hit a man.

"Aw, we had good eats den. Wish I has some of dem old ash-cakes now which was cooked in de brick oven or in de ashes in de fireplace. My mistress had a big garden, and give us something to eat out of it. We used to go hunting, and killed possums, rabbit, squirrels, and birds.

"We had home-made clothes 'till I was big boy. Dey was made from card and spin wheels.

"Our work was light; we got up at sun-up at blowing of de horn and worked till sundown. Sometimes we worked on Saturday afternoons when we had to. On Saturday nights we had frolics—men and women. Some women would wash their clothes on Saturday afternoons. Den at night we have prayer meetings.

"We had no church on our plantation, not till after freedom, but we learned to read and write and spell.

"De padderrolers didn't bother us; our master always give us a pass when we go anywhere.

"On Christmas Day master always give big dinners for slaves, and on New Year we had a holiday.

"I married Lila Davis at de Baptist Church in Newberry.

"When our slaves got sick we sent for de doctor. Some of de old folks in the neighborhood believed in giving root-herb tea or tea made from cherry barks or peach leaves.

"When freedom come de master told us we was free and could go but if we wanted to stay on with him, we could stay. We stayed with him for two years and worked by day wages.

"The Ku Klux was dere. I heard old folks talk about dem. Dey had white sheets over their heads and white caps on their heads.

"The Yankees went through our place and stole cattle.

"I thought slavery was all right, 'cause I had a good time. I had a good master.

"I joined the church when I was 21 years old because I thought I'd live better. I think all ought to join the church."

Source: Wallace Davis (88), Newberry, S. C.; interviewer: G. Leland
 Summer, Newberry, S. C.

United States

Project 1885-1
Folklore
Spartanburg, Dist. 4
Oct. 15, 1937
Edited by:
Elmer Turnage

# WALLACE DAVIS
## Stories Of Ex-Slaves

"I live in a little two-room house beyond Helena where I work a little patch of land which I rent. I don't own anything. I make a living working de land.

"I was born on Indian Creek in Newberry County, S. C. about 1856. My mammy was Rhody Davis and my pa was Ivasum Davis. We belonged in slavery to Bill Davis. He lived at de place called "Rich Hill". De old house is done tore down, but young Riser now lives in de new house on de place.

"Our master was good to us, but whipped us a little sometimes. He would not allow his overseer to whip any of us. He give us enough to eat and a fair place to live in. We didn't want fer anything. Dey had plenty to eat on de farm, and sure had good eatings. Dere was a brick oven which could cook good bread and cakes. We had a big garden which de mistress looked after, and she had plenty from it which she shared wid de slaves.

"De old spinning wheel was used lots of times and dey made all de clothes everybody on de place wore.

"We didn't have no church to go to, but dey sometimes made some slaves go to white folks churches where dey set on de back seats. We didn't have schools and couldn't learn to read and write till after freedom come; den some niggers learned at de brush arbors.

"Befo' freedom de patrollers marched up and down de road but didn't bother us. Our master always give us a pass when we went somewhere. On Christmas he give us big dinners.

"I married Lilla Davis at de white folks' Baptist church in Newberry.

"When slaves got sick some of dem took tree barks and made teas to drink, and some made tea from root herbs. We had doctors, too, but dey made lots of deir medicine from de barks and herbs.

"I can't remember much what de Ku Klux did, but heard about dem. Just after de war de Yankees marched through our place and stole some cattle and run away wid dem. In some places dey burned down de barns and gin houses.

"I had a good master and always had plenty to eat, so I thought slavery was all right. We didn't have nothing of any kind to worry about.

"I don't know nothing much about Abe Lincoln or Jefferson Davis."

Source: Wallace Davis (N. 88), Newberry, S. C.
Interviewer: G. L. Summer, Newberry, S. C. (9/15/37).

# United States

Project 1885-(1)
Prepared by Annie Ruth Davis
Place, Marion, S. C.
Date, August 20, 1937

# WILLIAM HENRY DAVIS
## Ex-Slave, 72 Years

"I born de first day of March in 1865 cause de white folks raise me mostly en dat how-come I know how old I ought to say I is. My father belong to de old man Jackie Davis, dat live not so far from Tabernacle, en den he fall to he son, Mr. William J. Davis. Dat whe' I was raise. My grandfather, old man Caesar, live dere too."

"I never been treated exactly as de other plantation peoples was as it just like I tellin you, I be round de white folks mostly. My mamma, she do all de cooking to de big house en dere be a division in de Missus kitchen for de cook en she chillun to stay in. Sometimes my Massa make my mamma feed all de small plantation chillun dere to de kitchen from de table. Dey want de chillun to hurry en grow en dat de reason dey give em good attention at de house. Dey give us milk en clabber en corn bread to eat mostly en give us fritters some of de time. Dat was fried wheat bread what some people call pancakes. Used to give me job to mind de cows en de calves when dey was put to grazing."

"All de other colored peoples live in de nigger quarter up on de hill. Just like de white people house here, de colored people house all be in row pretty much off from de big house. Oh, de people was meant to work in dat day en time. De white folks teach em en show em what dey look for em to do. Den if dey didn' do it like dey tell em do it, dey chastise em."

"It just like I tellin you, de people fare wid abundance of everything in dem days. Destroy much meat in one month den as de people gets hold of in whole year dese days. It was just dis way, everybody know to have fence round bout dey plantation den en de hogs could run anywhe'. All de field land was fence en de woods was for de run of de stock. Dey mark em en some of de time, dey hear tell of stock 10 mile away. Know em by de brand."

"Peoples didn' have heap of all kind of things dat dey have dese days, but somehow it look like dey have a knack of gettin along better wid what dey have den. Didn' have no stoves to cook on in dem days. Cook in clay oven en on de fireplace. Make up fire en when it die down, dey put tatoes (potatoes) in de oven en let em stay dere all night. My God, won' nothin no better den dem oven tatoes was. Some of de time, dey have wire in de chimney wid de pots hanging on dat. Folks used to make up a cake of corn bread en pat it on de hearth en when de fire burn right low, dey cover de cake all up in pile of ashes. When it get done, it be brown through de ashes en dey take it out en wash en rub all de ashes off it. Den it was ready to eat. Dat what dey call ash cake. Just seem like what de peoples used to cook be sweeter eatin den what dey cooks dis day en time."

"Oh, I beat rice many a day. Yes'um, beat rice many a day for my grandmother en my mamma too. Had a mortar en a pestle dat beat rice wid. Dey take big tree en saw log off en set it up just like a tub. Den dey hollow it out in de middle en take pestle dat have block on both it end en beat rice in dat mortar. Beat it long time en take it out en fan it en den put it back. De last time it put back, tear off some shucks en put in dere to get de red part of de rice out en make it white. Ain' nobody never been born can tell you more bout dem pestles en mortars den William Henry Davis know."

"Yes'um, used to go to corn shuckings en rye thrashings en pea thrashings plenty times. Oh, dey sing en have music en have big pot cookin out in de yard wid plenty rice en fresh meat for everybody. Dere be so many people some of de time, dey had to have two or three pots. Den dey have dem log rollings to clean up de land en when dey would get to rollin dem heavy logs, dey give de men a little drink of whiskey to revive em, but dey gage how much dey give em. O Lord, we had tough time den. After dey get through wid all de work, dey would eat supper den. Give us rice en corn bread en fresh meat en coffee en sweet tatoe pone. My Lord, dat sweet tatoe pone was de thing in dem days. Missie, you ain' never eat no pone bread? Dey take piece of tin en drive nails through it en grate de raw tatoes on dat. Den dey take a little flour en hot water en molasses en mix up in dem raw tatoes en bake it in de oven on de fireplace. Have lid to oven en put fire under de bottom of it en on de top to get it right done. Some of de time, dey put a little ginger in it fore it was baked. Cut it in big slices when it get done, but wouldn' never eat it till dey know it was cold. Missie, de older I gets de more I does sorrow to go back to dem old constructions dat dey used to have."

"Some of de colored peoples have bresh (brush) shelter whe' dey go to church in dem days, but all us go to de white folks church. Oh, de colored peoples go in ox carts, but us white folks have teams en carriage to ride in. I recollects Mr. Davis carriage look sorta like a house wid two big horses to pull it. De family would be in de inside en have seats whe' dey set facing one another. De driver have seat on de outside in de front en on de back of de carriage was de place to set de trunks."

"My daddy was de blacksmith for Mr. Jackie Davis en he could make plows en hoes en all dem kind of things. He have a circuit dat he go round en mend things on other white folks plantations. Some of de time, he bring back more den $100.00 to he boss dat he would make. Go all bout in dat part of Marion county dat be part of Florence county dose times."

"I hear some peoples say dey knows dere such as ghosts, but I ain' never have no mind in dat line. All I know bout is what my mamma used to tell us big chillun when she want us to stay home wid de little chillun en mind em. Say dere was Raw Head en Bloody Bones in de woods en if us go off, de child might set de house on fire. Such as dat was to make us stay home when dey was gone."

"It just dis way, I think freedom a good thing for some people while it a bad thing for de ones dat don' have a knack to shuffle for dey own self. When freedom come, some of de colored people didn' know what freedom was en dey just hang around dey white folks en look to dey Massa for what dey get right on. Wouldn' get off en make nothin for dey own self. Dat how-come I think it better for some not to be free cause so much of worryations ain' good for peoples. Colored peoples never had to worry bout nothin in slavery time."

Source: William Henry Davis, age 72, ex-slave, Wahee section
of Marion Co., S. C.

Personal interview, August 1937.

Project 1885-1
FOLKLORE
Spartanburg, Dist. 4
Aug. 24, 1937
Edited by:
Elmer Turnage

# ELIAS DAWKINS

## Stories From Ex-Slaves

"Sunday, Aug. 1, was my 82nd [HW: 84th?] birthday; so I was born in 1853. De very day I come into de world I do not know, but soon my marster, Starke Sims, begun to train me. Dr. Bill Sims, Marse Stark's son, was a doctor when I was born. A younger son was called Hal. When Hal was a boy he said he was gwine off, and when he got to be a man, dat is what he done; yes sirree, he got scattered off.

"Dr. Bill had done started to doctoring folks befo' I got into dis world. And first thing dat I recollects is how my marster teached me to address him. He addressed me as 'Elias, Johnny Elias'. I had to answer, 'Sirs', and dat 'S' always had to be dar to please de marster. All of his slaves had to address him de same way. Sometimes we would answer, 'Sirs Marster'.

"All de things my marster teached me are still a

great help to me. Dis younger generation does not have de quality dat we old niggers has, because dey refuse to take de teachings of dere parents and de good white folks. De main thing dat Marse teached his slaves was mannerableness. Dat I holds to dis day; 'specially to de white people. I allus tries to be mannerable to dem. Often I looks back on dat, but both white and colored is trying to do away wid dem things. Old training is de best, and I cannot fergit my manners. Never does raal folks fergit dere raising. Dats what shows up de quality in people. I likes quality in everything, and as soon as I sees strangers and hears dem talk and looks at dere action, I can tell how much quality dey got. Dat I sho can. I never is gwine to drap my raising, don't care what de style comes to. Dat's jest one thing dat my race and de white race, too, wants to do away wid. Dey don't hold up no manners and no ra'al raising.

"De school teachers tells de chilluns to say yes and no to me. Dey tells dem to say de same thing to white folks. Den dey teaches de chilluns to Mr. and Miss de own race and to call white folks by dere names widout any handle to it. Dat ain't gwine to work, and any niggers dat has self-respect jest ain't gwine to call no white folks by dere name. If you doesn't respect other folks, why den other folks ain't gwine to show no respect fer you. Why some of my grand chilluns sets up and says 'yes' and 'no' to me 'stead of 'yes sir' and 'no sir'. But I is right here to tell you dat my own chilluns don't say 'no' and 'yes' to me. I is strived wid dem and dey knows how to answer proper to dere elders and to white folks. I ain't got no time fer dese school teachers dat tells de pupils to answer in no sech insulting ways as dat. I likes manners and widout manners folks ain't quality; don't make no diffuns 'bout what color dey is or how far dey is gone in de reading books. Young'uns saying 'yes' and 'no' is jest plain ugly. It suits me to meet nice folks, and when I finds dat dey ain't got mannerableness about dem, den I concludes dat dey jest ain't nice.

"I gwine to dress up tonight and go to preaching at Mt. Zion. Dey done already started running meeting dar. I used to preach amongst dem at de big meetings, but I is retracting now.

"My old marse low to us, 'You is free now, yes sir, you is sho free niggers now. You is gwine out into de world on your own. Let me tell you dis: If you be's mannerable you will allus come out more dan conqueror.' I was young den, and I did not know what 'more dan conqueror' meant den. I is larn't now what it means. Thank God, I does, fer his telling me dat. I lays to de fact dat de reason I is never been in jail is dat I allus had manners. Young'uns acts biggety and den dey lands right straight in de first jail dar is.

"I sho never went to no war, but I worked at de house in de corn field a-raising corn fer de war hosses. I been in only two states, North and South Carolina. I travels jest according to common sense: lets other folks be my guide. I met up wid Indians; dey wanted to claim kin wid me, but I wouldn't claim kin wid dem. He tell me bout my high cheeks or something; den he low something 'bout my nose being long. Dey close thinking people, dem Indians is. Dey don't fergit nothing. He say he see I is mixed-up, but I never is knowed jest what he was driving at. I told him I was teached from de old generation, but dat dar wasn't narry drop of Indian blood in me. Cherokee Creek whar dat old Indian place is. Dey has all kinds of things to sell dat dey makes. I ain't no Indian and I does not feel dat way, no sir, not narry bit does I feel like I is a Indian.

"My mother died when I was a wee baby. Never is had no brothers or sisters. She left me wid her marster dat owned her mother, Kissy Sims. Marse Starke helped my granny to raise me. Kissy come from Virginia. Her Pa let a man buy her and three other chilluns. Marse Starke raised dem all up and dats how dey got his name.

"Dis here man standing here by me is Zack Herndon. We is de oldest niggers in Cherokee County dat I knows of. De other old ones is all dead now. Oh, you knows him, does you Zack?

"Never did so awful much work when I was coming up. Dey was priming me and training me. When dey call my name, I allus come. Often I hid myself to see de bad niggers whipped. Never had no 'buse in my life. Marse didn't 'low nobody to look at his niggers when dey was being whipped, kaise he hated to have to let any of dem be 'bused. Marse Starke sho never whipped no one dat was good. He never let his overseers 'buse nobody neither. I does not 'member much 'bout his overseers. One named a Briggs, one a Bishop, one a Coleman and Alley Cook was de last one; I 'members his name best.

"Marse Starke was a rich man. He had in de Quarter what was know'd as a chilluns' house. A nurse stayed in it all de time to care fer all de plantation chilluns. My granny 'Kissy' acted as nurse dar some. Aunt Peggy and aunt Ciller was two mo'. Ciller was de daughter of a King in Africa, but dat story been traveling ever since she got to dese shores, and it still a-gwine. All dese helped to nurse me. Dey fed us on milk, plenty of it. We had honey, lasses and lots of good things. When I was a little bit-a boy I had a big bowl to eat out of. And us chilluns et like hogs and got fat. We allus had fine food. My marster give me a biscuit sometime from his plate and I wouldn't have tuck 25¢ fer it. He allus put butter in it or ham and gravy. He would say, 'Dat's de doctrine, Be kind!' Nobody never got no 'borious beating from our master's hands.

"I been toiling here on dis earth fer a long time. De Lawd spared me to bring up a big race of chilluns myself. We is awful po' and ain't none of my chilluns got things as well as I had when my marster give it to me. My daughter and grand-daughter lives wid Mr. Nathan Littlejohn. He is rich. I stay in de house wid dem. Dey 'vides wid me dat what dey has. But dat ain't much. I has great-great-grand chilluns dat I ain't never seed. I have five chilluns living to my knowings. Last time I counted, I had 137 grand and great-grand chilluns. So you see I looks into de fourth generation of my own family.

"Me and Old man Zack went to a hanging one time. Both of us clamed up into a tree so dat we could look down on de transaction from a better angle. De man, I means de sheriff, let us go up dar. He let some mo' niggers clamb up in de same tree wid us. De man dat was being hung was called Alf Walker. He was a mulatto and he had done kil't a preacher, so you see dey was hanging him fer his wickedness, sho as you born dey was.

"While me and Zack up in dat tree a-witnessing dat transaction, peers like we become mo' acquainted wid one another dan we had ever been since us know'd one another.

"Sheriff 'low'd, 'You is got only fifteen minutes to

live in. What has you got to say?' Alf got up and talked by giving a lecture to folks about being lawful citizens. He give a lecture also to young folks who he 'low'd dat was not in sech condition as he was. He talking to dem 'bout obeying de parents and staying at home. Me and Zack exchange glances and Zack 'low, 'Alf ain't never stayed at home none since he been big enough to tramp over de country and he up dar fixing to git his neck broke fer his waryness, and trying to tell us good folks young and old how us should act. Now ain't he something to be a-telling us what to do.'

"Finally, Alf had done talked his time out and de sheriff 'low, 'Now you is only got two minutes, what does you want?'

Alf hollered, 'Mr. Sheriff, lemme shake hands wid somebody.' Sheriff say everybody dat wishes to may shake his hand. Me and Zack stayed up in dat tree, but some of de niggers went up and shaked hands wid Alf.

"Time out! You could-a heard a pin drap. I could hear my breath a-coming. I got scared. Zack looked ra'al ashy. Nobody on de ground moved, jest stayed ra'al quiet and still. Noose drapped over de man's neck and tightened. Some one moved de block from under his foots. Dat jerked him down. Whoop! All dem in de tree fell out 'cept me and Zack, dey was so scared. Alf Walker wasn't no mo'. Me and Zack sot up in dat tree like two cranks. Us sot dar as if it hadn't tuck no 'fect on us a-tall. All de other folks got 'fected. Zack tickled me when he saw me studying. He 'low 'you act awful hard-hearted.' I 'low, 'dat man telling us how to do jest now, and dar he is hanged. Us still a-setting in dis tree, ain't we? We ain't never wanted to see no mo' hangings, is we Zack?' Zack 'low dat we ain't.

"Onc't de guide low'd to de President, 'You raises your hat to a nigger?' President 'low, 'I ain't gwine to let nobody be mo' polite dan I is.' He never let nobody have mo' sense dan he did either. Dat was Washington.

"Me and Zack is gwine to tell you how it is. We is old and ain't no need fer old folks to try and fool. I is too shame to beg. I wants de pension. Is you gwine to tell me 'bout it? Dis de truth, I is took a chip fer food. If I could got to school and write fast as I can shake my fist, I'd be a-giving out dat pension right fast. I likes character and principle. I got a boy turned into 64 years. He got character and principle, and he still do what I say. I never put my mouth amongst old folks when I was young. Me and Zack often talks over old times."

Source: Elias Dawkins (84), Rt. 1, Gaffney, S. C.
Interviewer: Caldwell Sims, Union, S. C. 8/20/37.

Project 1885-1
FOLKLORE
Spartanburg Dist. 4
June 3, 1937
Edited by:
Elmer Turnage

# WILL DILL
## Stories Of Ex-Slaves

Upon learning where an ex-slave lived, the writer walked up to a house on Pickenpack street where two old colored men were sitting on the front porch. Asked if one of them was named 'Will Dill', the blacker of the two motioned to himself and said,

"Come here, come in and have a seat," at the same time touching the porch swing beside him.

He acknowledged that he lived in slavery days, "but was a small boy, walking and playing around at that time". His master was Zeek Long, who lived in Anderson County not far from "Three and Twenty Mile Creek' and used to ask him:—what the rooster said, what the cow said, what the pig said; and used to get a great deal of amusement out of his kiddish replies and imitation of each animal and fowl. From his own calculation, he figured he was born in 1862 in the home of his mother who was owned by Zeek

Long. His father, also, was owned by the same master, but lived in another house. He remembers when the Yankees came by and asked for something to eat. When they had gotten this, they went to the corn crib, which was chock full of corn, and took the corn out, shucked it, and gave it to their horses. All the good horses had been hidden in the woods and only two or three old poor ones were left in the stables, but the Yankees did not take these for they only wanted good horses. He remembers seeing the patrollers coming around and checking up on the 'niggers'. He had an uncle who used to slip off every night and go to see some colored girl. He had a path that he followed in going to her house.

"One night Uncle Bob, he started to go see his gal, and it was pretty late, but he followed his path. There were some paterollers out looking for him, and t'rectly they saw him. Uncle Bob lit out running and the paterollers started running, too. Here they had it up and down the path. Uncle Bob, he knew there was a big ditch crossing the path, but the paterollers didn't know it; so when Uncle Bob got to the gully, he jumped right over it and run on, but one of the patrollers fell into the gully and broke his neck. After dat, Uncle Bob, he stayed in and kept quiet, for he knew the paterollers had it in for him."

He asked the writer if he had ever heard a chicken talk. He said that he had, and described a scene at the house one day when a preacher was there. The chickens and guineas came around the house as usual to get their feed, but didn't get it. He "quoted" the rooster as saying; "Has the preacher gone yet?" A guinea hen answered, "not yet—not yet".

He said that he often heard turkeys talk. They would

ask each other questions, and another fowl would answer. He once heard a mule that was in the barn, say: "Lord! Lord! All I want is corn and fodder."

Being told by the negro who was sitting beside him, that he did not believe animals and fowls could talk, he at once said:

"Sure—roosters and gobblers can talk, one day there was a turkey hen and a lots of little turkeys scratching around a certain place on a hill, the little turkeys were heard to say, 'Please mam, please mam'. An old gobbler standing and strutting near, cried out, 'Get the hell out of here'. The turkey hen then moved to another place to feed."

He said that he gets out in his porch early in the mornings and whistles to the birds, and that soon a large flock of birds are all around him. Offering to demonstrate his ability, he began to whistle in a peculiar way. Soon thereafter, two or three English sparrows flew into the yard from nearby trees.

"See thar! See thar!" he said, pointing to them.

"When the war was over," he continued, "we stayed on at Marster's plantation for some time. I grew up, and was always a fellow who liked hard work. I have railroaded, was a tree doctor, helped dig wells and did a lot of hard work. The white people was always pleased with my work and told me so. I went down a well once to help clean it out. It looked like to me that well was caving in above me; so I hollered for them to pull me out. When I got out, I told them I wasn't going down no wells any more unless somebody threw me in."

He said that he had seen lots of wild turkeys when he was a boy. One day when he was going to get some "bacco" for his aunt, he saw a hen and a lot of little turkeys—

"I run after the little wild turkeys but I never kotched a one. That old mother hen would fly from one limb in a tree to another limb in another tree and call them. They was the runningest things I ever saw. I nearly run myself to death but I never did get one."

Every now and them, he said, one of the men on the plantation would shoot a wild hog and we would have plenty of meat to eat. The hogs ran wild in those days, he said.

"I never saw a ghost," he said, "unless it was one night when we boys was out with our dogs 'possum hunting. The dogs treed a possum in a little scrubby tree. I was always a good climber; so I went up the tree to shake the 'possum out. I shook and shook but the 'possum would not fall out of the tree. I shook so hard that my hat fell off and I told the niggers not to let the dogs tear my hat. That was no skunk in the tree, 'cause we couldn't smell anything, but when I looked again at the 'possum, or whatever it was, it got bigger and bigger. I scrambled down the tree right away, nearly falling out of it, but I wanted to get away. The dogs acted kinda scared; yet they would run up to the tree and bark. One old dog I had did not bark, he just hollered. We left the thing in the tree. I don't know what it was, but it warn't no 'possum, for I'd shook it out of the tree if it had been."

In further discussing the subject of fowls in talking among themselves, he said that he had often noticed a rooster and some hens standing around in the shade talking.

"The rooster will say something and the hens will listen; then answer him back, 'yes'. One day I heard a turkey hen say, 'we are poor, we are poor'. The old turkey gobbler said, 'well, who in the hell can help it.' Yes sir, they talk just like we do, but 'taint everybody can understand 'em."

He said that he had fifteen children by his first wife. He remained single for thirteen years after his wife's death, and never had any children by his second wife.

"Do you reckon we'll ever get a pension in our old age?" he asked. "It seems to me they would give us old fellows something to live on, for we can't work. How can we live now-a-days? When a man has done good work when he was able, the country ought to take care of him in his old age.

"I was a hand for hard work all my life. I was raised that way; but now, that I can't do nothing, it looks like the state ought to take care of me.

"My father told me when I was sitting up to a gal and I told him I was gwinter marry her, 'Son don't you never cut that woman across the back, for as sure as you do, that cut will be against you on Judgement Day."

"When I was laid up with the misery in my side, my feet swelled up and busted, and I had a awful hurting in my side and back. People wanted me to believe I had been conjured, but I did not believe it, and I told them I would eat all the stuff that a conjure man could bring. Anybody that believes in conjuring is just a liar. God is the only a person who can bring suffering on people. He don't want to do it, but it's because we do something He don't want us to when He makes people suffer. It is the bugger man that does it."

"Uncle" Will said that his father and mother were married by a "jack-leg" preacher who, when told that they wanted to get married, had them both to jump backwards and forwards over a broom. He then told them that they were man and wife.

Source: Will Dill, 555 Pickenpack St., Spartanburg, S. C.
Interviewer: F. S. DuPre, Spartanburg, Dist. 4 5/19/37

W. W. Dixon
Winnsboro, S. C.

## THOMAS DIXON
### Ex-Slave 75 Years Old.

Tom Dixon, a mulatto, is a superannuated minister of the Gospel. He lives in Winnsboro, S. C., at the corner of Moultrie and Crawford Streets. He is duly certified and registered as an old age pensioner and draws a pension of $8.00 per month from the Welfare Board of South Carolina. He is incapable of laborious exercise.

"I was born in 1862, thirteen miles northeast of Columbia, S. C., on the border line of Kershaw and Fairfield Counties. My mother was a slave of Captain Moultrie Gibbes. My father was white, as you can see. My mother was the cook for my white folks; her name was Malinda. She was born a slave of Mr. Tillman Lee Dixon of Liberty Hill. After she learned to cook, my marster bought her from her master and paid $1,200.00 for her. After freedom, us took the name of Dixon.

"My mistress in slavery time was Miss Mary. She was a Clark before she married Marse Moultrie. I was nothing but a baby when the war ended and freedom come to our race. I lived on my marster's Wateree River plantation, with mother, until he sold it and went into the hotel business at Union, S. C.

"My mother then went to Columbia, S. C., and I attended Benedict College. I became a preacher in 1886, the year of the earthquake. That earthquake drove many sinners to their knees, me amongst them; and, when I got up, I resolved to be a soldier of the cross, and every since I have carried the shield of faith in my left hand and the sword of the Word in my right hand.

"The night I was converted, the moon was shining brightly. We was all at a revival meeting out from Blythewood, then called Dako, S. C. First, we heard a low murmur or rolling sound like distant thunder, immediately followed by the swaying of the church and a cracking sound from the joists and rafters of the building. The women folks set up a screaming. The men folks set up a hollering: 'Oh Lordy! Jesus save me! We believe! Come Almighty King!' The preacher tried to quiet us, but we run out the church in the moonlight, men and women crying and praying. The preacher, Rev. Charlie Moore, continued the services outside and opened the doors of the church, and every blessed soul come forward and joined the church.

"I married Fannie Irwin, and God blessed us all the days of her life. My daughter, Maggie, married a Collins and lives in the Harlem section of New York City. My daughter, Sallie, lives also in Harlem, Greenville Village. Malinda, named for my mother, lives and works in Columbia, S. C.

"On the death of my wife, Fannie, I courted and married the widow Lizzie Williams. The house we live in is her own property. She had two children when we married, a boy and a girl. The boy got killed at the schoolhouse two years ago. The girl is working in Columbia, S. C. I am a superannuated minister of the African Methodist Episcopal Church, and receive a small sum of money from the denomination, yearly. The amount varies in different years. At no time is it sufficient to keep me in food and clothing and support.

"I have taken nothing to do with politics all my life, but my race has been completely transformed, in that regard, since Mr. Roosevelt has been President. Left to a popular vote of the race, Mr. Roosevelt would get the solid South, against any other man on any ticket he might run on. He is God Almighty's gentleman. By that, I mean he is brave in the presence of the blue-bloods, kind in the presence of the common people, and gentle to the lowly and despised Negro."

Project 1885-1
Folklore
Spartanburg, Dist. 4
Dec. 1, 1937
Edited by: Elmer Turnage
[HW: (Dorroh)]

## ISABELLA DORROH

### Stories From Ex-Slaves

"I live wid my daughter in a four-room house which we rents from Doc Hunter. He got it in charge. My husband died several years ago.

"My daddy was Harvey Pratt, and he belonged to Marse Bob Pratt in Newberry. My mammy was Mary Fair, and she belonged in slavery to marse Simeon Fair. When dey married dey had a big wedding. Marse didn't make slave women marry men if dey didn't want to. Befo' my mammy and daddy married, somebody give a note to take to Mrs. Fair, her mistress. Mistress wouldn't tell what was in it, but daddy run every step of de way, he was so glad dey would let 'em marry.

"Col. Simeon Fair had a big fish pond on his place down on de branch behind his house, and he had a milkhouse, too. (This is where the Margaret Hunter Park is).

"My great-grandmother come from Virginia. She was

bought by Marse Fair from a speculator's drove. Slaves had good places to live in and everything to eat. Old Marse sho cared for his slaves. He give 'em plenty of clothes and good things to eat. On Sundays dey had to go to de white folks' church and he made dem put on new clean clothes dat he give 'em.

"I was born about two years befo' freedom, and I lost my mammy right atter de war. I remember about de Ku Klux and Red Shirts.

"Everything we had was made at home, or on marster's big plantation in de country. Marse told his son, Billy, befo' he died to take care of his niggers and see dat dey didn't want for nothing.

"Marse made de slaves work all day and sometimes on Saturdays, but he never let 'em work at night. Sometimes on de plantation dey had corn-shuckings and log-rollings; den dey give de hands good dinners and some whiskey to drink.

"One old nigger had a weak back and couldn't work much, so he use to play marbles in de yard wid de kids most every day.

"Slaves couldn't go away from de place unless dey had a pass from de marse to show de patrollers when dey caught dem out.

"My daddy use to cook at de old Newberry Hotel. He was one of de finest cooks in dis part of de country. De hotel was a small wooden frame building wid a long front piazza. In de back was a small wooden two-room house dat servants lived in. Atter de war, de 'little guard house' stood jes' behind where de opera house now is.

"Some of de slaves learned to read and write. Marse didn't keep dem from learning if dey wanted to. Niggers used to sing, 'I am born to die'. Dey learn't it from Marse Ramage's son, 'Jock' Ramage. He learn't 'em to sing it.

"Atter de war, Marse told de niggers dey was free. Most of dem stayed on wid him and took his name. Slaves most always took de name of deir marsters.

"My mother married at Thomas Pope's place, and he had old man Ned Pearson, a nigger who could read and write, to marry 'em. He married lots of niggers den. Atter de war many niggers married over agin, 'cause dey didn't know if de first marriage was good or not.

"Marse Fair let his niggers have dances and frolics on his plantation, and on Saturdays dey danced till 12 o'clock midnight. Sometimes dey danced jigs, too, in a circle, jumping up and down. In dese times de young folks dance way into Sunday mornings, and nobody to stop 'em, but Marse wouldn't let his slaves dance atter 12 o'clock.

"Everybody believed in ghosts. Nobody would pass by a graveyard on a dark night, and dese days dey go to cemeteries to do deir mischief, at night and not afraid. Doctors used to have home-made medicines. Old Dr. Brown made medicine from a root herb to cure rheumatism. He called it 'rhue'. He lived in what is now called Graveltown. His old house has been torn down. He made hot teas from barks for fevers. He made a liquid salve to rub on for rheumatism.

"When freedom come most of de slaves stayed on. Some man come here to make a speech to de slaves. He spoke in Marse Fair's yard to a big crowd of niggers and told dem to stay on and work for wages. When de Yankees come through here, dey stole everything dey could git deir hands on. Dey went in de house and took food and articles. Marse put guards around his house to keep dem out so dey wouldn't steal all de potatoes and flour he had for his slaves. Ku Klux went around de country and caught niggers and carpetbaggers. De carpetbaggers would hunt up chillun's lands, whose daddys was killed and try to take dem. Dat was when Judge Leheigh was here, and Capt. Bone was postmaster. Dey was Republicans, but when de Democrats got in power dey stopped all dat.

"When I married John Dorroh I had a big wedding. We married at de Harp place in Newberry, jes' behind de big house, in a nigger cottage. White folks and niggers come. I was known amongst de best white families 'cause I served as cook for dem. I was married by Rev. J. K. Walls, a nigger preacher from Charleston.

"I think slavery ended through de work of Almighty God. My mother always said dat was it. My daddy left here and went to Memphis when I was five years old. He sent home $40. He was in de army wid Major James Baxter. He took care of de guns and things of de Major."

Source: Isabella Dorroh (N, 75), Newberry, S. C.
Interviewer: G. L. Summer, Newberry, S. C. 11/22/27.

Project 1885-1
Spartanburg, S. C.
May 31, 1937
Edited by: Martha Ritter

# LAURENCE DOWNING
## Folklore: Ex-Slaves

"I was born in Newberry County, S. C. below Prosperity on Capt. George De Walt's place. My daddy and mammy was Giles and Lizzie De Walt Downing. My daddy belonged to de Outz family, but changed his name to Downing—his master was Downing Outz. I was born about 1857. My mother had 16 children, some died young.

I was a little chap when the war was here, but I remember de soldiers coming home from de war. De Yankees went through here and stole all the cattle and all the eats. De Ku Klux marched down de road dressed in white sheets. Freedom come and most of the slaves went away, but I stayed on wid Marse De Walt. Daddy worked wid Downing Outz for wages. When I was 15 years old I worked in de fields like grown folks. I never learned to read and write. We had no schools then for colored people. De only church we had after freedom come was a small "brush arbor" church.

"We hunted rabbits, 'possums, squirrels, wild turkeys, doves and partridges there.

"I joined de church when I was 20 years old, 'cause I thought times would be better for me then. Of course, I kind of back-slided little afterwards, but always tried to do right.

    Source: Laurence Downing (80), Newberry, S. C.
    Interviewer: G. Leland Sumer, Newberry, S. C.

**Project 1885-(1)**
**Prepared by Annie Ruth Davis**
**Place, Marion, S. C.**
**Date, Jane 23, 1937**

# WASHINGTON DOZIER
## Ex-Slave, 90 years

"Dis heah sho' Washington Dozier. Dat is wha' de hard time left uv him. I born en raise dere in Florence County de 18th uv December, 1847. Don' know 'xactly wha' my father name, but my mudder tell me he wuz name Dozier. My mudder wuz Becky en she b'long to ole man Wiles Gregg dere on de Charleston road. I hab two sisters en one brother, but not uv one father. I s'ppose brother Henry wuz me whole brother en Fannie en Ca'oline wuz jes me half sister."

"Well, dey ne'er hab so mucha sumptin, but I recollect dey make dey own produce den. Oh, dey lib very well. We call it good libin' at dat time. Coase de bedding de colored peoples hab wasn't much cause dey jes hab some kind uv home-made stuff den. We raise in a t'ree room house wha' hab floor on two uv de room. Hab house right dere on de Gregg plantation. Family went from age to age in dat day en time wid dey own Massa name. I 'member my gra'mudder was name Fannie Gregg. Now, I tell yuh how

I 'count fa me hab de name Dozier, I jes s'ppose dat come from me father."

"Hadder do some sorta work in dem days lak hoe corn en replant en so on lak dat, but ne'er didn't do no man work. Wuz jes uh half hand, dat is 'bout so. Dey gi'e us plenty sumptin to eat den, but ne'er pay us no money. Coase dey didn't 'low us no choice uv wha' we eat at dat time. Hab plenty meat en corn bread en molasses mos' aw de time. Den dey le' us hab uh garden uv we own en we hunt possum many uh time en ketch fish too. Meat was de t'ing dat I lak mostly."

"Dey gi'e us good clothes to put on us back wha' dey hab make on de plantation en in de winter, dey gi'e us good warm clothes. Jes wear wha'e'er de white folks gi'e us. Didn't take no 'ffect tall 'bout Sunday clothes."

"Fust time I marry I hab uh very good wedding. Marry ole man Gurley daughter o'er in Florence County. Don' know 'xactly how ole I was den, but I c'n tell yah dis much, I wasn't in no herry to marry. Aw colored peoples hadder do to marry den wuz to go to dey Massa en ge' uh permit en consider demselves man en wife. I recollect dat we hab a very good wedding supper dere. I marry Georgeanna de second time en I hab four head uv chillun by me fust wife en four head uv chillun by me second wife. Ne'er couldn't tell how many gran'chillun I got."

My Massa en Missus wuz mighty pious good people. Dey go to preachin' dere to Hopewell Presbyterian Chu'ch aw de time. De man wha' wuz de preacher dere den wuz name Frierson. De colored peoples go dere to dat same chu'ch en sot en de gallery. Yuh know dere spirituals hymns en dere reels. I c'n sing one uv dem dat I use'er sing in my slumberin' hours. It go lak dis:

> Chillun, wha' yuh gwinna do in de jedgment mornin'?
> Chillun, wha' yuh gwinna do in de jedgment mornin'?
> Oh Chillun, wha' yuh gwinna do in de jedgment mornin'
> When ole Gable go down on de seashore?
>
> He gwinna place one foot in de sea
> En de udder on de land,
> En declare tha' time would be no more,
> Chillun, wha' yuh gwinna do?
>
> Chillun, wha' yah gwinna do in de jedgment mornin'?
> Chillun, wha' yah gwinna do in de jedgment mornin'?
> Then chillun, wha' yuh gwinna do
> When ole Gable go down on de seashore?
>
> He gwinna place one foot in de sea
> En de udder on de land,
> En declare tha' time would be no more,
> Then chillun, wha' yuh gwinna do in de jedgment mornin'?

"Now de angels sing dat to me in my slumberin' hour en dey sing it dat I might gi'e it to de libin' heah on dis earth. Well, I know right smart uv dem song cause accordin' to my 'sperience, de hymn book wha' to fence de human family in. I got ah good set uv lungs en I wuz de one wha' lead de flock den. Dere jes one grand reason why I can' sing right well dis a'ternoon, yuh is take me on de surprise lak."

"I was jes uh chap in slavery time en I hadder stay dere

home aw de time whey dere didn't no harm come 'bout me. Dey le' we chillun play marbles en ball aw we wanna den. Jes chunk de ball to one annuder o'er de house. Dat how we play ball in dem times. My white folks didn't do nuthin but stay home en go to chu'ch meetin's. Dey ne'er didn't punish none uv dey colored peoples en didn' 'low no udder people to do it neither. I couldn't tell yah how many slave dey own but dey hab more slave by de increase uv dey families. Dey hab so many dat some uv de time dey'ud hire some uv dem out to annuder plantation. Ne'er didn't see em sell none uv dey colored peoples. I know dis much, dat wuz uh right good place to lib."

"I heared tell uv trouble 'tween de whites en de colored peoples, but dere wuzn't none uv dat 'round whey I stay. Dey say some uv de slave run 'way fa bad treatment en stay in de woods. Didn't hab no jails den en when dey'd ketch em, dey'ud buff em en gag em en hoss whip em. Now, I ne'er see none uv dat but I heared tell uv it."

"My Massa ne'er didn't work us hard lak. Coase uz de day' ud come, de hands hadder go up to de big house en go 'bout dey business, but dey al'ays knock offen early on uh Saturday evenin' en le' everbody do jes wha' dey wanna dere on de plantation. Ne'er didn't use no horn to wake dey colored peoples up en didn't wake em work en de big Christmus day en New Years' neither. Ne'er hab no udder holidays but dem two. My Massa gi'e aw his colored peoples uh big Christmus dinner to de white folks house. Jes hab plenty uv fresh meat en rice en biscuit en cake fa eve'ybody dat day."

"Dey hab funeral fa de colored peoples den jes lak dey hab dese days 'cept dey ne'er hab no preacher 'bout. Aw de slaves stop workin' fa de funeral en dey'ud jes carry de body en permit it to de ground uz wuz de usual t'ing dey do. Coase dey hab plenty singin' dere."

"Dem t'ing wha' people call ghostes, dey is evil walks. I know dis much, de sperit uv de body travels en dat de truth sho' uz I libin' heah. Coase I ain' ne'er see none uv dem t'ing en I ain' scared uv nuthin neither. Don' ne'er pay no 'ttention to no black cat en t'ing lak dat. Ain' bother wid none uv dem charm neither. De peoples use'er hab dey own doc'or book en dey search dat en use wha' it say do. Dey ne'er use no me'icine tall den but calomel en castor oil en turpentine."

"I sho' 'member when de fust gun shoot dere to Fort Sumter. Us fer uz I c'n recollect, it wuz in June. De Yankees come t'rough dere en to my knowin', dey 'haved very well. Jes ax my Massa fa sumptin to eat en dat wuz aw dey done. Dere sho' wuz uh rejoicing 'mongest some uv de colored peoples when dey tell em dey wuz free uz de white folks wuz. Some uv dem leab dey Massa plantation jes uz soon uz dey know'd dey wuz free, but we ne'er do dat. Jes stayed right on dere wid Mr. Gregg en work fa one-third uv wha' dey make. Coase de white folks furnish aw de wear en tear uv eve't'ing."

"Dey ain' ne'er hab no schools fa de colored peoples no whey 'bout whey I stay 'fore freedom come heah. Won' long a'ter de war dat free schools wuz open up dere. It jes lak dis, I ain' bother wid dem schools mucha den, but I c'n read right smart. Jes ketch it uz I come 'long en wha' I kotch, I put dat to work. I is went to one uv dese night schools dey hab 'bout heah not long gone."

"Mr. Abraham Lincoln, I ain' ne'er see him, but I know he wuz de President uv de United States. Ain' ne'er see Mr. Jefferson Davis neither. Dey wus oppositionalist den, I sho' know dat."

"It jes lak dis, I t'ink dis uh better day we lib in dese times. When we b'long to de white folks, we lib, en a'ter we wuz free we lib right on. I t'ink being free de best time to lib. Better to be loose den tied cause don' care how good yo' owner, yuh hadder be under dey jurisdiction. Ain' dat right?"

Source: Washington Dozier, age 90, colored, Pee Dee, Marion
Co. (Personal interview, June 1937).

Project 1885-1
Spartanburg Dist. 4
Sept. 22, 1937
Edited by:
Elmer Turnage

## ALICE DUKE

### Stories From Ex-Slaves
[Hw: Duke]

"Vinie Wilkins is my daughter's name dat live wid me. My son owns dis house and he keeps it up fer me and his sister. I's born on de bank of Cherokee Creek, but I jest 'members how many years I stayed dar. Atter Freedom had been a long time, we moved to Mr. Chesterfield Scruggs' plantation whar we share cropped. It was on de old Spartanburg road from here to Spartanburg.

"I was purtty good-size chile when de Ku Klux come and tried to git my daddy. Dey whipped him; den he run off and stayed off fer over seven years. Dem Ku Klux was in all kinds of shapes, wid horns and things on dere heads. Dey was so scary looking dat I ain't never fergot dem. Dem's de awfulest 'boogers' I is ever see'd befo' or since. I was in de bed and so was Pa, but dey broke in our do' and got him. I kivvered up my head and did not make narry a sound. Dat's all dat I can recollect now."

United States

Source: Alice Duke (72), 401 Woods St., Gaffney, S. C.
Interviewer: Caldwell Sims, Union, S. C. 9/16/37

Project, 1885-(1)
Prepared by Annie Ruth Davis
Place, Marion, S. C.
Date, June 9, 1937

# AUNT SILVA DURANT
## Ex-Slave

"I don' know 'xactly when I wuz born but I hear my white folks say dat I wuz born de fust (first) year uv freedom. I I c'n tell yuh dis much dat I wuz uh grown 'oman when de shake wuz. Aw de older peoples wuz at de chu'ch en ha' left us home to take care uv aw dem little chillun. Fust t'ing we is know de house 'gin to quiver lak. We ne'er know wha' been to matter en den de house 'gin to rock en rock en rock. We wuz so scare we run outer in de yard en eve't'ing outer dere wuz jes uh shaking jes lak de house wuz. We ne'er know wha' to do. Den we heared de peoples comin' from de chu'ch jes uh runnin' en uh hollerin'. Didn't nobody know wha' make dat. I tellin yuh jes lak dat wuz, de jedgment ain' ne'er been no closer come heah den when dat shake was."

"My mudder wuz name Clorrie en she b'long to Miss Millie Gasque up de road dere. I born in Miss Millie yard en I stay dere till I wuz six year old. My pa say I wuz six year old. He been ole man Vidger Hanes en b'long to Mr. Wesley White o'er dere 'bout laughin 'fore freedom 'clare. A'ter dat we move on de hill en my pa hire me dere to Colonel Durant to wash dishes en help 'bout de kitchen. Den dey put me to do de washin' en I been uh washin' en uh washin' mos' e'er since. Dats de way I done till I ge' so I ne'er couldn't make it en den I hadder quit offen. Dat how come I hab aw dese pretty flowers. Miss Durant gi'e me aw dem dahlia wha' yuh see in dat yard right dere. Dat how I ge' wha' little bit uv money I hab dese day en time. Dem white folks up dere in town comes down heah en begs em from me."

"Dey tell me some uv de peoples ge' 'long good en den some uv dem ge' 'long bad back dere in slavery day. Don' care how good peoples is dere sho' be uh odd'un de crowd some uv de time. Dey say some uv de colored peoples'ud run 'way from dey Massa en hide in de woods. Den dey slip back to de plantation in de night en ge' green corn outer de white folks field en carry em back in de woods en cook em dere. I hear Tom Bostick tell 'bout when he run 'way one time. Say he use'er run 'way en hide in de woods aw de time. Den de o'erseer ketch him one time when he been come back en wuz grabblin' 'bout de tatoe patch. Say he gwinna make Tom Bostick stay outer de woods ur kill him 'fore sun up dat day. Tom say dey take him down 'side de woods en strip he clothes offen him. (I hear em say dere plenty people bury down 'side dem woods dat dere ain' nobody know 'bout). Den he say dey tie him to uh tree en take uh fat light'ud torch en le' de juice drap outer it right on he naked body. He say he holler en he beg en he ax em hab mercy but dat ne'er didn't do no good. He mock how de tar make uh racket when it drap on he skin. Yuh know it gwinna make uh racke't. Dat t'ing gwinna make uh racket when it drap on anyt'ing wha' fresh. Ain' yuh ne'er hear no hot grease sizzle lak? Yas'um, hear Tom Bostick tell dat more times den I got fingers en toe."

"Den dey'ud hab sale en sell some uv de colored peoples offen to annuder plantation hundred mile 'way some uv de time. 'Vide man en he wife. Dey sho' done it. I hear pa tell 'bout dat. Make em stand up on uh stump en bid em offen dere jes lak dey wuz hoss. Pa say dey sell he brother Elic wife 'way wid de onlyest child dey hab. Ne'er didn't see dat wife en child no more."

"Coase de le' de colored peoples visit 'round from one plantation to annuder but dey hadder hab uh ticke' wid em. Effen dey meet em in de road en dey ne'er hab dat ticke' somewhey 'bout on em, dey hadder take wha' follow. Ne'er 'low em to hab no udder paper 'bout em no whey. Effen dey see em wid uh paper, dey ax em 'bout it en effen it ne'er been uh ticke', dey mighty apt to gi'e em uh good t'rashin'."

"Dey tell me some uv de colored peoples use'er take t'ing from dey Massa, but I ain' ne'er see em do none uv dat on my white folks plantation. Ne'er hadder take nuthin dere. Ge' 'nough meal en meat dere to de big house eve'y Friday to las' em aw t'rough de week. Reckon de ration wuz more wholesome den in dat day en time cause dey take time en cook dey t'ing done. Hadder cook in de fireplace. Dat how dey done. I 'member wha' good t'ings my ole mammy use'er cook in dat spider. Jes set it on de coals en keep uh turnin' it 'bout wid de handle. Dere ain' ne'er nuthin eat no better den dat ash cake she use'er make fa we chillun. Yuh ain' ne'er hear tell 'bout dat. Jes ster (stir) up uh nice hoecake en wrap it up in oak leaves wha' right sorta wet. Den yuh rake uh heap uv ash togedder en lay yuh hoecake on dat en kiver it up wid some more ash. Yuh le' it cook right done en den yuh take it up en wash it offen en it ready to eat. Us chillun lub dat den."

"Annuder t'ing dat eat right smart in dem days wuz dat t'ing call big hominy. Dey jes ge' some whole grain corn en put it in de pot en boil it long time. Den dey take it offen de fire en pour lye water aw o'er it. Dey do dat to ge' de husk offen it. Soak ash outer de fire en ge' dat lye water. Den dey hadder take it to de well outer in de yard en wash it uh heap uv time to ge' dat lye outer it. A'ter dat dey season it wid salt en pepper en cook it annuder time. No 'mam, dey ne'er eat it wid no butter. Jes drap it in de grease wha' left in de pan a'ter dey fry de meat en make it right brown lak. Dat de way dey cook dey big hominy."

"Folks don' hab time to do t'ings in de right way lak dey use'er cause de world gwine too fas' dese day en time. Dese people comin' up 'bout heah dese days ain' gwinna ne'er quit habin' so mucha belly ache long uz dey ain' stop eatin' aw dem half done ration dey is eat. Coase de peoples wiser now but dey weaker. De peoples wuz more humble in dem days. When dey didn't hab no rain, dey ge' togedder en pray fa rain en dey ge' it too. I tellin' yuh peoples gotta work effen dey gwinna ge' to de right place when dey leab heah. Effen de peoples ne'er didn't go to chu'ch in dem days, dey stay home. Ne'er see chillun in de road on Sunday eve'y which uh way lak yunnah see em dese days. My pa say yuh mus' train up uh child in de way he oughta go en den effen dey stray 'way, dey sho' come back a'ter while. I tellin' yuh de peoples ain' lak dey use'er wuz. Dey sho' wickeder en worser in dis day en time den when I raise up. Dey wuz more friendly den en do more favor fa peoples. It jes lak dis, I ain' gwinna do nobody no harm. Effen I can' do em no good, ain' gwinna do no harm en ain' gwinna 'buse em neither."

Source: Aunt Silva Durant, colored, Marion, S. C.
Personal interview, May 1937.

United States

Project, 1885-(1)
Prepared by Annie Ruth Davis
Place, Marion, S. C.
Date, October 21, 1937

## SYLVIA DURANT

### Ex-Slave, 72 Years

"Well, I tell you just like it been. Dat was an unexpectin trip when you come here dat day en I wasn' thinkin bout much dat I had know to tell you. It been kind o' put me on a wonder."

"You see, child, I never didn' see my grandfather cause when I was born, dey had done sold him away. I hear tell dat sometimes dey would take de wife from dey husband en another time dey would take de husband from dey wife en sell dem off yonder somewhe' en never didn' see dem no more neither. Yes, I sho know dat cause I hear my father speak bout dat plenty times. Yes, mam, dey sold my uncle's wife away en he never didn' see her no more till after freedom come en he done been married again den. Speculators carried my mother's first husband off en den she married again. Cose I was born of de second husband en dat ain' been yesterday."

"I hear talk bout dat didn' none of de colored people have nothin in slavery time en heap of dem wasn' allowed to pick up a paper or nothin no time. Often hear dem talk dat some of de niggers was freed long time fore dey know bout it. Hear dem say some white folks hold dem long time till dey could make out to get somethin for demselves. Don' think so. Don' think so. No, mam, don' think so. Dey might been intended for dem to get somethin when dey was freed, but I never learn of nobody gettin nothin. Cose I often heard my father say some white folks thought more bout dey colored people den others en hope dem out more. Hear tell dat didn' none of dem have no clothes much den. No, mam, colored people won' bless wid no clothes much in dem days. I remember dey had to wear dese old big shoes, call brogans, wid brass all cross de toes here. Nobody don' wear nothin like dat now. Dey was coarse shoes. Some say plenty of de people had to go barefooted all de time in dem days. Reckon dat would kill de people in dis day en time. Couldn' stand nothin like dat. Yes, mam, see Tom Bostick walk right cross dat field many a day just as barefooted as he come in de world en all de ground would be covered over wid ice en snow. De people get after him en he say, 'Well, I had worser den dis to go through wid in slavery time.' Say he come up dat way en he never know no difference den dat he had thick shoe on his foot."

"Well, you see, some of de white folks would spare dey colored people so much ration when dey knock off work on a Saturday to last dem till de next Saturday come. Hear tell dey give dem a peck of meal en a little molasses en a hog jowl en dat had to last dem all de week. Dem what use a little tobacco, give dem a plug of dat en give dem a little flour for Sunday. Didn' nobody have to work on Sunday en den dey would allow dem two days off for Christmas too. I tellin you bout how my white folks would do, but dem what had a rough Massa, dey just got one day. I hear dem say dey always had a little flour on Christmas. Don' know what else dey give dem, but won' nothin much. I know dat. Sho know dat."

"I hear say two intelligent people didn' live so far apart en one never treat dey colored people right en being as dey wasn' allowed to go from one place to another widout dey had a ticket wid dem, dey would steal somethin en run away. Say de just man tell dat other man dat if he would feed his niggers right, dey wouldn' have no need to be stealin so much things. No'um, I does hate to tell dat. Cose dey say dey done it. Say de overseer would beat dem up dat never do what he tell dem to do mighty bad en wouldn' be particular bout whe' dey was buried neither. Hear talk dat dey bury heap of dem in a big hole down side de woods somewhe'. Cose I don' know whe' dat word true or not, but dat what dey tell me."

"Oo—oo—yes, mam, dey sho whip de colored women in dem days. Yes, mam, de overseer done it cause I hear dem say dat myself. Tell dat dey take de wives en whip de blood out dem en de husband never didn' dare to say nothin. Hear dey whip some so bad dey had to grease dem. If de colored people didn' do to suit de white folks, dey sho whip dem. No, mam, if dey put you out to work, ain' nobody think dey gwine lay down under de bresh (brush) en stay dere widout doin dey portion of work. Yes, child, hear bout dat more times, den I got fingers en toes."

"Oh, de times be worser in a way dese days. Yes, mam, dey sho worser in a way. De people be wiser now den what dey used to be, but dere so much gwine on, dey ain' thinkin bout dey welfare no time en dat'll shorten anybody days. Oh, honey, we livin in a fast world dese days. Peoples used to help one another out more en didn' somebody be tryin to pull you down all de time. When you is found a wicked one in dat day en time, it been a wicked one. Cose de people be more intelligent in learnin dese days, but I'm tellin you dere a lot of other things got to build you up 'sides learnin. Dere one can get up to make a speech what ain' got no learnin en dey can just preach de finest kind of speech. Say dey ain' know one thing dey gwine say fore dey get up dere. Folks claim dem kind of people been bless wid plenty good mother wit. Den another time one dat have de learnin widout de mother wit can get up en seem like dey just don' know whe' to place de next word. Yes, mam, I hear dat often."

"What I meant by what I say bout de wicked one? I meant when you found a wild one, it been a wild one for true. I mean you better not meddle wid one like dat cause dey don' never care what dey do. People look like dey used to care more for dey lives den dey do dese days. Dat what I meant, but you can weigh dat like you want to. You see, dere be different ways for people to hurt demselves."

"Oh, my soul, hear talk bout dere be ghosts en hants, but I never didn' experience nothin like dat. Yes, mam, I hear too much of dat. Been hearin bout dat ever since I been in a manner grown, you may say. I hear people say dey see dem, but I ain' take up no time wid nothin like dat. I have a mind like dis, if such a thing be true, it ain' intended for everybody to see dem. I gwine tell you far as I know bout it. I hear dese old people say when anybody child born wid a caul over dey face, dey can always see dem things en dem what ain' born dat way, dey don' see dem. Cose I don' know nothin bout what dat is en I is hate to tell it, but I hear lot of people say dey can see hants en ghosts all time of a night. Yes'um, I hear de older people say dat, but I don' know whe' it true or no. I know I don' see nothin myself, but de wind. Don' see dat, but I feels it."

"Oh, my God, some people believe in dat thing call conjurin, but I didn' never believe in nothin like dat. Never didn' understand nothin like dat. Hear say people could make you leave home en all dat, but I never couldn' see into it. Never didn' believe in it."

"Yes, mam, I see plenty people wear dem dimes round dey ankle en all kind of things on dey body, but never didn' see my mother do nothin like dat. I gwine tell you it just like I got it. Hear talk dat some would wear dem for luck en some tote dem to keep people from hurtin dem. I got a silver dime in de house dere in my trunk right to dis same day dat I used to wear on a string of beads, but I took it off. No, mam, couldn' stand nothin like dat. Den some peoples keeps a bag of asafetida tied round dey neck to keep off sickness. Folks put it on dey chillun to keep dem from havin worms. I never didn' wear none in my life, but I know it been a good thing for people, especially chillun. Let me see, dere a heap of other things dat I learn bout been good for people to wear for sickness. Dere been nutmeg dat some people make a hole in en wear it round dey neck. I forget whether it been good for neuralgia or some of dem other body ailments, but I know it won' for no conjurin."

"Honey, pa always say dat you couldn' expect no more from a child den you puts in dey raisin. Pa say, 'Sylvia, raise up your chillun in de right way en dey'll smile on you in your old age.' Honey, I don' see what dese people gwine expect dey chillun to turn out to be nohow dese days cause dey ain' got no raisin en dey ain' got no manners. I say, I got a feelin for de chillun cause dey parents ain' stay home enough of time to learn dem nothin en dey ain' been know no better. Remember when my parents went off en tell us to stay home, we never didn' darsen to go off de place. Den when dey would send us off, we know we had to be back in de yard fore sunup in de evenin. Yes, child, we all had to be obedient to our parents in dat day en time. I always was sub-obedient myself en I never had no trouble nowhe'. Yes, mam, when we went off anywhe', we ax to go en we been back de hour dey expect to see us. Yes, mam, chillun was more obedient den. None of us didn' sass us parents. Won' raise dat way. I remember when I was young, I used to tote water en make fire to de pot for my mother to wash plenty times. Den dey learn me how to use a hoe en when I was married en left home, won' nothin strange to me."

"No, mam, I didn' have no weddin when I was married, but everything was pleasant en turned out all right. Yes, mam, everybody don' feel so good leavin home, but I felt all right, I was married over dere in Bethel M. E. Church en served a little cake en wine dere home afterwards en dat ain' no weddin. Didn' have nothin but pound cake en wine. Had three plain cakes. Two was cut up dere home en I remember I carried one wid me over Catfish dere to de Reaves place."

Source: Sylvia Durant, ex-slave, age about 72, Marion, S. C.
Personal interview by Annie Ruth Davis, Oct., 1937.

## Transcriber's Note:

To reflect the individual character of this document, inconsistencies in formatting have been retained.

[HW: ] denotes a handwritten note.

www.ingramcontent.com/pod-product-compliance
Lightning Source LLC
Chambersburg PA
CBHW071645160426
43195CB00012B/1360